OUR LIFE STORY

Roy Rogers
and Dale Evans

with Jane and Michael Stern

SIMON & SCHUSTER
New York × London × Toronto × Sydney × Tokyo × Singapore

SIMON & SCHUSTER
Rockefeller Center
1230 Avenue of the Americas
New York, New York 10020

Designed by Irving Perkins Associates
Manufactured in the United States of America

1   3   5   7   9   10   8   6   4   2

Library of Congress Cataloging-in-Publication Data

Rogers, Roy.
Happy trails : our life story / Roy Rogers and Dale Evans ; with
Jane and Michael Stern.
p.   cm.
1. Rogers, Roy.   2. Rogers, Dale Evans.   3. Actors—
United States—Biography.   4. Singers—United States—Biography.
I. Rogers, Dale Evans.   II. Title.
PN2287.R73A3   1994b
791.43′028′092—dc20
[B]   94-35133
                                                          CIP

ISBN: 0-671-89714-4

WE DEDICATE THIS BOOK OF "happy trails" to our children, in the order of their ages:

Thomas Fox
Cheryl Barnett
Marion Swift
Linda Johnson
Roy Rogers, Jr.
Mary Sailors

and to our deceased children:

Robin Elizabeth Rogers
John David Rogers
Deborah Lee Rogers

Each child has given us blessed responsibility, joy in their maturity (however long or short), and gratitude for the privilege of housing them and for "training them up in the way they should go" (Proverbs 22:6). We have been grateful for the biblical promise that, though they stray, when they are old they will not depart from it.

We thank the friends we have made in and out of show business across the years. Our sincere appreciation to Dr. Billy Graham, Dr. Jack MacArthur, Reverend Harley Wright Smith, and Reverend O. William Hansen—all ministers of the Gospel of Jesus Christ—whose spiritual guidance has blessed and strengthened our lives since 1948.

We thank our friends in the entertainment industry, who allowed us to participate in entertainment for the families of our nation.

Finally, we offer thanks to God the Father of our Lord Jesus Christ, and to His Holy Spirit, for the guidance we have experienced.

—ROY ROGERS AND DALE EVANS

Contents

PART I
Leonard and Frances:
The Earliest Years 9

PART II
Leonard and Dale:
The Road West 49

PART III
Roy and Dale:
Fame and Misfortunes 87

PART IV
Roy and Dale:
Happiness, but Not Without Pain 135

PART V
Roy and Dale:
A Large and Loving Family 185

PART VI
Roy and Dale:
Just Us Two 235

PART I

Leonard and Frances: The Earliest Years

*T*HE UNITED STATES has no king as head of state; but on rare occasions our culture provides a hero so great that the royal title fits: Elvis, King of Rock and Roll; Kitty Wells, Queen of Country Music; Babe Ruth, Sultan of Swat. In 1943 Republic Studios declared Roy Rogers King of the Cowboys. It was an audacious marketing ploy, but it worked. The tuneful sagebrush superstar from Duck Run, Ohio, fit the silver-saddle throne like no man before or since. As a movie buckaroo, he was the best there ever was: he shot the straightest and rode the fastest (on Trigger, "The Smartest Horse in the Movies") and yodeled the sweetest and strummed hypnotic sagebrush tunes about tumbling tumbleweeds on his guitar. He was invincible: when it came to fisticuffs, he could outbox any one man or any four, always fighting cleanly even if they did not. He was fabulously well-dressed in fringe and fancy leather, and he was a man who never seemed to need a shave. His partner in many of the movies he made was just about the prettiest cowgirl there ever was—Dale Evans, "Queen of the West." When Roy crinkled his eyes in a smile, girls fell in love and boys smiled right along with him. Children especially adored him because even though he was a grown-up, Roy Rogers seemed never to lose his boyish enthusiasm for life's adventures.

At the peak of his career, from the early 1940s to the mid-1950s, he made as many as six pictures a year, which were seen annually by more than 80 million Americans—over half the population of the country. In 1950 there were more than two thousand Roy Rogers fan clubs around the globe; the one in London had fifty thousand members—the biggest such club then for anyone, anywhere on earth. In 1951 Roy Rogers moved to television and starred for six years on "The Roy Rogers Show" along with his wife, Dale Evans. They also created several long-running radio series that featured their singing duets and dramatic sketches, and they regularly rode in all the biggest parades and performed at all the grandest rodeos throughout the nation.

Roy Rogers and Dale Evans were simply the most popular cowboy and cowgirl the world has ever known. Their West was a magical American landscape full of promise and hope in which goodness was always rewarded and bad guys always got what they deserved. They reigned at a time when the cowboy ideal seemed to signify everything decent about a nation in which all things were possible if you were a good guy with a solid handshake and a sense of honor. They were, in the words of H. Allen Smith, "purity rampant" at a time when we Americans wanted heroes pure and yearned to believe that dreams come true. They fought fair and didn't swear or even grumble when the going got tough. The adventures they had were thrilling and fun and wholesome, filled with rollicking songs, mile-a-minute horse chases, and a dash of fresh romance (but not too much mushy stuff). Whatever trouble came along, you knew that Roy and Dale could handle it—with skill and certainty, good humor, and grace. The mythology known as pop culture doesn't make heroes like them anymore, which is why Roy and Dale have become American icons bigger than their fame as performers and celebrities.

For many of us who grew up with them, they have always felt so much more personal than other Hollywood royalty. In their fanciful movie and TV dramas, but also in the very real and sometimes tragic struggles of their private lives, they took their position as stars to heart and always tried to set a good example. They cared about the influence they had on all the little pardners in their thrall, and they weren't embarrassed to tell us so. Dale often liked to tell her own children as well as the rest of us, "Your life is the only Bible some people will ever read"; and for us youngsters who adored them, Roy and Dale truly were an inspiration of near-biblical significance. If our own parents weren't around to help or maybe sometimes didn't provide such good examples, the King of the Cowboys and the Queen of the West were there to show us how to live: how to make a slingshot from the prongs of a vining maple tree, how to shoot straight and ride smooth, how to be brave at times when we were scared, how to be decent human beings in the face of bushwackers and bad guys.

Some of us fell in love with them. A neighbor of ours who runs a Western wear and tack store recalls gathering around the TV with her three sisters to watch "The Roy Rogers Show" every Sunday evening at 6:30. "We sat as close to the television set as our parents allowed," she says. "And whenever Roy came on, we took turns jumping up to kiss the screen." She asks us, "Is he really as nice as he seems? Are they truly in love?" When we tell her that Roy and Dale in person today are as kind and bright and charming and plumb *good* as she remembers from forty years ago, she beams with delight, looking like a little girl with stars in her eyes.

Another woman we know says that she liked Roy and Dale because of the relationship they had. "Dale sometimes told Roy off," our friend recalls with a wistful smile, "and he liked it! They liked each other so much; you could see that. Dale was my role model when I was growing up because she showed you could be a cowgirl with a fast horse and be pretty, too. I think the biggest thrill of my childhood was when my father took the whole family to the rodeo at Madison Square Garden. We didn't know it until we got there, but Roy Rogers was the headliner. He was there with Dale and his sidekick Pat Brady. They sang songs and put on a show, but what I remember most is the end of the performance when Roy went all the way around the edge of the tanbark, riding Trigger in a sidepass and reaching down to shake hands with the audience. We were in the tenth row, and it seemed like there were a thousand other boys and girls in front of me. As he pranced along and came closer, I bent forward and held my hand out as far and high as I could. Everyone was yelling—all my brothers and sisters and the other kids—but I swear he looked my way when he heard me call his name. He spurred Trigger to move closer so the horse's breast pressed against the stands. Roy stood in his stirrups, leaning forward and extending his right hand—I watched the fringe swinging from his gauntlet—and as he passed, I reached impossibly far above the crowd and into the air. His hand grabbed mine, he looked me in the eyes, and he said, 'Howdy, Pardner.' At that moment, I felt there was no one else in the arena but us, and all he cared about was me."

—J. & M. S.

CHAPTER 1

Roy's Story

Trigger quivered underneath me like a rocket ready to lift off. As we waited for our cue in the arena at Madison Square Garden, my legs hugged the palomino's sides and my spurs skimmed the hair on his flanks. We heard the sounds of an eager audience: screams and whistles, children crying out with excitement, vendors hawking souvenirs and pictures of me. It was October 1943, and the World Championship Rodeo had come to New York City.

I was King of the Cowboys, Hollywood's number-one Western star. *Life* magazine had put me and Trigger on its cover, rearing up over the skyline of Los Angeles. Republic Studios bought billboards all across the country to advertise me. More than four hundred different products had paid for my endorsement. Fan mail was delivered to me by the ton and truckload. Tonight I was the headliner at the richest rodeo on earth.

The timpani sounded and the drum rolls began. I heard my name rumble through the crowd in whispers, shouts, and laughter. I eased a little slack into Trigger's reins and pulled my white Stetson low so the blast of speed when we entered wouldn't blow it off my head. Bright colored spotlights circled the darkened arena, and my rhinestone cowboy shirt started shooting glints of spangled starlight. My outfit was custom-made head to toe, and at seven thousand dollars, it was the finest buckaroo gear money could buy. Trigger's saddle, bit, and bridle were encrusted with inlaid gold and silver.

The drums lowered and the announcer's voice boomed forth, echoing through the loudspeaker system. "Ladies and gentlemen, Madison Square Garden and the World Championship Rodeo of 1943 are proud to present to you the King of the Cowboys, Mr. Roy Rogers!" At that, I tapped my spurs into Trigger's sides and he leapt off his mark into the arena at a full gallop, his flaxen mane and tail streaming out behind him like a picture from an Arabian fairy tale.

Mothers and fathers held their children aloft. Hands waved to me from every direction. We thundered in a fast circle, then I slid to a dead halt in the center of the arena. With a slight tug on the reins, Trigger rose up on his hind legs, pawing skyward with his front hooves as I raised my hat in the air to salute the crowd. The cheers swelled so loud they seemed to penetrate my bones. The stallion's hot breath sounded like a piston, and he was all I heard above the roar of the crowd. It was a special moment for me. To have reached this point, to have gotten to this place—it was amazing that something like this could actually happen. I looked around the big arena. At that moment, time slowed to a stop. My thoughts spun back into the past, to the life I had lived. I thought of where I came from, and wondered how in heaven's name I got to where I was.

I never set out to be King of the Cowboys, and certainly never thought I would wind up a movie star of any kind. When I was a kid growing up in the last house in the "holler" in Duck Run, Ohio (population fourteen), I got to see about one picture a year. My dream, if you could call it that, was to be a dentist. I know, it seems kind of funny now to think of ol'

Roy Rogers dressed in a white dental coat instead of a white Stetson hat, but you have to remember I wasn't Roy Rogers then. I was Leonard Slye, a backwoods country boy who knew firsthand that a toothache meant you had to go to the dentist, who grabbed a pair of pliers, pushed his knee into your chest, and yanked your jaw teeth straight from your head. I guess before I learned about cowboys, I believed a hero was someone who could take out your sore tooth without it hurting too bad.

Before my folks moved all of us out to Duck Run, I was born in Cincinnati, Ohio—412 Second Street to be exact. You won't be able to find my old home if you go lookin' for it, because where I first popped out and took a look around is now second base on the baseball diamond of Riverfront Stadium. The wrecking crew that toppled my birthplace probably didn't give it a second thought. It sure wasn't much to look at—just a four-story red-brick tenement with fire escapes in the front and some stores on the ground level. My folks lived there not because it was pretty, but because it was near the United States Shoe Company. That's where my pop worked.

My pop, Andy Slye, had been born in Portsmouth, Ohio. He was a small man who probably didn't weigh much over 125. The older I get, the more I look like him; I've even got the same squinty eyes he did. Dad was part Choctaw Indian, and like me he was an easygoing fella and a self-taught musician. He was also a dreamer, always looking for something better for himself and his family down the line. He had held a lot of jobs before the one at the shoe factory, working for a while as a carnival roustabout, an acrobat, and a showboat musician who played guitar and mandolin for vacationing folks. Pop was outgoing, and gentle in his heart. He wouldn't kill a fly, and as a city boy growing up in Portsmouth he never learned to hunt or do farm chores.

My mother, Mattie, was as shy as Pop was outgoing. She

was born in Kentucky, and when she was two years old she came down with polio, or as the country people called it back then, "the white swelling." It left her crippled for life, and she never could walk without bending down and holding her weak leg tight around the knee for support. She never had any crutches or braces back then, and the polio made it so she couldn't even walk well enough to get to church or do the kind of farm work we needed done. What a thrill it was for me once I became a movie star to bring her to the hospital at UCLA where the doctors fixed her up in a wheelchair. She went out shopping with my three sisters and had a ball wheeling herself through the aisles of stores. She was like a little girl, wanting to go everywhere and look at everything, doing the things she hadn't had the freedom to do before.

My birth on November 5, 1911, brought the Slye family to five. My two older sisters are Mary and Cleda; my younger sister's name is Kathleen. I am told that after having had two baby girls, my father came home from work at the end of that day and just couldn't believe he finally had a son. "Prove it," he said, and made my mother pull down the blankets I was swaddled in to show the evidence.

Even though my father was raised in the city himself, it wasn't what he wanted for his family, so he came up with an improbable scheme to move us to greener pastures. Teaming up with his brother Will, Pop began to build a houseboat that would sail us down the Ohio River from Cincinnati back to his hometown of Portsmouth. I guess it never concerned Pop too much that his brother Will was completely blind; they just set about the work, rounding up heaps of scrap lumber and salvaged materials, fashioning the boat the best they could. Sails for its mast were made from mother's bedsheets stitched together by hand, and the houseboat soon became the talk of the neighborhood. It was dubbed "Andy's Ark" by well-wishers and neighsayers alike, and after Pop hammered the last nail in, the squat whitewashed barge pushed off the muddy banks of the Ohio River in July of 1912. I suppose it sure wouldn't have won any awards for beauty, but amazingly, it got us where we had to go.

It's a good thing that Pop and Mother were strong country people, because the first day out a fierce storm kicked up on the river. It ripped the sails right off the homemade boat and broke all of mother's china dishes in the kitchen. We even collided with another boat nearby. My folks patched things up pretty good and continued their slow journey along the river undismayed. Along the way, Pop worked at odd jobs, anchoring long enough to help out fishermen in exchange for a tow further down the river. We docked at a landing in Portsmouth and spent four years afloat there.

If I had to put a finger on my first real childhood memory I guess it would be something that happened while we were living on the houseboat. Pop had moored us to the riverbank at one of the many stops we made on our way down to Portsmouth. I was just a little kid at the time, no more than a year and a half old, and I was bored. Right at my fingertips was this nice big river where another boy might have had some lawn growing. Since I didn't have any stones to throw, I found the next best thing: my mother's silverware. One by one, I threw knives, forks, and spoons into the muddy Ohio just to hear the splash they made and see the silvery shapes disappear into the wetness. I remember my mother walking slowly around the boat, looking everywhere for her silverware. Later, when the water went down, she spotted a whole set of knives, forks, and spoons sticking straight up out of the sand.

Sometimes I wonder if Pop had had a premonition of things to come when he decided to build his ark. Anyone who knows about Ohio River history can tell you about the great Portsmouth flood that happened shortly after we arrived there. It lasted thirteen days and was so famous a disaster that people still talk of it today. My folks told me stories of watching their neighbors' houses rise right up off their foundations and float away. The flood came along just after Pop had moved the houseboat inland to a site he had found and started making it into a permanent home. He had put up a white picket fence and we even had a few chickens scratching in the grass outside. When the waters came, up we went, chickens and all, sailing right down Water Street. As we floated by our neighbors' houses, Pop used a pole to maneuver close so he could help pick folks off their rooftops. It's curious how a child's mind works, but the thing I remember most of all was not the people who were in trouble, but how horrible it was to see one of our chickens flopping around in the raging water. I started to cry until Pop saved him, too. Like I said, he had a tender heart.

When the flood waters receded the houseboat was again moored on dry land in Portsmouth, and Pop took another job at a nearby shoe factory. Thinking back, I reckon his return to Portsmouth must have been something of a disappointment for him. After battling nature's tempests to get there, he and his family were still living in a city. It wasn't as big as Cincinnati, but the city had nearly 60,000 residents in those days—hardly the rural paradise he had envisioned for us.

In a way, I take some credit for Pop once again pulling up roots and getting grass under his children's feet instead of concrete. The final straw happened when my family was called to the local police station to bail me out of trouble. I was all of five years old when my pal Bob Stevenson and I hitched a ride on an ice wagon. Well, it was hot that day and we helped ourselves to hunks of ice to suck on. The no-nonsense driver of the wagon deposited us at the local hoosegow, where the policemen, faced with two bawling kids, located our parents to come pick us up. Getting a call from the police about his son must have felt to Pop like a bad omen of what kind of life I would have if we stayed in the city. So pretty soon after my trip to jail, we packed most of what we owned into a second-hand Maxwell car and headed deep into the countryside to Duck Run, a good twelve miles out of town. We were finally home, and here we stayed until I was a teenager.

Duck Run wasn't really a town—just a few farms and cabins. We lived so far away from everything that you had to pipe in sunlight. We lived in the last house in the holler. There was no plumbing or electricity, and no radio to listen to until I got older and built a crystal set. I didn't wear shoes all summer when we lived there, unless it was Sunday. Never having been a farmer himself, Pop knew he couldn't make enough of a living working the land to support all of us, so he moved back to Portsmouth where he lived alone for two weeks at a time, coming home to visit every other Saturday and Sunday. Today, to travel twelve miles sounds like nothing, but back then it was a day's trip along a rough country road.

For me, the most startling thing about moving to Duck Run was that at age six I suddenly became the man of the family. With Pop gone for two weeks at a time I was plunked down in the middle of nowhere with a whole heap of farm chores to do. The outcome didn't look promising, with a crippled mother and three sisters as my only helpers, but I have always believed that the surest way to learn something fast is when your life depends on it. And that's what I did: I learned fast, figuring out things as I needed to. I figured out farming, figured out hunting, figured out riding mules and horses and raising pigs and chickens and planting vegetables. I guess I figured it out pretty much like I figured out playing the mandolin and guitar. No one ever taught me how to read music, but I picked out what I needed to know.

It was hard work to keep our little farm going. I hauled wood using our mule, Tom, with my sisters and mother helping as best they could. We'd walk into the woods, cut down trees, split 'em up, and try to gather enough cords to last through the winter. One of the first things I learned when we moved out to Duck Run was how to plow behind a mule. I was a little fella then, so I had to reach way up to get hold of the plow handles, and I had to take great big steps to keep up walking behind ol' Tom as he made the furrows.

Later on, in addition to Tom, we had two other mules—Barney and Jack. For a long time Barney was the closest thing I had to a horse, and it was on him I first learned to ride. I used to ride him everywhere. I'm not ashamed to say that Barney was my best friend back in the holler. We went everywhere together. But thinking about him also reminds me of one of the worst moments of my childhood. As I said, Pop just wasn't a country boy, so he didn't really know his way around animals. He didn't know that when you approach one, you always say a few words so you let the critter know you're coming and you don't spook him. Well, one weekend Pop had come home from Portsmouth and he wandered into the barn around feedin' time. All of a sudden I heard this awful hollerin' and I rushed into the barn and saw him rollin' on the ground holding his knee. He was squirtin' blood and the clear liquid that holds your knee joint in place. Barney had been busy eating his dinner when Pop walked up behind him and surprised him. That ol' mule just hauled off and kicked him square in the knee. I knelt down and wrapped Pop's leg up real tight with rags and we were able to get him to the hospital where they sewed up his leg and managed to save it.

Pop's injury was bad enough, but what followed has made me ashamed of myself for years. When I got back from the hospital I stormed into the barn, picked up a pitchfork, and stuck it right into Barney's butt. Looking back on it all, I knew ol' Barney hadn't acted mean; he was just being a mule. But at the time I was so mad at him for hurting my father that I just lost my senses. I don't know if mules accept apologies but I often think I owe one to Barney.

In the country, you're real close to animals. I learned to track raccoons and to know every bird in the woods by its call. I had a pet skunk, a groundhog, and a rooster that I trained to sit on my shoulder and crow. If there was ever a sick or injured animal out there, I couldn't help but bring it home and see what I could do for it. One time I found a puppy with a broken leg—must've been abandoned—that I took home and tried to fix up. I made her a splint, fixed her a bed from an old quilt, and fed her warm milk. After some time, I unwrapped the leg and the puppy stepped free. The bone had mended, but the pup still walked with a limp. After that happened, I decided that rather than become a dentist, I ought to be a doctor so I could fix a puppy's broken leg right.

Living on the farm I learned how to hunt. Not the fancy kind of sport hunting rich folks do with beautiful rifles and such. This was hunting to eat. A lot of people don't understand that for country folks like us, dinner was what you see in the iron sights of your .22. Before I got a rifle, though, I whittled myself a slingshot with my old Barlow knife and went out each day to try to catch a rabbit or a squirrel. If I got one, we ate real well that night; if not, supper was beans and cornbread. I believe my early training with that slingshot is why I always had a good aim. I fashioned a bow, too, and got pretty sharp with bow-and-arrow hunting, then finally Pop gave me a single-shot rifle. Once I got that rifle, we ate pretty well around the Slye house.

When I wasn't working on the farm I was at school—a little schoolhouse where children from the first through the eighth grades were taught. I don't recall there being more than four or five kids in class, and no matter how far away they lived, everybody walked to school. Most of the boys wore overalls, white shirts rolled up to the elbows, and tweed newsboy caps on their heads.

School was the first place I recall having to fight for my rights, and my adversary was, of all people, my teacher. I was a skinny little eleven-year-old when I had a teacher who was a pistol if ever there was one. He wouldn't touch the girls in class, but partner, he'd give it to us boys. He beat us up every day. You didn't have to do anything to get beat up either— just show up for school. I grew pretty tired of going home every day covered with welts and bruises, so one day it all came to a head. During recess a girl in the class threw my cap up in the air and it landed on the school roof. To get back at her, I grabbed her hat and threw it up there, too. She went running in and got the teacher, who came out and started yelling at me to get her hat down. I believe in fair play, so I said, "I'm not going to get her hat until she gets mine." I stood my ground as he glared at me. Finally I scrambled up on the roof, grabbed the girl's hat, and went running with it to a little creek behind the school. I waded in and held the hat out for him in the middle of the stream, calling, "Come and git it!" He turned red with rage and stormed back into the schoolhouse. A few seconds later, out he came with a wooden switch eight feet long, waving it at me in a fury. He waded into the water and got in one good lick. I reached down, picked up a rock, and let him have it—but good.

I regret having come to blows with him, but after that day, he stopped picking on me. Without a father living at home and no brothers, I had to learn at a young age to settle my own fights. The funny thing is that when I was no longer skinny little Len Slye, but Roy Rogers the movie star, wouldn't you know that one day when I was performing in front of a big crowd back in Ohio, I looked out and there was that same teacher who had made my life so miserable standing there waiting for an autograph. He looked at me kind of shyly, and said, "Well, Len, I heard you were in town."

"I'm glad you're here," I told him. "I'm sorry about what happened back then." We shook hands and I signed a picture for him. I'm glad I saw him again. It took all those years of hate out of my mind.

Life in Duck Run wasn't all work and school. I had lots of fun, too, but it was a different kind of fun than kids have nowadays. In that time before video games and trips to Disney World, families made their own fun. For the Slye family, about the most fun we could have together was singing. My whole family was musical. Pop played the mandolin and mother played guitar, and my sisters and I all joined in. On weekends when Pop was home, we made harmony long into the night. Sometimes on a Friday night, we all went to the square dance—even Mom, though she had such a hard time walking. I was shy, but when the music played, I didn't feel so bashful. Pretty soon I learned how to call the dances. I loved to call, "Swing your partner, do-si-do, and allemande left!"

I think one of the best things that I ever did when I was young was join the 4-H Club. That happened thanks to a teacher I had named Guy Baumgartner. He was just the opposite of the teacher I had the fracas with—one of the kindest, most caring people I ever met up with. Just looking at him made me feel good, as he always had a smile on his face, and he had a way of making even schoolwork seem like fun. Two weeks after he got there, he had all us kids eating out of his hand. He had heard about the trouble we were having with that other schoolteacher, so he was extra nice. He started a baseball team and a basketball team and used to take us kids out on nature walks, pointing out different creatures that we saw. I loved that! He also started a 4-H Club, which he encouraged me to join.

Mr. Baumgartner, or Guy as he preferred his students to call him, suggested that we buy baby pigs and raise them for our pig club. I got myself a newborn black baby pig, named her Evangeline, and raised her up as well as I could. To get her ready for the Scioto County Fair in Lucasville, Ohio, I had to hold her in my lap, which was fun. I brushed her until she shone like ebony and I manicured her toenails. I guess I did a pretty good job because Evangeline took the grand prize. That included a trip to the state capital—Columbus, Ohio—which was farther away from home than I had ever imagined going.

When Mr. Baumgartner came to pick me up to leave for the trip, I nearly didn't get out of the house for all the worrying my family did. Each of my sisters gave me ten kisses apiece and my mom was hugging me so tight I could hardly breathe. I remember Mr. Baumgartner out on the porch, calling, "Hurry up, Len, or we'll never get to Columbus!" Finally, I was hugged and kissed enough by all the ladies in the family to satisfy them, and away we went. That was some adventure, let me tell you. I got to see the Ohio State University and the Ohio State Penitentiary all in one day. At the old Neil House Hotel, I encountered the first elevator I ever saw. I spent nearly the whole first day we were there riding up and down in it, amazed.

I liked farming and it kept me plenty busy, but I had other interests, too. I played the clarinet a little; I liked sports, especially baseball, and for a while there, I thought I might have a future as a pitcher. Because he thought it would help me get over my shyness, Guy Baumgartner encouraged me to try out for the school play. To my horror and dismay I was cast as Santa Claus, which meant I had to stand up in front of a crowd of people patting my padded belly and saying, "Ho, ho, ho!" As if that weren't bad enough, I then had to sing a little song about Santa heaping the stockings high and carrying toys in a sack on his back. You would have thought I had to deliver a Shakespearean speech, I was so terrified with stage fright. My knees knocked, my teeth chattered, and my mind went blank with panic trying to remember what I was supposed to say. I guess I did manage to croak out the words and the tune and made it through the play, but if anyone told me back then that I would make my fame and fortune as an actor I would have laughed out loud. Nothing could have seemed less likely.

Christmas at home with the family was a wonderful time. We didn't have much money for presents, so I whittled little things out of wood for my sisters and my folks. I made whistles and little boxes for their knickknacks, and we all got together to make ornaments for the tree out of paper and cardboard and strings laced through popcorn and cranberries. We found our tree in the woods out back of our house, and I went out and killed a chicken (Dad never could do that), which Mom cooked up with vegetables she had put up during the fall.

Pop was thrifty, a trait I inherited from him along with squinty eyes. But he could also be mighty kind. The best gift he ever got me was a horse when I was eleven years old. Her name was Babe and she was a little ex-sulky racer. Boy, was I in seventh heaven; I thought I had me a race horse! First time I got on, Babe threw me onto the seat of my pants. But I dusted myself off and tried again, and soon enough we were a team. I even taught her a few tricks, like saying yes and no and bowing, and I was convinced she was the smartest animal on earth. After a while, I learned to ride Babe from Duck Run into Portsmouth, where I visited my father. When he had an extra dime, sometimes he gave it to me so I could see a movie. That's where I saw my first Western, one starring Hoot Gibson in his tall Stetson hat. It was fun to watch Hoot's adventures, but I never imagined myself a movie cowboy. The wild West seemed just pure fantasy, and my own future was too far off to think about. My main concerns in those days were sleeping as late as I wanted and eating as much as I could eat and riding my horse as fast as she could go.

Even with Babe to boost my ego, my skills with girls were dismal. I fell in love with pretty ones from afar but was too afraid to speak to them. When I did manage to muster the courage to go out on a date, my conversation skills were pretty much limited to saying yes or no while I looked down at my feet. I've always been that way, and I guess I still am.

Even after all those years in Hollywood, having my face plastered on a million posters and lunchboxes, I still get bashful around people. I'm fine with kids and with horses and animals, and of course with my family, but when I have to be with strangers, I still feel a little like that bashful kid trying to be Santa Claus in the school play.

Despite the good memories I have when I think about my childhood, it wouldn't be true to say that life on the farm in Duck Run was as perfect as a Norman Rockwell picture. Sure, it's easy to look back on those times and think of the good fun and family togetherness we enjoyed and to forget that we tilled the fields and worked that land until our bodies ached, and that no matter how hard we struggled, we always seemed to come up short financially. Pop grew weary of commuting to see us, and the weeks without him at home were lonely and long. My dream of becoming a dentist or a doctor seemed more impossible each year. By the time I graduated from the eighth grade in Duck Run there was no place else there for me to go, so I had to travel four miles each day to a high school in the town of Mc-Dermott, where I studied as a freshman and sophomore.

When I was seventeen I made a decision that my mother dreaded, but ultimately went along with. I quit school. The whole family moved back to Cincinnati, and I got a job alongside my father there at the U.S. Shoe Company, working in the insole department. I was earning about twenty-five dollars a week, which sure helped pay the bills. To appease my mother I agreed to go to night school. But working all day and going to school at night were more than I could handle. I remember the shame I felt during a class session when I was so exhausted I rested my head in my arms for what I thought was a moment, only to wake up to find the classroom empty and the class long over.

Life had come full circle, and not for the good: I was back again in Cincinnati, making parts for somebody else's shoes.

Pop and I both were older, not much wiser, and certainly not any richer. My sister Cleda had married and she and her husband were living back on the farm in Duck Run. My older sister Mary had also gotten married and she had moved to California. Her letters to us made California seem like another world, and each day as Dad and I hunched over the machinery in that grimy factory, her picture of a sunny Promised Land out West filled our heads. Dad's health was starting to suffer. Never one to complain, he developed bad headaches when it came time to go to work in the morning; and there were some mornings when he just couldn't get out of bed.

I had never been west of Ohio. The closest I had ever come to knowing about the West at all was from a little crystal radio set I had fooled around with on the farm in Duck Run, where sometimes I could pick up some cowboy singing about "home on the range." And I had seen maybe half a dozen cowboy movies back in Portsmouth. But all of that could have been life on Mars as much as it affected me. Still, I began to think: if the family could go out West, maybe Pop and I could find jobs driving trucks in California. We would have it made!

Early one morning in 1930, I watched Mom pressing a damp cloth to Pop's aching head as we were getting ready to go to work. He was gray-faced and sad. As I looked at him, I thought of the small bundle of bills I had managed to stash away from work. I was eighteen and eager for a change. "Dad, I have ninety dollars saved," I said. "I bet you've got at least a hundred. Why don't we head out to see Mary in California? Look around, see what's there?"

Watching Pop's face was like seeing the hands of a clock tick backwards. His headache faded away, his eyes grew bright again. We began to pack that very day, loading up the family's old rattletrap 1923 Dodge for the long trek out West. The Joads in *The Grapes of Wrath* or the Beverly Hillbillies had nothing on us Slyes as we hit the highway. You never saw such a rotten-looking vehicle, piled to the top with rickety junk. About the only precious things we had to our names were our dreams, which were bright enough to keep us heading west toward the setting sun.

CHAPTER 2
Dale's Story

Little girls dream fantastic things. When I was young, I used to sit by the banks of the Nueces River in South Texas and dream that Tom Mix would marry me. Old Tom was the greatest movie cowboy of his day—so handsome and tall in his glittering silver saddle. He was everybody's hero; adults admired him and children adored him. Saturday afternoon we went to the picture show where I watched him ride the wild West with his trick horse, Tony. I worried terribly for them when they got in trouble; I cheered for them when they saved the day; and I ached for Tom to be mine. He was a full-grown man, but that didn't matter to this wide-eyed little Texas girl. I was quite certain he would wait for me to grow up, and that he would never change. I was going to make him mine. We would have six children together, then gallop our horses through the sagebrush, and the world would be as sweet as it could be.

I never met Tom Mix. A lot of things have happened in my life that I sure never expected when I was a girl of five sitting by that easy-flowing river. There have been more tears and pain than any young child could possibly imagine. But I'm not here to complain or to tell you of my disillusionments. Because, you know, as things turned out, that crazy South Texas dream about my handsome cowboy hero and all those kids we'd raise and the happy trails we would ride together really did come true.

It took me a long time to wake up, and I am not talking about my spiritual state of mind. I am talking about being born. My mother used to say I spent my whole life making up for the first three days after I came into this world. It was in my grandparents' home in Uvalde, west of San Antonio—in those days women didn't go to the hospital to have a child—and the doctor had given my mother an anesthesia called "twilight sleep" to help her through her labor. Trouble was, it not only knocked her out, but me, too. On October 31, 1912, I was born sleepy—deathly sleepy. For three days after my birth, I did not cry or make a sound. My parents, Walter and Betty Sue Smith, began to worry that I wasn't right. But when I came to, I made enough of a racket to let the world know I was fine. Since then no one has ever accused me of being the quiet type.

I was born Frances Octavia Smith. Being the first grand-child in my mother's family, I never lacked for attention. Six loving aunts doted on me. My uncle Byron and aunt Annie Merle had no children of their own, so when I visited them it was a special occasion. They had a ranch—acres and acres of South Texas paradise, or so it seemed to me. Visiting them was so romantic. All of Texas seemed like a grand romance in those days—so wild and free. I rode forever on their land. If there was a pony around, I rode that; if not, I found a goat to ride. I rode anything I could get astraddle. And when I wasn't riding across the plains or toward the foothills of the Anacacho Mountains, I swam the Nueces, which was so clear you could see the fish below and the rocks at the bottom.

I worshiped my uncle Byron. But of course I did: he was the kind of man I have always liked—good-looking, strong-willed, and courteous. He was a gentleman in a cowboy hat, a Texan through and through. I remember to this day what a great coffee drinker he was. He drank it all day long in little demitasse cups, and he liked it STRONG. "Texas style," he called it: "Too thick to drink and too wet to plow." My aunt was a fabulous cook; she had graduated from Columbia University in New York with a degree as a dietician. But she used to make her chili the way Texans like it—with beans on the side. Uncle Byron took a handful of those red-hot Mexican peppers they used to grow—real gut-busters—and chopped them up over his beans. Hot peppers and black coffee, for pity's sake! Now, he was a rugged individual.

One relative I think I take after—for better and for worse —is my great-grandfather. He was a man who went his own way and stood on his own two feet, no matter what. I remember him when he got old and his eyesight became so poor that he couldn't see across the front porch. Still, he never let anyone drive him to Wednesday night prayer meetings. He was going to make it on his own, don't you know! He walked straight down the middle of the street, leaning on his cane. Even when he did something completely crazy (which he did aplenty!), you couldn't help but admire the man's grit. There was one time he decided to pause in his walk about town smack in the middle of the railroad track just as a train was about to pull out of the station. The brakeman got down and asked if he would kindly move, but for reasons known only to the old man and to God, he refused. He didn't budge until the brakeman fetched the stationmaster, who was a good friend of Great-grandfather's, and the stationmaster finally convinced him to saunter off the track. I remember him reaching out with that cane of his to hook me about the neck and pull me close. I complained and said I didn't like him doing it, but if I could talk to him today, I would tell him that I knew it was a loving gesture all along, and deep inside I appreciated his affection. The man had backbone, if you know what I mean.

My father lived on a farm that belonged to my grandfather. He and my mother's brother ran a hardware store in Italy, which is about forty miles south of Dallas, and which used to call itself "the biggest little town in Texas." When it came time for my brother to be born, three years after me, my dad decided to take me back down to Uvalde, which I liked so much, and where I wouldn't be in the way when the new baby was brought to the house. Aunt Annie Merle was coming through by train on her way back there, so we went down to the railroad station in horse and buggy, me dressed in my Sunday best for the trip. But it was raining like mad, and when it rains in Texas, the mud is something else. The earth turns to glue. We slogged through the knee-deep muck, and finally I stood in the rain with my dad, holding his hand, waiting eagerly for Aunt Annie to whisk me down to the ranch I adored. I was thrilled when I saw the huge headlight barreling down the tracks from afar and I heard the train whistle blow. My dad lifted me up in his arms. He was going to hand me to my aunt in the observation car when the train stopped for water. The train *always* stopped in Italy for water. But the rain had slowed its schedule down, and that conductor had no intention of stopping. The engine barreled through the station, its whistle shrieking like a banshee, and I remember one short glimpse of my aunt standing there with her arms outstretched as my dad held me up. He told me that he thought for a moment that he might be able to throw me into her arms as she sped past, but the train was moving too fast. As I watched my aunt recede into the distance I let out a wail and squalled all night long. The next day my dad got on the train and took me to Uvalde himself.

At first I loved my little brother Hillman, who was named after the founder of Hillman College, the Baptist school where my father had been educated. Because he was the firstborn boy, Hillman was always known as Son; even when he was middle-aged, my grandkids used to call him Uncle Son. Soon, though, I learned to hate him. I had been queen of the castle up until my little brother's arrival, and all of a sudden I had to share my empire with this squirt (who, adding insult to injury, used to fight with me because he considered Hoot Gibson a better cowboy than Tom Mix). I soon became convinced that the little devil was going to steal all my parents' and grandparents' affection. There was only one solution: I ran away from home. At the age of four, I would fend for myself in the wilds. My grandmother caught up with me in a wooded glen behind the farmhouse and tanned my hide with a switch.

That whipping didn't cure me of my sorrows; it only convinced me that I wasn't loved, and that all hope was lost. One day when my parents were too busy pampering *him* to pay sufficient attention to me, I decided to abandon the human race altogether and join the family of newborn pigs we kept behind our house. There I cuddled in among the piglets, soothing my grief, oblivious to the mother sow who was eyeing me with increasing curiosity and suspicion. When, finally, my parents missed me, my father came looking and found me in the pigpen. He stepped ever-so-gingerly toward me, realizing that the wary mother was beginning to feel protective about her litter, which by now included me. Praying that neither I nor any of the little porkers would squeal before he could lift me away from the glare of the fierce mother's eyes, he scooped me up and out of harm's way. He hugged me with relief, which was, I suppose, what I had been after all along; but then he took me across his knee for a firm laying on of hands—the kind that has nothing to do with religious spirit.

I was a born show-off. If ever I got a new dress, I would pirouette through the house in it, and I used to burst into song recitals at the slightest provocation. At Sunday School, I was far more interested in what the other little girls were wearing than in the lessons. I remember coming home one Sunday when I was especially proud of a new dress I was wearing. My father asked me what I had learned about Jesus in school. "Oh, he wasn't there today," I said, thinking of how nice I had looked. In church, I couldn't help swishing my skirts with glee during the gospel singing, and on some occasions I got so carried away with the spirit of the occasion that I danced wildly down the aisles, singing gospel *a cappella* and showing off my pirouettes and pretty dress. I loved to dance, which is something I must have inherited from my father. He loved to dance, but was forbidden by his religion. Visits to my grandparents' house in Centerville, Mississippi, were always rollicking fun. The floorboards in that old place literally rocked with laughter and fun. And yet it's strange: my father's family were strict Baptists, and if you asked them, they would tell you that they frowned on frivolous dancing, particularly in church. How well I remember after one of my impromptu Sunday morning recitals when my father escorted me next door to the fire station and taught me a lesson about vanity via my backside.

Music was always in my soul, and performing came naturally. I was encouraged by all my aunts, who had taught me to read, recite, and sing early on. By the time I was five years old, I was reading everything I could get my hands on, and when I enrolled in school I was so precocious that I skipped half the first grade and all of second. At home, when one of the aunts gave me a new dress or hat (which was often!), I put it on and danced around reciting poems and stories I had learned. At any family gathering, all the relatives used to delight in coming up to me and saying, "Frances, recite something." I thrived on these command performances—a born ham. One year when I had just learned "The Night Before Christmas," I went around repeating it to anyone who would listen. Over and over and over: I recited it so much that my brother finally got a bellyful. I was getting all the attention, as usual, so one evening he stood up and announced to all my aunts and uncles, "Hush! Let Bubba talk!" My mother said, "All right now, everybody be quiet. Frances, you sit down. We will now let Son talk." Well, Son got up and took a deep breath and, loud and forceful as you please, proclaimed, "SPEECH, SPEECH, SPEECH!" then sat down, satisfied that everyone had paid attention to him for once. He was a terrific, terrific boy.

My dad was one of those men who always believed the grass was greener somewhere else, so when I was seven he turned the farm in Italy back to my grandfather, sold his interest in the hardware store, and set off for Osceola, Arkansas, on the banks of the Mississippi River. His brother already lived there in a big, two-story house, and he had convinced my pop that he would enjoy the sure-fire profits of long staple cotton-growing if he moved there to join him. Dad took the money that he'd gotten from the hardware store and sank it all into a farm. Unfortunately, that year it rained . . . and it rained, and it rained—it rained all year long. Levees broke, and the fields turned into mud. Boll weevils ate the cotton, and I remember the evening sky turning dark with swarms of mosquitoes. It was the worst crop ever, and we lost everything.

Still, I have fond memories of living in our little frame house in the country between Osceola and Luxora, Arkansas. We had no electricity, and my brother and I had very few toys, but we found our fun in simple things. How well I recall the smell of the rich earth. I can see my little brother and me playing with a black boy and his sister, the children of the tenant farmers on the place my dad had rented. I had a garden planted with mustard greens, onions, and radishes. I got a toy iron stove and a little iron pot, and my brother and I and those two children would build a fire and cook our greens and our produce over it. It smoked like the devil, but the aroma was heavenly. Then the four of us ate our children's meals together, just like grown-ups. We had such a good time. But when company came to their house or to our house, we had to break up the fun and go our separate ways.

None of us knew why, because we were children, but neither their parents nor ours wanted the company to see us playing together. Oh, I used to be furious about this and I would argue with my dad no end. "When you're older, you will understand," he told me. I'm eighty-one, and I still don't understand. But that's just the way my father had been raised. In Mississippi segregation was a way of life. He allowed that it might be all right to play with the little colored children outdoors, but never inside.

One time I was at the barber shop—in those days, little girls got their hair cut by the barber, just like little boys, a bob with bangs in the front—and the barber parted my hair and said to my father, "Mr. Smith, come here, I think you ought to see this." He showed my father that I had little nits crawling on my scalp. Well, my daddy stormed home and said to my mother, "See, I told you not to let them play with the colored children." But it turned out that it wasn't the colored children's fault at all. I had spent the night with a little white girl the week before. I had borrowed her cap, and gotten the head lice from her. Her parents confirmed this, and don't you know I sure never let my dad forget that!

My Arkansas cousins lived in a big house where we used to chase each other up and down the great stairway and wrestle in the front hall. Their cook, Liney, was a very religious woman who didn't know how to read or write, so she had my cousin Quentin read the Bible to her every day. At night, when she went to bed he sat beside her and read Scripture as she nodded and "Amen'd" and cried, "Yes, Lord!" to the great truths of the Book. I didn't know it then, but this woman, with her deep and unabashed spiritual feelings, had a profound influence on me and on all us children growing up. Many years after I left the Deep South, Liney was found dead on her knees by the side of her bed. She had died in prayer. I always thought that was the way she would have wanted to pass on.

My first-grade teacher, Miss Blanche, had a paddle. And if one of us sassed her or misbehaved, believe me, she *used* it! Every day she lined up the class scoundrels in a row and applied it—not brutally, but strong enough so we remembered . . . and behaved. I was cautious to avoid becoming a career criminal in that class, but on one occasion I was called into the lineup—I don't recall exactly why—and I was a clever enough girl that I managed to talk myself out of a beating. "Miss Blanche," I said in a fearful voice, "if you spank me, I'll have to tell my parents that you spanked me, which means I will get another spanking when I get home!" She took pity on me, and she hung up her paddle. What relief I felt that day! But in retrospect, I wonder if it wouldn't have been better if she had gone ahead and applied the paddle. It might have taught me a lesson I sorely needed to learn. Acting on impulse was becoming a bad habit with me, as it is for so many children; in my case, it got me into trouble fast and at an early age.

My mother used to say I was "born grown" because I was so impatient to grow up. I wanted adventure! I wanted to see the world and be sophisticated. I was aggressive, smart, and extroverted—too much so for my own good. Skipping early grades put me with older children, and I think because of that I missed some of the easygoing times of childhood. I loved music so much that I started piano lessons when I was eight years old, but soon I grew impatient with them, too— all those boring scales and exercises—and I began improvising my own compositions. This drove my poor teacher to distraction until finally she informed my parents that she could no longer teach me anything and stalked out of the house. From that point on, I played by ear, turning to voice to express myself musically. My first public solo was in church. I sang "In the Garden," accompanied by the organist. In high school we had a band in which girls played ukuleles and I played piano: "Five-foot-two, eyes of blue . . ." That kind of fast jazz song was more to my liking then.

I had a nervous breakdown when I was eleven years old. I had skipped another grade—the seventh—and the pressures to do well in school as well as extracurricular activities took their toll. I collapsed, physically, and I was compelled to spend a whole summer in bed recuperating. But even this enforced idleness didn't do a thing to slow me down. My stars, I wanted to do *everything*. I wanted to be a singer, I wanted to be a dancer, I wanted to be an artist—I used to draw and paint, you know, free-style—and I think most of all I wanted to be an actress. I wanted to do anything that involved performing. But my family wanted me to be a piano teacher or an elementary school teacher. Oh, no, that wasn't nearly enough for me!

At the age of twelve I was a freshman in high school but too young to attend the public dances at the town courthouse in Osceola with a date. I looked and acted older than I was, and boys asked me out, but my parents wouldn't allow me to accept their offers. What I did was this: I managed to cajole my mother into becoming a chaperone, which meant I could go to the dances with her. Everyone in town was there, and once the music started I could dance to my heart's delight. At age thirteen I had my hair permed and borrowed a dress with a pouf of real ostrich feathers from my aunt Rose, and I felt like a grown-up.

It was at one of the courthouse dances that I met my first steady boyfriend, Thomas Fox, from the neighboring town. Tom was dashing and handsome with dark, serious eyes. And he was so mature in my young eyes—all of eighteen years old, with a Chrysler roadster. My, how we used to do the Charleston! I loved dancing with Tom. Soon we went everywhere together. When my parents realized what was going on they forbade me to see him. An old bachelor uncle of mine offered to send me to Switzerland to study music to get my mind off teenage romance. But it was too late to reel me in. Rebellion flared in my soul; Tom and I met secretly at friends' homes. One night, when I was supposed to be rehearsing an operetta at school—I had a leading part because of my high, almost lyric soprano voice—we eloped. Tom had gotten a marriage license by lying about our ages. We were married in a Baptist minister's home. I broke a lot of hearts that night; I was young and thoughtless. Afterwards, we sped across the state line in his roadster to Tom's mother's house in Humboldt, Tennessee. We spent our honeymoon there— one weekend with his mother and his aunt. I was fourteen years old. We then moved in with my husband's father and stepmother.

When I was fifteen, I had a baby: Tom Jr. We were living in Memphis at the time. We had moved there from Blytheville when I was pregnant, and for the first time in his life, Tom worked for someone other than his father. I didn't know anything about keeping house, I didn't know anything about *anything.* I would try to cook for us, but it was awful: lumpy cream gravy, burnt hamburgers. I tried, I did the best I could, but I wasn't much more than a child myself. Tom had to sell his car to pay the bills, and he grew very resentful. We moved back to Blytheville where he could work in his father's dry-cleaning operation, but that didn't help the situation for him. One spring day, when the baby was six and a half months old, Tom's brother and his brother's wife took me to visit my mother, who now lived in Memphis. It was Easter time. They said they would come back in a week to pick me up and bring me home. I was supremely happy that Easter. Tom Jr. was such a pretty little boy, and I was with my mother. But three days later I got a letter from my husband in which he wrote that we were too young to be married, and he needed to be free. He said we should get a divorce. It broke my heart. I was stricken. It felt like I was being killed. I wasn't yet sixteen years old.

My mother, bless her heart, agreed to help raise Tom. She even suggested she adopt him, freeing me to be young again.

But I couldn't do that, not even for my mother. Still, as Tom learned to speak he called her Mom. Me, he called Sassie because "Frances" was too difficult for the little boy to pronounce. As a baby he had such severe ear problems that for a while we thought we might lose him. They operated and my mother stayed up two days and two nights with little Tom, applying icepacks to keep the swelling down. I believe he might have lost his life if it weren't for her.

I had no diploma, but my grades had been good, so at age sixteen and a half I was able to enroll in business school. I soon got a job as a secretary in an insurance firm. My boss was the claims agent, and my job was filling out and filing forms. Far more interested in show business than in the insurance business, I spent a great deal of time at my desk writing. First I tried short stories, but the rejection slips flooded in; then I tried song writing, which was easier. In fact, one time I personally took a song I wrote to a Memphis publisher and sang it to him. He said it had possibilities and he would consider publishing it. "Leave the music with me," he said, "and I will get back to you with a decision." I was thrilled. I waited months to hear from him. Then one day when I was in a Memphis music store I saw my tune in sheet music—only slightly altered—with the name of someone else on the music as composer. I was miserable; nothing was going right.

I sat at my desk alone in the office one day with an accident claim form in the typewriter and my hands resting idle on the keyboard. I was thinking, but not about the form; I was trying to come up with lyrics for a tune I had just composed. As I thought, I started singing. I didn't notice my boss walk in. He stood there awhile, listening to me and watching the accident report form gathering dust in front of me, then he exploded. "Miss Fox, what *are* you doing?" he demanded. Shaken from my creative reverie, I flew to the keyboard and my fingers began moving like mad. "What are you doing?" he asked again. I admitted that I was trying to write lyrics for a song. "You sing well," he said. I assumed I was about to be fired.

"I love to sing," I confessed. "I've always loved to sing."

"How would you like to sing on the radio?" he asked.

You're kidding me, I thought.

"I have an interest in a paper stock company on a local station and we sponsor a fifteen-minute program every Friday night. If you can accompany yourself on the piano, I would like you to sing for me. I think, Miss Fox, you are in the wrong business."

Trumpets blared! Bells rang! The heavens opened before my very eyes! That Friday night, Frances Fox made her radio debut. I sang the old song "Mighty Lak a Rose," dedicated to my little son. I was elated when the station offered me a regular spot on a thirty-minute weekly program. Listeners phoned in requests and I sang whatever they wanted, dedicated to whoever they named. Within a few months, I moved up to WMC, the big commercial station in town. I was on the air with a sports announcer named Bucky Harris. Between his sports reports and commentary, I sang and played the piano.

Civic organizations invited me to perform at luncheons and banquets. Some of them paid—as much as twenty dollars from the well-to-do groups; for most such performances, though, the pay was in chicken croquettes and peas. I welcomed it all; it was a great experience. I learned to perform in public, in front of all kinds of people. In the evenings I often went with a date to dances on the roof of the Peabody Hotel. This was a very chic and cosmopolitan venue—the heart of social life in the mid-South—and I thought I was quite the sophisticate just going there. Sometimes, when the big dance bands came to town, I would be invited up to join them. I sang through a big old megaphone, like Rudy Vallee, and I was in seventh heaven. Soon I went to the local CBS station—WREC, which broadcast from the Peabody Hotel—and I got my own half-hour program. My name was up there. I was in popular demand. I was somebody.

Still, I wasn't making enough money as a singer to get by, so I kept a day job. I was employed by Clarence Saunders, founder of Piggly-Wiggly, which was a kind of novelty back then—the first self-service grocery store. One day I walked out of the office with the other girls on our way to lunch and there was Tom, my husband, sitting in his car, waiting for me.

"Frances," he called out, "come here. I want to talk to you."

I left the girls and went over to the car. I hadn't seen him or heard from him in months.

"See if you can get off work this afternoon," he said. "Let's go over to the State Theater, let's catch a show."

I was dumbstruck. Our divorce wasn't yet final, but it was about to be. What was he doing there?

"Frances, come back to me," he said.

I loved him very much. I never had stopped loving him, even when I felt abandoned. And for a few hours that day, I *was* going to go back to him. In the evening I went home to prepare to leave. I was planning to slip out of the house at midnight, taking little Tom with me, and meet my husband on the corner. Long about twilight that day, I looked at my mother and I looked at that little boy, and I began to weep. I knew that mother would always be there. If I faltered, she would stand by my side. I thought about how much she had done for me, and how she had stayed with the boy day and night when he needed her, and I made a decision. When Tom called at twelve o'clock, I told him I wasn't going with him. It was tough, but it was the right thing to do. For little Tom, and for me.

I had made it to the top in Memphis, and I therefore reasoned that I could succeed in a bigger market, too. So I set off to conquer Chicago. I started as a file clerk at Goodyear—

their biggest branch, on the South Side. Remember, these were horrendous times, the height of the Depression. While I was there the banks closed, people were jumping out of windows on LaSalle Street in Chicago just as they did on Wall Street in New York. I was making twenty-five dollars a week doing all the filing for the branch. My salary went for rent, a babysitter to watch Tom when he came home from school, heavy coats to protect us from a kind of winter we had never known, and food. It was a struggle to make ends meet.

I took the electric train in from the South Side to the office, which was a huge set of filing cabinets arranged like a horseshoe, two stories high. I filed upstairs and downstairs, up and down all day long. I also relieved the switchboard operator for one hour at lunch and in the morning and afternoon; we had fourteen lines coming in and fifty interoffice lines. And I took dictation from five men including the operating manager, who traveled to universities and interviewed young men who wanted to get into the rubber industry. Whenever I had a free moment, I went to auditions, but nothing seemed to click. No matter how hard I tried, I couldn't make the grade as a performer. Not in Chicago. My mother came to help with Tom, but after a while she went back down to be with the family in Texas.

I was nineteen, working hard, with bleak prospects as a singer. Not long after my mother left us, my health broke. There simply wasn't enough food, so I had been depriving myself to feed Tom, and I was under such pressure at my job and going to auditions that I developed malnutrition and something close to pernicious anemia. My hemoglobin was just zilch, nothing. I applied for health insurance and they turned me down flat. They said, "You're a sick woman. You'd better take care of this or you'll die." So for the first time in my life, I asked my mother for money. I had come to crack Chicago, but Chicago had cracked me.

We were a miserable pair, Tommy and I, as we rode the train back to Texas. I couldn't stand up without feeling dizzy. Two weeks in the hospital on liver and iron, then three months' rest on the family farm had me on my feet again. When I left home this time I went to Louisville, where I managed to land my first job with really good pay, at station WHAS. My mother wanted Tommy to stay behind with her on the farm, but I insisted he come with me.

When I first went to WHAS, I auditioned using the stage name Marion Lee. A lot of women were using Lee or Leigh or Marion at the time, and I thought it sounded rather glamorous. But the station manager called me into his office and said, "Your name is trite! I want you to have something different." So the next morning when I came to work he called me in and told me that my name was Dale Evans.

"Dale Evans?" I said. "Dale is a boy's name! And what does Evans have to do with me?"

"First of all," he said, "the woman I like the most on the screen, in silent pictures, is named Dale. And as for Evans: your name is concocted for radio announcers. It is a very euphonious name. It cannot be mispronounced, and it is hard to misspell it. So, that is your name, Dale Evans." I wasn't very happy, because it wasn't swank and sophisticated, but I must admit, it stuck!

As Dale Evans, I became a featured singer on a program with three boys who were called the Romeos of Song and a radio announcer named Joe Pierson who played piano. We had a five-piece band and we went on the air at six-thirty in the morning. They called us Honey and the Flapjacks. A lot of country people came up from Nashville to be on that program, some, like the Log Cabin Boys, from the Grand Ole Opry. They all performed for free, just to advertise where they were doing a concert that night. Why, sometimes when we did our show we had so many performing guests that the whole corridor outside the studio was lined with guitars as far as you could see. I liked my work, and I liked having a stage name. To me, it was a sign I was on the road to success.

Tommy and I were living in an apartment out of Louisville. One afternoon when I arrived home from work, the lady who had been taking care of him said he had been vomiting most of the day. His arms and legs were wracked by awful pains that made him scream. I turned white with fear. Kentucky was raging with a polio epidemic, which was the most dreaded disease of that era. It struck fear into parents because it crippled and killed thousands of children. Doctors suspected that Tommy had contracted polio, and the only way to know was to put him in the hospital for a spinal tap. The test proved negative; my boy would be all right. Then and there I promised God that I would be a better person, that I would read my Bible every day . . . but I was young, and my musical ambition was stronger than my spiritual devotion, and my promises were soon forgotten.

Bad as the polio scare had been, it took a different kind of fright to send us packing from Louisville. This one happened around Halloween. A friend of mine had a beautiful child for whom she had made a crepe-paper costume covered with ruffles. This little girl went downstairs into the yard where a man was burning autumn leaves. Her dress caught fire. The mother heard screams and looked out the window to see her daughter going up in smoke and flames. She leaped off the second floor to try to rescue her—broke her ankle doing so—but the little girl died on the way to the hospital. At that moment I decided that Tommy needed to be much safer than I had been keeping him. He needed a place that would nurture him . . . and I, once again, needed to restore myself. Back we went to Texas.

How Tommy loved the family farm, and how he thrived with my brother and sister-in-law and the close-knit community of Texans they were part of! He chased chickens until both he and the birds couldn't run anymore. He had a dog, he attended a good school, and he went to church every Sunday. He breathed fresh air and he blossomed with good health. I looked at the roses in his cheeks and for the first time in that boy's young life, I felt secure knowing that he was safe and happy.

As for me, I had no idea when I once again retreated back to Texas to lick my wounds that I was about to see my career take flight. I found a job near home on the staff of radio station WFAA in Dallas, close enough so that I could come home every weekend and be with my family. I was the band singer on a show there called "The Early Birds." We had a big orchestra and two comedians; I sang songs like "Shine On, Harvest Moon" and "Mockingbird Hill." Listeners began to know Dale Evans and to like her. In August 1938, I was the cover girl for *Rural Radio* magazine, which showed "Tune Tumbler Dale Evans" wearing a sunbonnet and a short skirt, dipping my toes in the waters of Turtle Creek in Dallas and holding a fishing pole. *Rural Radio* billed itself as "The Only Magazine Published Exclusively for Rural Listeners," but pretty soon I found myself singing at the Adolphus Hotel with Herman Walman's orchestra and performing at the Meadowbrook Country Club out of St. Louis, Missouri, which was hardly hayseed. I remarried—a pianist and orchestral arranger from WHAS in Louisville. He was on his way to the West Coast. He stopped in Dallas and we were married there. From Dallas, once again I set off to conquer Chicago. This time, I made all the right connections, and before I knew it I was Hollywood bound.

PART II

Leonard and Dale: The Road West

*T*HERE WAS A TIME when to many Americans, California seemed like an exotic place, as foreign and exciting as any land on earth. It was a land of sunshine, clear skies, and purple mountains, of salty surf crashing on pristine unpopulated beaches, of elegant vaqueros riding swift ponies across the ranchlands of the great old Spanish land grants. In the southern part of the state, curious deserts sprouted fascinating palm trees, and even lush palm springs like magical oases from the Rubáiyát of Omar Khayyám. "Health, rest, and beautiful surroundings!" one old brochure promised travelers, singing of the road to Los Angeles as "a modern Arabia . . . a winter wonderland without the winter. The mind pictures it lovingly; the spiritual ear can hear the crisp rattle of the palm leaves in the breeze. And the actual physical viewing is rest and balm to the tired body after the long trek over the desert. To lie at night and watch the moonshine shimmer up and down the leaf blades of the lordly palm trees is like a dream come true."

The Golden State was America's dreamland, and not because the movie colony was there. Hollywood's motion picture business was at most a minor curiosity for the carloads of optimistic families who headed West during the Depression. For those in search of tomorrow, California appeared to be a land of opportunity where, if nothing else, at least there would be salubrious weather and elbow room—relief from the stinking, crowded cities of the East or the barren Dust Bowl of the Plains. It was the fertility of the land, not the glitter of bright lights, that attracted them. In California, even the deserts blossomed with rainbows of wildflowers and trees heavy with sweet dates!

It was in the 1930s that Route 66 became known as the Mother Road, on which thousands of families who had left their old lives behind took flight with the dream of finding open space to live and clean air to breathe and good work that didn't kill your soul. For many wiped out by hard times, it was a desperate journey—their only hope. The Slye family wasn't that bad off. They had a home back in Ohio, and they had jobs. But they wanted more. Andy Slye was a man who had always wanted more, and when his daughter's letters told him of the wonders of the West, he was ready to make the trip. The Slyes headed West just to visit and look around, they told themselves, but like so many who felt the promise of California when it was young, its charms proved irresistible. For young Leonard, whose greatest travel experience had been a week in a hotel in Columbus, Ohio, and all the elevator rides he could stand, the long journey along Route 66 to the land of milk and honey was as thrilling as a trip to Shangri-la.

Dale Evans's California dreaming had been of movies: of her girlhood hero, Tom Mix. But by the time she was a teenager, silver-screen cowboys had been relegated to a childhood memory. For this ambitious girl, the West was not an exotic location, it was home; and her fantasies were of the sophisticated East, of Broadway's bright lights and a world far from West Texas dust and California sunshine.

For most Americans, the idea of heading West was an exciting one, and not only because of the Great Depression. The very idea of leaving old ways behind and following the sun has enthralled this nation since it began. That's what the frontier is all about—starting fresh, in a new land, free of all restrictions and the burdens of the past. It's the greatest American dream: to shuck your old life and find a new one, just over the horizon. Leonard Slye of Duck Run, Ohio, and Frances Smith of Uvalde, Texas, thought they were headed in opposite directions, but they were both on their way to California to reinvent themselves.

—J. & M. S.

CHAPTER 3

Roy's Story

The old Dodge sputtered to a halt in Magdalena, New Mexico. It had been choking and bucking its way across country for the whole trip, and we kept fixing it with parts from a junker car that we found in a yard and towed behind us nearly the whole way. Traveling out West during the Depression sure wasn't what travel is like today. It was long before well-paved superhighways; Route 66 was nothing but a two-lane road, and if your car broke down, you had to hope you found a part somewhere to patch it up. Along the way there weren't any comfy motels or nice restaurants. And even if there had been, the likes of the Slye family couldn't have afforded them. No, at night when it came time to bed down, we pulled far off the road, laid our blankets on the ground by the side of the car, and slept under the stars.

I'll tell you one thing, though: we weren't alone. Along the way we met dozens of families just like us, fleeing the Dust Bowl or some other misery, heading for the Golden State and hoping for something better, their old jalopies piled high with everything they owned. I remember how much those other families looked like us, too—hungry, tired, their clothes dusty from the long road, their shoes patched near as much as some old quilt. It had been exhilarating to leave Ohio on a bright June day, but once we got out onto the broad prairies and plains of the Southwest, we started feeling mighty puny against this big land. California sure seemed far away.

It took more than two long weeks to make the trip, and by the time we got to Lawndale, where my older sister Mary and her husband lived, we were bone-weary. But she was a good cook, and after a few days' rest, her husband got Pop and me jobs loading and driving gravel trucks. It was sweaty, hard work, but I liked it a whole lot more than the shoe factory. At least I got to feel the sunshine on my back, and see the broad blue sky overhead. I liked California; it felt good to be there, like I belonged. Even though I wasn't doing anything more than hauling gravel, just being there really seemed like the big adventure I had hoped it would be. Pop and I worked as truck drivers for four months, after which he decided his "vacation" to see Mary was over and it was time to return to Ohio, and to our old jobs at the shoe factory. I hated hearing those words, but Pop made some sort of promise about returning to California in the future, so we loaded up the car and pointed ourselves East.

I wasn't happy back in Ohio, cooped up in the factory. I especially wasn't happy when the weather started to turn cold that fall. With winter coming on, I kept thinking of the California sun and recalling warm, easy evenings singing songs with the family on my sister Mary's porch. So late in the year when Mary's father-in-law decided to move out to join her, I offered my services to him as co-driver. He agreed to let me come along. I said "Happy trails" to my folks and headed West again, this time to stay. Once Mary and I were both in California, Mom and Pop soon made the decision to give up working at the shoe factory. They sold the farm in Duck Run and joined us.

Life sure looked sweet: I managed to get my old job back driving trucks filled with gravel. I had it made! But a few weeks after I settled in, I arrived at work to see all the dumptrucks being towed away. The boss had gone bankrupt. I was out of work with no prospects of a weekly paycheck any-where, for in those days you couldn't beg, borrow, or steal a regular job. So, I did what lots of other poor, displaced folks did back then. I became part of the army of migrant workers, picking peaches or whatever other crops were coming up, moving with the harvest and getting paid by the bushel. Along with my pop and my cousin Stanley Slye, I picked peaches in Bakersfield for Del Monte and grapes and everything else for anybody else who would hire us. We never did work for any of the WPA camps that President Roosevelt set up: I guess we were never lucky enough to find one. You could say that we were too busy starvin' outside the system.

When one job finished we would load the family up in our battered old truck and make camp with a whole bunch of other poor strangers near another orchard that needed pick-ing. The only thing more scarce than money in those days was food. Even if you got a little ahead on feeding yourself, the hungry faces of those around you in the labor camps made it so that a full belly didn't set so well. I remember once hunting us up a rabbit for supper—got it with my trusty slingshot—and as we cooked it in a frying pan over a camp-fire the aroma brought a whole herd of hungry, sad-faced children to where we sat. They didn't beg or anything—just stood to the side, watching the rabbit cook like they'd never seen anything so pretty. Even though Pop and I were caving in from working the fields all day, we couldn't eat with those starving little ones all around. So we Slyes wound up having nothing but bitter black coffee for our evening meal. We cut the ol' rabbit into as many pieces as we could and the kids feasted on it like it was a T-bone dinner at Delmonico's. Afterwards, Stanley and Pop played their guitars and I sang some songs for the little ones. Our family did a lot of singing in those days, even when we were alone, just to keep our spirits up.

The people in those camps were scraping hard to make ends meet, but it wasn't all hunger and misery. There were times we managed to get a whole crowd of folks to join our family singalongs, and on some occasions the men were able to lay down enough boards so we had a fitting dance floor. With the moon full and the stars shining bright on a clear California night, we kicked up our heels, you bet! I was able to put all the square-dance calling I learned back home to good use. I remember at one of those camps there was a fellow named John Steinbeck going around taking notes on what he saw. He never did speak to me directly. I was probably too shy to have anything to say to him, and there was no reason he would have noticed me: I was just another grape picker. I did eventually read the book he wrote about us, *The Grapes of Wrath,* and he sure did get it down right.

Picking fruit wasn't getting us anywhere. I'll never forget the day Pop came over to me and said that he had heard about a shoe company in Los Angeles that might be hiring. The look of defeat on that man's face made me want to cry. When he asked me if I wanted to come along with him, I said no. He didn't force the issue, and I couldn't tell him not to go. For myself, though, I had another idea. I thought that I'd talk my cousin Stanley into joining up with me as "The Slye Brothers" and playing music at dances and social get-togethers in the area. We tried it for a while, and we did play at a few parties around town, but never for pay. The only money we made was what party-goers tossed into the hat that we put down on the floor in front of us. After a few weeks, though, Stanley decided he needed a job with a regular paycheck, so we abolished the Slye Brothers. I joined up with another musical outfit called Uncle Tom Murray's Hollywood Hillbillies. We didn't get much work, and when we did, good ol' Uncle Tom Murray told me that instead of money, my pay would be the valuable experience of playing in public. I was going nowhere with my musical career.

My older sister Mary used to harmonize with me a lot at family get-togethers, and she was the one who was always pushing me to get up and sing for people other than my own kin. I didn't mind calling square dances, or singing among a few friends in the camp, or playing with little groups of musicians at local dances of people that I knew, but I was still bashful about standing up and singing in front of large numbers of strangers. Still, Mary didn't let up, finally talking me into going to a little radio station in Inglewood, KMCS, where they had an amateur show called "The Midnight Frolic." With my twenty-dollar guitar and a clean new patchwork shirt Mary made for me herself and pants that Ma had ironed specially for the occasion, I showed up around midnight, when the show began. It lasted till six in the morning, and I figured that with those hours there wouldn't be too many people listening, so that made me feel a little better.

When they pointed to the microphone and announced my name, I felt like I was in that school play in my Santa Claus suit all over again. I mean I was so fearful I couldn't move. I sat in my chair clutching the neck of the guitar like it had frozen in my hand. Mary came over and looked down at me, fixing my frightened eyes with hers. "Now you get up, get up there and sing," she commanded. And I did. I stood before the small audience of people who cared enough to come down to a no-account radio station in the middle of the night to hear a group of nobodies sing, and I played some old hillbilly songs for them. I guess they liked me enough because they applauded pretty good and the people at the radio station took my name down before I left.

The next day, as the red from my blushing face was still draining away, the pay phone near where we were staying rang and someone picked it up. It was for me—a call from a man who identified himself as the manager of a musical group called the Rocky Mountaineers. He said he had heard me singing on the radio show and wanted to know if I had any interest in joining the band. He said the band played regularly on a radio station in Long Beach, which was swell; but he also said that the radio job didn't pay anything. All it did was give them a chance to announce that they were available for parties and dances. Just what I needed—more work and less pay! But I can't lie: it was a thrill to get the call and to think of myself being in a real musical outfit. And the fact is that a life of picking fruit all day in the blazing sun wasn't exactly my idea of a great career. Besides, I figured my stomach couldn't get much emptier than it was. I told the fella on the phone that I would be delighted to join his band.

When I met them, I saw why they were so eager to have me join up: they didn't have a singer. There were whole bunches of all-instrumental groups around in those days, but the Rocky Mountaineers had gotten a lot of requests to sing, and none of them could. I suggested that in addition to me, they would need to hire another singer, too, for the harmony, and they agreed to the idea. We placed an ad in the *Los Angeles Herald-Examiner* saying, "Yodeler wanted for old-time act; tenor preferred," and a fellow named Bob Nolan answered. It's hard to forget Bob when he walked in the door—barefoot, holding a pair of brown shoes in his hand! You see, he was a lifeguard down in Santa Monica—you could tell that right away by his good physique and his golden tan. Each of his feet had a big blister on the heel, and I reckon his beach job didn't require much in the way of a business wardrobe. Financially, lifeguarding was probably only one step above fruit picking, and when Bob learned what we paid (nothin'!) his face fell; but like me, he was game to try. He was a great singer with a rich, honeytone voice, and a fine musician who played fiddle and guitar. Before too long, Bill Nichols, a tenor, joined the group and the three of us made a well-blended trio.

I'm surprised we lasted the eight months that we did together. We played pretty regularly on the radio, but the problem was that times were tough and nobody could afford to hire us. We made no money, and in order to get by we mooched off the banjo player and his wife for a roof over our heads and for meals. We used to take their couch and put it next to the day bed and we would all sleep across it that way. After a while, Bob Nolan couldn't take it anymore. He quit the group to become a caddy at the Bel Air Country Club. For the sake of musical history, I'll tell you here and now he didn't do that forever. Bob went on to be a great songwriter, coming up with some classic Western tunes, including "Tumbling Tumbleweeds." I've sometimes wondered if he thought of that one while hauling some rich man's golf bag over the smooth grass at the Bel Air Country Club, where there was nary a weed at all.

When Bob Nolan left the group, we placed an ad in the paper for a harmony yodeler who could also play guitar. Tim Spencer answered. Like me, Tim had come West to seek his fortune. He was from Oklahoma—a fine singer and a first-rate yodeler, with a terrific talent for songwriting. He, too, went on to write some of the classics, including "Pioneer Mother of Mine" and "Roomful of Roses," which Mickey Gilley revived as a number-one hit not too long ago. But all that success was far in the future. In the early 1930s, we sometimes thought we would never get a break. There was no money coming in at all; all we had was our dreams, which we held on to with the tenacity of a barnacle. We tried every way we knew to retool the group and get noticed. We dropped the name Rocky Mountaineers and joined up with Benny Nawahi's International Cowboys. Despite this high-flown moniker, there wasn't really a whole lot that was international about us; we liked the name because each member of the group had such a different ethnic background. But our home was still a makeshift campground on the floor of someone's living room, our meals were what we could manage to scrape together or get ourselves invited to. At least people seemed to like to hear us sing. We were invited to play over the radio, and in 1933 we performed at the Warner Theater in downtown Los Angeles. That was one show I'll never forget.

Just as we were introduced a big earthquake hit and the audience ran for the doors. One man remained in his seat. To this day, I don't know if he really wanted to hear us perform, or if he was so scared he couldn't move. Whatever the reason, when even one person wants to hear you play (and has paid for it!), you play. We launched into "Tumbling Tumbleweeds" as the giant chandelier overhead swayed like crazy and the whole theater vibrated with aftershocks.

By this point, I was darn near convinced that the International Cowboys had about as much chance of making it as a thirsty man in the desert. A phone call from a booking agent made it seem that there might be some hope. He asked us if we would be willing to take our act on a tour of the Southwest, where the type of music we played was most popular. He suggested barnstorming into such places as Yuma, Arizona; Roswell, New Mexico; and Lubbock, Texas. The boys and I sat down and discussed it, and we figured that we didn't have a lot to lose: might as well starve to death in a part of the country we hadn't seen. We called the man back and said, "Let's go!" To make it a fresh start, we gave ourselves a new name, taken from a famous old ranch brand that we felt had the right sound for traveling through the heart of cowboy country. We became the O-Bar-O Cowboys—Tim Spencer, Bill "Slumber" Nichols, Cactus Mac, Len Slye, and a fiddle player known as Cyclone. Cyclone was the one with the car, an old broken-down Ford. In June of 1933, we strapped our instruments to the roof and hit the road to find our fortune.

The O-Bar-O Cowboys' tour of the Southwest made my family's trek out from Ohio look like a first-class holiday. We knew when we left Los Angeles that we weren't going to be playing in glamorous places like New York or Chicago, but no one had told us that Miami, Arizona, where we were booked one night, was now a ghost town, population zero. Down the road in Yuma, the good citizens there had never been told we were coming, and not a single person had ever heard of us. When we stood up to perform, it was in front of an audience of none. We figured we'd better learn how to drum up business, so we went to a pawn shop and found us a megaphone. Whenever we arrived in a new town, we drove up and down the street leaning out the window of the car, using the megaphone to tell everyone that the O-Bar-O Cowboys were in town. Not many people cared. We had to pay the bill at one tourist court with my wristwatch. On those occasions when actual living people showed up to hear us, we took in maybe three or four dollars apiece. Most of that money seemed to get put back into fixing the rotten old heap of a car we traveled in. We spent more time under the car then aboard it looking at scenery. Even the silver clouds had dark linings. Cactus Mac, the leader of the band, was a native of Willcox, Arizona, so when we rolled into that town, we got a hero's welcome. Boy did that feel good for a change! People turned out in droves to hear us that night. We couldn't go anywhere without getting our hands shaken and backs slapped. The townspeople were so danged friendly, however, that Cactus Mac decided he never wanted to leave home again. He quit the band on the spot, pulling his guitar out of the car and waving good-bye as we drove out of town, one member short.

When we had seven flat tires between Willcox and Roswell, New Mexico, Cyclone the fiddle player decided that he had had enough of this tour, too. He wanted to drive straight back to Los Angeles. But we had one more town to hit—Roswell—and he agreed to hang on till we finished up there.

This time, it really did seem like the end. In order to eat, I borrowed a rifle from the man who ran the radio station. I

shot a stringy jackrabbit for supper, and we were happy to
have it. The next night, when I couldn't find a jack, we had
to make do with a hawk I shot off a telephone wire; and the
third night we ate a wild blackbird I remember being nothing
but gristle and bone. We tried to brew up some gravy to cover
these miserable offerings, but it was so thick you could stand
a fork in it.

When you get hungry enough, you spend lots of time imagining what you would eat if you had your choice, so we boys
in the band sort of cooked up a game in which we imagined
our dream meals out loud. We'd debate for hours about
whether it would be a T-bone or a plump turkey, and whether
there'd be pie or chocolate cake for dessert. When we showed
up to sing at the Roswell radio station one night, visions of
pork chops were dancing in our heads. One of us had a bright
idea: maybe if we spoke on the air a bit about what food we
liked, some nice listener might help us out. It was all planned
ahead; the boys and I figured out a real full meal. Slumber
Nichols said he liked fried chicken best; Cyclone rhapso-
dized over homemade biscuits; and I sang the praises of
lemon pie (which was no lie)!

The scheme worked! The phone at the radio station rang,
and a woman on the other end of the line said that if I sang
"The Swiss Yodel" the next night we were on the air, she
would bake us a lemon pie and bring it down to the station.
Talk about motivation! Back at the motor court I stayed up
practicing all night. My tonsils were vibrating by the time I
got to the microphone, and I sang the best "Swiss Yodel" you
ever heard in your life. But when the show was over, no
woman and no pie had shown up, and man, was I disappointed! We drove back to the tourist court, and we weren't
there long before a car pulled up and an older lady and her
daughter stepped out holding two warm-from-the-oven pies.
She introduced herself as Mrs. Wilkins, and said her daughter's name was Arlene. Being a healthy young male, I

couldn't help but notice Arlene. She was pretty—five foot nine, ash-blond hair, with a gentle manner. But good-looking as she was, we could hardly wait for those ladies to hand over the pies and go away. We positively inhaled them. Oh, boy, they were good, with meringues as tall as Hoot Gibson's ten-gallon hat. We ate them both, including every crumb— everything but the plates they came on.

I guess Mrs. Wilkins felt real sorry for us because she invited us over for fried chicken dinner the next day. We almost fell to our knees with happiness at the prospect. Over dinner, when I was able to relax a little, I really got to looking at Arlene. I guess if there is such a thing as love at first sight, this was it. The band spent two weeks in Roswell, and I saw her nearly every day I could. When the time came to leave, it wasn't easy to drive away from her.

I left that town feeling a whole lot different about my life. I was better fed than I had been in months; I was in love; and despite the O-Bar-O Cowboys' lack of success, I had a sense that my career blues just might start to turn around. Back in Los Angeles, the singing group split up: Tim Spencer went to work bagging groceries at Safeway, Slumber Nichols landed a job at a radio station in Fort Worth, and I joined a group called Jack and His Texas Outlaws. I also spent a lot of time exchanging letters back and forth to Arlene Wilkins; and the more I got to know her the more I wanted to be with her.

I wasn't particularly happy with Jack and His Texas Outlaws, so I got in touch with Bob Nolan, who was still slingin' around other people's golf bags in Bel Air, and twisted his arm a little until he agreed to give his singing career another shot. When I went to talk with Tim Spencer, he pointed out to me that he was enjoying the regular meals he could afford now that he had a real job; but as I stood there watching him stack cans of beans and bags of flour, it didn't take a whole lot of convincing to get him to untie his clerk's apron and come along with me and Bob. We called ourselves the Pioneer Trio, and pretty soon we got a regular spot on the Warner Brothers radio station KFWB in Los Angeles. The pay was nothing—literally—but they let us advertise that we were available if anyone wanted to hire us.

Inchworms would have grown bored measuring our success. But at least we had beds to call our own instead of sleeping on other people's living room floors and couches. We found a boardinghouse at Carlton and Bronson in Hollywood for nine dollars a week (three meals a day included) only a short walk from KFWB. Other than our performances on the morning radio show and the occasional party or dance we played, I didn't have much of a life. I ate, I slept, I wrote letters to Arlene and waited anxiously for hers, and all the other hours in the day I spent rehearsing songs. I thought that it would be a good idea to join the musicians union because it seemed to me that they would help us find work. But when I went to them, they turned me down. The reason? I couldn't read music. I played by ear. Six months later, once the band started getting some good work, I remember some fella from the union coming up to me and saying that I couldn't play unless I was a union member. I told him I *still* couldn't read music. He said that didn't matter; I had to pay dues. To this day, I've never had much use for that kind of organization.

The *Los Angeles Herald-Examiner* had a writer named Bernie Milligan who wrote a column called "Best Bets of the Day." Mr. Milligan heard us play somewhere and put us in his column. He started to mention us pretty regularly, saying we had the finest arrangements and were a good singing trio. We were doing mellow, three-part harmony yodeling, which was pretty novel in those days. The yodeling was put together with some jazzy fiddle playing and syncopated singing—kind of an early version of what they later called Western swing. Well, folks liked it a lot. And once Mr. Milligan started writing about us and we were getting that daily exposure on KFWB, things began to fall into shape. We worked harder than ever perfecting the smooth harmonies and wistful Western sound that would soon become our trademark, leading off nearly every show with a song Bob wrote called "The Last Roundup." Another columnist named Ray De O'Fan heard us sing that song and wrote, "Eating, sleeping, driving, working, or playing, this haunting melody seeks me out and taunts me."

Suddenly, we had no trouble getting bookings all around the town. The radio station actually offered us a contract, for money: thirty-five dollars a week, apiece, paid by our sponsor, the Farley Clothing Company! I thought I was going to swallow my tongue; thirty-five dollars was like a million to me then. We did two shows a day—one in the morning as the Gold Star Rangers, and one in the afternoon as the Pioneer Trio. One day early in 1934 announcer Harry Hall introduced us as the *Sons* of the Pioneers. We were so flustered by that, we hardly could perform, and after the show we all gathered around Mr. Hall and asked to know what kind of trick he thought he was playing, introducing us wrong. "You're all young guys," he explained. "You don't look like pioneers." It made sense to us; I mean we didn't want the radio audience to think we were grizzled old men with long gray beards. That name stuck, and life just kept gettin' better. The only thing that didn't change much was my problem with being bashful in public. Although there wasn't a live audience, there were always five or ten people hanging around the station listening to us. To this day I'm still scared to death the first half hour I get up on stage.

The phone in our boardinghouse was ringing morning and night. All the popular radio shows of the day wanted us to perform, and to top it off we even got invited to a benefit for the Salvation Army in San Bernardino. That came about because Will Rogers had personally requested that we appear! Will Rogers was my hero. He went through hardships and came out with his wit intact. He looked at America from the poor man's side of things, not from the point of view of the rich bankers and powerful politicians who usually get their thoughts heard. After the show Will Rogers visited with the band awhile and shook our hands one last time, telling us that he and his airplane pilot Wiley Post had to get going because the next day they were heading off for Alaska. That night would be the last time anyone saw Will Rogers on stage. His plane crashed on that trip, killing all aboard. Years later I traveled to where the plane had gone down at Point Barrow, Alaska, to pay my respects. Tim Spencer wrote a song about it. It went something like:

> 'Twas the fifteenth day of August, year of 1935
> In Alaska's frozen land of ice and snow
> Will and Wiley looked around just to set the old ship down
> And to howdy with the native Eskimaux . . .

Anyway, I'm sure glad to have met Will Rogers when I did.

Western groups were getting pretty popular around Los Angeles, although a lot of people still thought of what we were doing as old-fashioned hillbilly music. I remember groups with names like the Arizona Wranglers, the Texas Wranglers, Jimmy LeFevre and His Saddle Pals, and Stuart Hamblen's Lucky Stars. There was one bunch back then that called themselves the Beverly Hill Billies. Their story, believe it or not, was that they had been discovered in the backwoods of Beverly Hills by the managers of radio station KMPC, who convinced them to come down from their holler and sing on his station. They wore floppy backwoods hats and went by the names Zeke, Lem, and Ezra. Their yarn was a windy one, but they were probably the most popular Western group in the area when we were getting started with the Sons of the Pioneers.

There was some friendly competition among us Western singers. One time the Lucky Stars challenged the Sons of the

Pioneers at a local rodeo—not to try and outsing each other, but to ride wild broncos. I was sure we'd win; those Lucky Stars were no cowboys, and I knew I could sit a horse pretty well. I sure was surprised when the Lucky Stars beat us hands down. Turns out they had recruited a bunch of sure-'nuf cowboys and dressed them in Lucky Stars clothes for the contest!

The Sons of the Pioneers were becoming such a hot commodity that a new outfit named Decca Records wanted us to go with them and do some recordings on the West Coast (which was then kind of a novelty; most recordings were made back East). We signed a deal that guaranteed us a penny for every record we sold, and went for our first studio session in August 1934. We recorded "Way Out There," "Tumbling Tumbleweeds," "Moonlight on the Prairie," and "Ridin' Home." Pretty soon Liberty Pictures cast us in a cowboy movie called *The Old Homestead.* We sang "Wagon Wheels" and "Tumbling Tumbleweeds." We also sang in some Charles Starrett Westerns called *Mysterious Avenger, The Old Wyoming Trail,* and *Gallant Defender.* We appeared in one big-budget movie over at Paramount, Bing Crosby's *Rhythm on the Range,* which also featured Martha Raye and Bob "Bazooka" Burns, and in four of Gene Autry's earliest singing-cowboy pictures. The whole country was cottonin' up to singing cowboys and the smooth harmonizing sounds of Western music. I guess we were in the right place at the right time. It just took us awhile to get there.

In 1936 the boys and I were invited to perform at the Texas Centennial. It was a good job, but when I accepted I had more on my mind than the show. I had been keeping up my letter writing to Arlene Wilcox during the two years since we met, and my thoughts never strayed far from her. I was no longer the struggling, hungry kid who had eaten her lemon pie in record time, and with some measure of success under my belt I felt ready to ask her to marry me. On the way to Texas,

I detoured to Roswell, New Mexico. We stood hand-in-hand in the living room of her mother's house and pledged our love to each other on June 14, 1936. We were now man and wife.

Marrying Arlene made me even more eager to make something of my life. The Sons of the Pioneers were getting good work and being paid for it, but I got to hankering for greener pastures. We went to radio KHJ in Los Angeles, and we became regulars on Peter Potter's Hollywood Barn Dance on KNX. Early in 1937, we signed a deal with Columbia Pictures to appear in a series of Westerns. In those days, a movie deal was considered the Holy Grail; it meant you were a big name. But in nearly all the pictures we made, we were only interludes in the action or voices in the background. I did manage to land a few bit parts in movies that involved a little more than singing; in *The Old Corral,* I was the bad guy and had a fistfight with the hero, Gene Autry. When Gene won, he forced me to sing a song at gunpoint, which was supposed to be a humiliating moment for me.

I wasn't very good at playing bad guys. I guess I wanted to win the fights; I wanted to be the hero, and I wanted to be the one whose name was on the movie marquee outside. By this time, Gene Autry's pictures were a big success, and nearly every studio in Hollywood was looking for its own singing cowboy. I heard that Universal was casting and managed to actually get a screen test there. But I lost out to Bob Baker, who went on to make quite a few musical Westerns back then. They told me I wasn't right to be a movie cowboy hero because the camera made me look like a teenager.

In the fall of 1937 I walked into a hat shop in Glendale to pick up my white Stetson, which I had left there to be cleaned and reblocked. While I was standing at the counter a big guy, about the size of John Wayne, came running through the door, wild-eyed and in a hurry. "What's all the excitement about?" I asked him. He said that Republic Pictures was holding auditions the next day for a new singing cowboy, and he needed a hat fast so he could look the part. Now, Republic already had Gene Autry, but Gene's contract was up for renewal and the word around town was that he was hoping to go to the mat to fight for the great big raise he thought he deserved. To put the pressure on Gene to keep his contract demands in line, Republic had set up these auditions to find another singing cowboy.

I didn't have an appointment, but I went anyway, unaware that the guard at the gate had orders to let in only those people with a gate pass. The guard told me to get lost. I walked away but didn't leave, lurking around all morning hoping to figure out a plan or see someone I knew going in. Around the end of the lunch hour, I saw a large group of studio workers heading for the gate to return to work. I slipped into their midst, collar up and Stetson hat pulled down low so the guard wouldn't recognize my face and, sure enough, I got past him. About ten yards inside, though, I heard him call out for me to stop. I froze, ready to get the bum's rush. But before the guard had a chance to turn me around, I heard a friendly voice.

"Len, Len Slye! Hello!" It was Sol Siegel, the producer, who saw the guard coming toward me and knew I was about to be expelled. He remembered me as one of the Sons of the Pioneers. "I assume you're here to try out for the singing cowboy screen test," he said. "I've tested seventeen men already, and don't feel good about any of them. If you have your guitar, come on in and give it a try." I had left my guitar in my car, several blocks away. "Go get it," he said. "Don't worry, I'll make sure you get back in," he called to me as I sprinted away.

When I returned and caught my breath, I sang "Tumbling Tumbleweeds," which was the theme song of the Sons of the Pioneers, and "Haddie Brown," which is a fast-paced ol' country song with a lot of flashy yodeling.

By the smile on Mr. Siegel's face I could tell he liked my work. "Len, come back in the morning and let's do a screen test," he said. He later told me that as much as he liked the music of the Sons of the Pioneers, he had never once considered me when thinking of hiring a new singing cowboy. It was only when he saw me there walking through the gate that it dawned on him that I might be right for the role. If he hadn't been walking by just when the guard was about to nail me, who knows what ever would have happened to young Leonard Slye?

I floated out the gates of Republic humming a tune, too happy to notice the suspicious "Ain't-I-seen-you-before?" look in the guard's eyes.

On October 13, 1937, I became a contract player at Republic Pictures.

CHAPTER 4

Dale's Story

"She'll die hard, with her head up," my grandfather had predicted when he first laid eyes on me lying in my crib. I don't know exactly what he saw, but I do believe his words were prophetic. Life has bowed my head many times, but I have always managed to find the strength to endure, then to lift up my eyes and carry on.

I had foundered miserably in Chicago when I first went there; when I returned in 1939, I was determined to succeed. I registered with every booking agent in town and auditioned every chance I got. Finally I found work as a jazz singer with an orchestra at the Edgewater Beach Hotel, which was a kind of high-society establishment along the lake shore. I was glad to do it—it was a job! But it was the wrong job. The Edgewater Beach Hotel featured a dignified ballroom that attracted a sedate clientele; my jazz songs simply didn't click; another girl, who sang pretty ballads, got all the applause.

I auditioned for Anson Weeks's orchestra and landed the job as his female vocalist. What followed was a whirlwind of one-nighters throughout the Midwest—in ballrooms, nightclubs, supper clubs, and small hotels. We were on the road constantly, sometimes traveling hundreds of miles between engagements. We even did two months in Los Angeles, at the Ambassador Hotel. While on the West Coast, I was offered the opportunity to do a screen test. I turned it down: not interested! By this time I was well up in my twenties—way too old to start a movie career. That's what I thought, or at least that's what I thought *producers* would think. Besides, there was Tom. He was ready to begin junior high school, which would make me an ingenue with a teenage son. Impossible. A movie career was out, as far as I was concerned. I was resolved to make it as a singer—in clubs or, if fortune smiled, on Broadway.

I missed Tom. I decided to leave the band so he could come to Chicago and visit me more often. I sang almost every evening in nightclubs such as the Balinese Room at the Blackstone Hotel, and I especially looked forward to Wednesdays in the Panther Room at the Sherman Hotel. That was the night Fats Waller sat in on piano. We did New Orleans jazz, "Honeysuckle Rose," songs that he was famous for—and let me tell you, he gave my voice a workout! Ol' Fats had a saxophone player named Cedric—a great player, just terrific—who was black, really black as night. I recall one night Cedric was up there blowing his heart out, but the lighting crew simply wasn't paying attention. It was dark in the room, and a single puny spot could not do its job on a fella with Cedric's complexion. Fats was furious to see his saxophonist in the shadows, so he stood up at his piano, grabbed a microphone, and boomed out, "Put the moon on the man!" They added plenty of light, and finally those folks saw Cedric blow.

I knew something about singing on the radio and in dance halls and country roadhouses, but I had a lot to learn about club music. When I performed at Chez Paree, which was then the jewel of Chicago's nightlife, Ray Bolger was the headliner. One night he came into my dressing room and said, "Honey, you've got a nice voice, and you've got a nice personality, but you need some special stuff. You need songs that nobody else knows, something different so people will think of you when they hear it." Well, it was leap year, when a gal can ask a guy out on a date, and I had written a little song for the occasion, called "Will You Marry Me, Mr. Larrimee." It went:

> *Will you marry me, Mr. Larrimee?*
> *Will you carry me far away?*
> *Will you marry me, Mr. Larrimee?*
> *Will you marry me TODAY?*

It seems modest enough by today's standards, but back then it was scandalous for a woman to be so forward with a man. Ray Bolger looked at me and he said, "You can't do a bawdy lyric. You're not the type." He said, "You go home and figure out a second set of lyrics, lyrics that are just on the line. Say the same thing, but in a more demure way. A little naughty, maybe, but nice." So I did. Ray Bolger liked the new version so much he said, "I'll stooge for you." He came on stage when I sang that song and he was just great, so funny. I held his hand and pretended to propose to him while I sang. He got all red and made his Adam's apple bob up and down. That little song kept my job at Chez Paree for three more weeks, which turned out to pave the way for my lucky break.

The head of the Columbia network—that's CBS—happened to come in one night and hear me sing. Their Chicago station, WBBM, needed a new singer for their staff. The executive liked what he heard, so I was hired. They called me "That Gal from Texas." I did everything: announced, talked, and sang. I wrote "My Heart Is Down Texas Way" for the show, but a lot of what I sang was in Spanish, to give the repertoire a south-of-the-border flavor. I didn't speak any Spanish, though, except what little I learned from a Cuban bartender at the Balinese Room. I sang all those songs phonetically. The show did well, and I was becoming a popular performer. I was suddenly in demand at Chicago's finest hotels and nightclubs, which were quite soigné in those days—

the Balinese Room, the Drake Hotel, Chez Paree. I even did an audition for a commercial with a group of cowboy singers from California that came through town calling themselves the Sons of the Pioneers. Finally, good things were coming my way.

Those WBBM broadcasts were carried on the network, which meant people heard them coast-to-coast. Out of the blue I got a telegram from a Hollywood agent who had heard me and wanted some photographs to see if I would be right for a screen test. Well, I laughed long and loud about that! I was no actress, I knew that—remember, I had turned down my first shot at a screen test. Besides, I had no desire whatever to go to Hollywood. Aside from being too old, I believed I wasn't pretty enough for movies, and furthermore, movies weren't sophisticated enough for me! All along my ambition had been musical comedy—and on stage in New York, thank you very much. Actually, I had been pretty well disabused of that goal in Chicago when I had the chance to be in *Hold Onto Your Hats,* a musical that came to town starring Al Jolson, Ruby Keeler, and Jack Whiting, a great dancer. Ruby and Al had a spat; she was going to leave the show, and they wanted to put me in her place. I was a good ballroom dancer, but not tap, not solo! "No problem!" they said. "You can learn her routine in three weeks." I turned them down, pretty much bidding farewell to my musical theater aspirations. Likewise, I ignored the telegram from Hollywood. But the agent didn't give up: he sent more, sometimes one each day. Finally, when I had gotten a stack of wires, my program director suggested I play along. "Go on out there," he said. "Take yourself a vacation at their expense. Have fun. Do it!"

I went to the studios of Maurice Seymour, who was the big glamour photographer in Chicago, to put together a portfolio. I sent pictures to the agent, Joe Rivkin. Mr. Rivkin and another agent out there, Danny Winkler, had been listening to me every Sunday on a show sponsored by Dairy-Rich. They were casting a movie called *Holiday Inn* at Paramount and needed a new face. Well, they liked mine, at least as it appeared in Seymour's glamour photos, so Mr. Rivkin wired me to take a plane immediately to California. I got tickets for the sleeper: in the air all night from Chicago to Burbank, arriving first thing in the morning.

I had never taken a long flight before. Approximately one minute after takeoff I developed a throbbing earache that lasted through dawn. In those days, cabins weren't pressurized, and stewardesses—who were all required to be trained nurses—dropped warm oil into passengers' ears to ease the pain. The oil didn't help me, though, and by the time we arrived, I was nauseated, my head was spinning, and my ears throbbed. As the plane taxied to the gate I looked out my window and saw a man pacing back and forth, looking between his wristwatch and the airplane. I had read in a book that all agents were nervous, so I knew this must be mine. I was so sick I could barely walk down the staircase to the tarmac, but I managed to drag myself over to him. "Are you Joe Rivkin?" I asked.

"My God," he gasped, looking at my greenish complexion, watery eyes, and furrowed brow. "Are YOU Dale Evans? You certainly don't look like your pictures!"

I wanted to run back on the plane, but the thought of another flight was even worse than the prospect of listening to more of his critique.

As he drove me down the road toward Hollywood, he continually glanced at me with undisguised revulsion. "I don't like your lipstick," he said. "Don't wear it anymore. And we'll have to do something about your hair. You'll lose weight, too." Then he asked, "How old are you?" I lied and said twenty-five. "No," he answered. "You're twenty-one. Understand?" He took me to my hotel, the Hollywood Plaza, where we went straight to the beauty parlor. "Do something with her," he told an operator. "Put some blood in her face.

We're due at Paramount in an hour." By this time, all I wanted was rest! I didn't give a hoot what Mr. Rivkin or anyone else in Hollywood thought of me. They tinted my light brown hair auburn and slapped and pinched and rubbed my face until I developed some color, after which I went upstairs to dress. I put on an ensemble that I thought would make a good impression at lunch: a sheer dark dress, the one fur I owned, and a pair of white gloves.

"Who died?" Mr. Rivkin asked when he saw me. "What's with the black shroud?"

Well, I should have popped him then and there, but instead I drew myself up with as much hauteur as I could muster and informed him, "Sir, this is proper dress for a business meeting at noon."

"Sister, you are not in Chicago anymore," he reminded me. "In Hollywood, you wear bright colors, flowery things, casuals." He shook his head in disgust, then grabbed my hand and dragged me toward the car. "Aw, it's too late now. Let's go!"

The commissary was filled with stars. I remember seeing Dorothy Lamour and Betty Hutton there, but most of all I remember heads craning and eyes staring to look at me—*the new one*—as Mr. Meiklejohn, the casting director, led me to a chair. "How old are you, Dale?" he asked.

"She's twenty-one," Joe Rivkin shouted above the din.

Mr. Meiklejohn looked long and hard at my face. "She'll photograph older," he said. Then he announced, "I'm a little worried about the nose. It's too long for the chin."

"Don't worry, we'll have some of the nose taken off," my agent volunteered.

"Dale, do you dance?" Mr. Meiklejohn asked.

"She makes Eleanor Powell look like a bum," Rivkin piped in.

Enough of this, I thought. "No, Mr. Meiklejohn, I can't dance." I confessed, "I cannot even do a time step." I told him about turning down *Hold Onto Your Hats* back in Chicago. Joe Rivkin was fuming and his face was the color of a beet when I started to confess my flaws. Mr. Meiklejohn did a slow burn and looked daggers at my agent. It could not have been the first time an agent tried to sell him a bill of goods, but even so, he laced into Joe Rivkin, and good! I am not even going to tell you what he called him except to say that it had something to do with the conjectural nature of his ancestry. He then explained to me that the role they were casting in *Holiday Inn* was opposite Bing Crosby and Fred Astaire. Yes, indeed, they needed a new face, but they needed one that could dance up a storm.

Still undismayed, Joe promised that I would be delighted to learn all the dancing I needed in a jiffy.

Mr. Meiklejohn gave me a sympathetic glance and explained that I was not right for *Holiday Inn*. He did confess, though, that he liked my face, wrong nose or not. "We have a whole roster of singers here," he said. "But I'd like to test you anyway." I was taken to Wardrobe, where Edith Head outfitted me with a dress and a fur muff that Barbara Stanwyck had worn. The drama coach then selected a scene from *The Blue Angel* and told me I had two weeks to learn my part.

For those two weeks, Joe Rivkin watched me like a hawk eyeballing a chicken; he monitored what I ate, who I saw, what time I came home, and what time I woke up in the morning. "Work hard, go to bed early, keep yourself in good shape, and don't get mixed up in your private life," he intoned over and over again. He was right, but by the day of the screen test, I had become a nervous wreck. The deception about my age didn't sit right with me. And I had another, bigger secret that made me feel like I was about to blow up with tension. As I sat in the studio watching the crew adjust lights for the test, I suddenly got cold chills. I felt I had to come clean. I walked over to where Joe was sitting and faced him, hands on my hips.

"Mr. Rivkin, you know I am not twenty-one. I am twenty-eight. What you don't know is that I have a son. He is thirteen years old."

His jaw dropped. He shot out of his chair and began to pace, deep in thought. "Send him away to school," he said.

I told him that if Tom could not come with me to Hollywood, we would stay in Chicago.

"No, no, no, that's no good," he replied and began to pace again. Then he stopped, spun on his heel, and announced, "I've got it!" He walked right up to my face and said, "Tom is your brother. Understand? Your kid brother."

At least that scheme would permit Tom to be with me. "If it's all right with Tom, it will be all right with me," I said. I rationalized the deception by telling myself that the money I might make in Hollywood would buy Tom a fine education. Besides, chances were good that nothing would come of the screen test, so why worry? It wasn't easy to tell a thirteen-year-old boy that he would have to masquerade as his mother's brother. I had always tried to teach Tom the importance of honesty. When I told him the plan, he said that it sounded pretty silly, but he would play along just as long as he didn't have to out-and-out lie.

The test was a short scene in which I played opposite Macdonald Carey. I was supposed to get angry at him, slap his face, and storm off camera in a huff. The problem was, I didn't know anything about a screen slap. So when the director called "Action!" we went into our dialogue and I hauled off and really let him have it—hard. His face began to throb. I was so embarrassed, I about died on the spot.

Paramount was not impressed. They rejected me. Joe Rivkin managed to take the test over to Fox, where Darryl Zanuck liked what he saw. He offered me a year's contract at four hundred dollars a week—more than twice what I was making in Chicago. Unheard of! In 1941 I packed my bags and left Chicago for good. I was accompanied by Tom and my mother. She brought along some words of advice from Dad: "Don't let anybody kiss you on the screen and don't show your legs." My husband and his parents drove out from Chicago later.

When I arrived in Hollywood they wanted me to do another screen test. Tom Moore, a kindly old-time actor from the silent-film era, was to direct it. He was the dramatic coach at 20th Century–Fox. For my test, he decided I ought to read selections from *The Hound of Heaven,* by Francis Thompson. I asked him why he chose this particular material and he said, "Dale, there's a spiritual quality about you. I want to capture it in the test." I didn't know what the heck he was talking about. I was just all gung-ho, career-wise; I certainly wasn't thinking about anything spiritual. So I read the words about fleeing the Hound of Heaven down the arches of the years and the labyrinthine ways of my own mind . . . Well, the test was miserable, a big goose egg. I didn't know what I was saying. The words signified nothing to me. I had not suffered enough at that time to know what Mr. Moore saw in my face . . . and probably in my future. Much later, after I became a committed Christian, someone anonymously sent me *The Hound of Heaven.* I read it once again, this time with many more of life's tears having been spilled, and it meant so much to me. But at that time, I didn't know about the Hound.

Darryl F. Zanuck had a fetish about women's teeth. He wanted every woman to have a smile like Jeanette MacDonald's. I was sent to the dentist, where I spent my first week's salary having my front upper teeth shaved perfectly even and buying temporary caps—the kind they paste on—to put on the top of my teeth. I was then shipped off to a health club where I was pummeled, pounded, massaged, steamed, and exercised until I lost twelve pounds. I was then ready for my first starring role.

The studio announced that Dale Evans would play the lead

in a college musical called *Campus in the Clouds.* I truly was walking on air; all my reservations about a movie career had evaporated. Dale Evans, movie star, was about to set the world on its ear. Then the Japanese bombed Pearl Harbor and World War II began. Frivolous movies were out of fashion for the time being. *Campus in the Clouds* was shelved, and I was left to twiddle my thumbs. I took the opportunity to study with Flossie Friedman, the well-respected British voice coach. Well, she just about keeled over when she gave me some Rudyard Kipling to read. "Darling, you have got to be kidding with that accent!" she declared. "I'm afraid we shall never be able to eradicate it." She did her best, and I dropped enough of my drawl that my parents didn't even recognize my voice when they heard me on the radio after those lessons. But you know something funny: as soon as I got into Westerns, it came right back. I guess Texas is the sound of my true self.

I did nearly five hundred shows during the war for the USO and the Hollywood Victory Committee. Before each one, I liked to survey the audience, hunting for a bashful-looking serviceman toward the front. When I came out on stage, I called him up and began my act by singing "Will You Marry Me, Mr. Larrimee." The proposal and his red-faced reaction were always a great icebreaker. The boys really liked that.

Working alongside some of Hollywood's best talent in the USO shows taught me about the obligation real entertainers feel toward their audience. I remember once working with Marlene Dietrich at a camp in Northern California. It was far from Hollywood's movie studios, on a poorly lit stage in a muddy field. The weather was miserable that day, and we were all dog-tired from a rugged travel schedule. Yet Miss Dietrich prepared herself for the show as if she were giving a royal command performance: false eyelashes, slinky sequined gown, the works. When she went on stage to sing, she gave it everything she had. She was a performer who simply didn't know how to give less. And let me tell you, those boys appreciated it. Many years later when I went to Vietnam to entertain the troops, there were so many occasions when I was so exhausted I felt I couldn't go another step. Then I would meet a young soldier who so desperately needed comfort from home. In those boys' longings I found my strength.

During my year's tenure at Fox I got exactly two walk-on roles—blink and you'll miss me—in movies. The trouble was, if you can believe this, they told me I looked too much like Betty Grable—even to the legs. I was told, "You'll never get anywhere on this lot because there is only one queen, and that is Miss Grable." That was very bad news indeed. The four hundred dollars a week they were paying me was way too much for a bit player. I grew certain that when the contract was over it wouldn't be renewed. I was right.

At the same time, my home life was turning ever more painful. Tom, bless his heart, was growing into a very wise, very good boy. Playing my kid brother didn't suit him. Whenever there was studio-related publicity going on around our house in West Los Angeles, he quietly disappeared. He understood that my deceit about him was hard for me to bear, but the only way I then knew to cope with the situation. He was willing to be invisible, he said, but not to lie. "I am a Christian," he told me. "Christians do not lie." Oh, Lord, that stung; but my ambition burned hot enough to overwhelm my guilt; and I continued to rationalize that I was doing it out of love for him, to insure his future. My self-deception was not entirely successful. My nerves were ragged; I felt a deep emptiness. I began to read every book I could find about peace of mind and help for nervous tension: psychology, Eastern mysticism, self-help galore. Nothing touched what ailed me, certainly not my perfunctory Sunday visits to church, where I considered I was doing the Lord a big, fat favor by taking time out of my busy schedule to be there. I reasoned that once I became successful, *then* I would be able to devote more attention to my son and to my faith. Until then, though, my career came first.

Dr. Harold Proppe, our minister at the First Baptist Church in Hollywood, didn't make it easy for me to delude myself with such logic. He would deliver a sermon about people with God-given musical talents who used them out in the world, but not in God's house. I've always said that at such moments I felt Dr. Proppe was throwing out spiritual shoes, saying, "If the shoe fits, wear it!" Well, sir, those shoes did fit—so tightly that my toes ached. I left church pouting and angry, resentful that neither Dr. Proppe nor the Lord seemed to understand just how demanding show business is.

I yearned to get back to radio, where I believed I was better appreciated. Joe Rivkin had gone into the army, so I found a new agent named Art Rush. Art was a strange man indeed for an agent. He had once planned to be a minister, and his conversation was laced with references to the Bible, whose lessons he tried to apply to his work. We talked religion all the time; and although my heart and soul weren't really in it at this point in my life, I talked a pretty good game. I didn't know it at the time, but those talks and Art's true spirituality were helping to keep me afloat; I had so little sense of bearing on my own.

Art found me a terrific audition: for the girl singer on "The Chase and Sanborn Hour," starring Edgar Bergen and Charlie McCarthy as well as Don Ameche and Ray Noble. I knew I had the job after I sang a number and heard Charlie McCarthy let out with a long, appreciative whistle through his wooden mouth. I did forty-three good weeks with that show. Edgar Bergen was a master of comedy, and I learned so much about timing watching him. Later, when I was in all those Westerns with Roy and Gabby Hayes, I was able to put it to use in the funny scenes: slow takes, pregnant pauses, little bits of business that perk up a scene. "The Chase and Sanborn Hour" was a great experience, but I was dropped after an advertising executive wanted to play footsie with me. I refused. He warned that I would never get anywhere in the business if I didn't go to lunch with him. I stuck to my guns and, sure enough, I was fired.

To make matters worse, Art Rush didn't seem to have much time to think about me anymore. I needed guidance, I needed help, I needed a job! All he wanted to do was talk about this wonderful client of his, a fast-rising young singer named Roy Rogers. Earlier, Art had introduced me to his pet star during a USO show at Edwards Air Force Base. We shook hands and said hello. I thought Mr. Rogers was a very attractive guy, but awfully shy. I probably would have forgotten all about him, except for Art talking about him so much. After a while Art's enthusiasm started to really grate on me and I began to hate the very mention of Roy Rogers's name. So I did what seemed like the logical thing: I told Mr. Rush that I was fed up with him and his singing cowboy. As far as I was concerned, he could devote all of his attention to his favorite client. I was leaving him. I intended to find myself an agent who put me and my career first. Even at the time, I knew I was losing a good friend—Art was so much more than an agent to me—but I was too hungry for success to have second thoughts.

In 1943 my new agent, Danny Winkler, got me a year's contract at Republic Studios, and two weeks after signing, I starred in a country musical called *Swing Your Partner* with Lulu Belle and Scotty from the "National Barn Dance" and Vera Vague from the "Bob Hope Show." I liked Republic. It was a small studio, and it felt like a family place; you were part of a crew there, all working together, and nobody had the time or energy to play prima donna. I worked so hard I met myself coming and going; and after a year they picked up my option. In twelve months, I made nine pictures including *Here Comes Elmer* and *Hoosier Holiday*. I wasn't in the running for an Oscar yet, not by a jugful, but I was busy, and I always had hope that my big break was just around the corner.

Things were going along swimmingly until Herbert Yates, the head of the studio, went to New York to see *Oklahoma!* That stage show put a bee in his bonnet: he wanted to produce Westerns with the full *Oklahoma!* treatment—not just songs, but production numbers with dancing, choreography, a big cast, and a female lead who had more to do than just be a pretty damsel in distress. He said he thought I would be just right to star in such a picture. He planned to cast me opposite my old nemesis Roy Rogers. Danny Winkler didn't like the idea of my doing a Western. In fact, I had been slated to be in one of Roy Rogers's earlier pictures, right after I made *Swing Your Partner,* but Danny had gone to Mr. Yates and gotten me out of it. "She's not going to look well," he argued. He was worried about those big, horrible reflectors they use out on location; he was certain that I would be unable to keep my eyes open in the glare, and that they would make me look sick and pale.

As for me, I never had thought of myself doing a Western. Sure, I had liked cowboy pictures as a child, but that was *as a child.* As a professional actor, my goals were grander than that. I thought I wanted to be in a sophisticated musical comedy—something debonair, urbane, and adult. But I didn't argue with Mr. Yates, who was certain that with my real Texas background I was the right gal for the part of Isabel Martinez in *The Cowboy and the Señorita,* to be directed by Joe Kane. I was supposed to be a raven-haired beauty, and as "the señorita" I had to speak with a heavy Spanish accent. Mr. Kane used to kid me about my delivery, saying it sounded like "*Si, si,* you'all!"

Of course, Mr. Yates and everyone else just assumed I knew my way around a horse, being from Texas and all, but I had not ridden since I was seven years old. The fact was: I couldn't ride worth beans. To make matters worse, they gave me a big horse with the disposition of a convict breaking out of prison—frisky to the point of being downright mean, and with a mind of his own. He was the kind of horse cowboys call cold-jawed, meaning you can pull and tug on those reins all you want and the horse will do what it chooses and go where it wants to go at whatever speed suits its mood at the time. I'd get on him for a scene and we'd start galloping somewhere, and all I could do was hold on and hope. In one scene I was supposed to come cantering down a hill with Roy riding Trigger in front of me and Guinn "Big Boy" Williams on his horse in back. How I stayed on my horse, I will never know. I bounced so hard in the saddle that my temporary caps just flew out of my mouth—those teeth Zanuck had made me buy. And Big Boy Williams's horse trampled right over them. That was the end of my lovely caps; to tell you the truth, I was glad to be rid of those pesky things.

When I finally managed to stop the horse, Roy came over and said, "I never saw so much sky between a woman and a horse in all my born days." He suggested that if I wanted to stay alive, I ought to take a few riding lessons, which I did at Pickwick Stables in North Hollywood. Roy was a natural on a horse and gave me pointers whenever he had a chance. He taught me how to take the action in my knees when I galloped, and how to take a deep seat and lean back when we shuttered to a stop. After some time I got to the point where I could sit a horse pretty well. I *had* to ride well by the time I got Buttermilk, that pearl-colored quarterhorse with black mane and tail. He became *mine,* just as Trigger was Roy's; but let me tell you, that was one feisty cayuse. He had a head on him that was something else. He had been used for roping quite a bit, so he was nimble and could turn on a dime— which he sometimes did without any forewarning; why, one time he dumped our horse trainer Glenn Randall just to prove he could do it. Buttermilk grew camera-wise, and as soon as he heard the buzzer go off—the one that sounds when they say "Roll 'em"—he'd be on the move. I remember that Pat Brady, who was a darn good horseman himself, had to gallop somewhere on Buttermilk in a scene in one of our pictures. After he got off he came over to me and said, "Shoo, girl, you gotta ride every minute you're on that horse."

One day while we were filming *The Cowboy and the Señorita,* I was sitting aboard the willful horse they had given me. I was dressed in city clothes and high-heeled shoes. Roy warned me to be careful with those shoes; he said that if the heels ever caught in the stirrup when I was getting on or off, I could get hung up there and dragged to death. Well, I thought I knew it all, so I didn't pay much attention to what he had said. I was busy listening to Gabby Hayes practicing some dialogue, laughing at the way he twisted that wrinkled old face of his when he spit out his words. At one point I laughed so hard that I threw my head back and slapped my side. The horse took my sudden reaction as a signal to bolt— and bolt he did, like he was shot from a cannon! I wasn't even sitting square in the saddle. I was sideways, and sure enough, one of my heels caught in the stirrup as I was sliding off. I reached up and grabbed the saddle horn to keep myself from falling to the ground, but I was hanging on for dear life as that horse hit a gallop.

"Grab her, Roy!" Gabby called out. Roy jumped on Trigger and came after me. He drew alongside as I was about to lose my grip, reaching over and hefting me from the side of the runaway horse, pulling me up close to him on Trigger's back. For me, no movie scene could have been so breathtaking. And no make-believe movie cowboy was ever as heroic as Roy Rogers appeared to me at that moment.

PART III

Roy and Dale: Fame and Misfortunes

*H*OLLYWOOD WAS BUILT on Western movies. After *The Great Train Robbery* of 1903 based its plot on a Butch Cassidy holdup three years earlier in Wyoming, frontier adventure became not only the meat and potatoes of the movie business but the paradigm for all action pictures. By 1910 one out of five movies made was a Western, and Bronco Billy Anderson became Hollywood's first star, playing a cowboy hero in over five hundred two-reelers, made at the rate of one each week. Although *The Great Train Robbery* had been filmed in New Jersey, moviemakers soon settled in Southern California, where they found easy access to high desert locations, cactus fields, ranch land, and a culture rich with such photogenic skills as riding, roping, and cattle punching. Early directors feasted on the West because it offered everything audiences wanted: fast action, wondrous scenery, moral lessons, bad guys to hiss, fair ladies in distress, and manly men to admire. It is impossible to imagine what American movies would have been if there hadn't been a lore of the Wild West to inspire them.

Long before Roy Rogers and Dale Evans were born, the hard realities of the American frontier had already been swallowed up into a rousing epic tale of horsemen, covered wagons, Indian wars, and an awesome untamed landscape. The facts of history became material for a saga that combined the moral purpose of King Arthur's knights with the bravura of Greek mythology. No fictional world ever created has been so elaborate in its detail or so rich with potential for allegory. The star of this national morality play was the cowboy, who had been transformed from what he actually had been—a hired hand on a horse—into America's greatest hero, a handsome paladin always ready for adventure, free as the wind, honest, and good.

The West became America's national fable at a time when this country needed a new mythology and a hero to match. The frontier had been declared closed by historian Frederick Jackson Turner in 1893; and as the twentieth century promised bigger cities with crowded streets and noisy cars and grimy factory jobs and an ever-more-intrusive government to control it all, America turned to the wide open spaces of the West for spiritual reassurance, and to cowboys for a moral compass. For young Leonard Slye, who got to see a cowboy movie when his father, working at the shoe factory, had a spare dime, and for Frances Smith, who imagined riding off into the sunset with her cowboy hero, the Wild West was less history than it was a fabulous vision of paradise lost—American style.

In Buffalo Bill's Wild West shows, as well as in rodeos and dime novels, the story of the frontier had become a beloved epic adventure bristling with all the good, simple ideals that twentieth-century life seemed to threaten—bravery, self-reliance, and the eternal promise of open range. In Owen Wister's best-selling book *The Virginian,* published in 1902, America first met the quintessential cowboy protagonist: a strong, silent gent who was wily, tough, dangerous, and gallant. Most important of all, the Virginian lived by what became known as the Code of the West—ironclad rules of honor and conduct that arose from the real details of frontier life but were fit for a citizen of Mount Olympus. America's cowboy hero, by the time he became a staple of the movies, was already considered virtuous and invincible—a mounted warrior with Victorian standards of right and wrong and frontier survival skills.

The power of this ideal, which stayed a fundamental part of cowboy pictures for a good half century, could be magical. Take the case of William Boyd, the movies' Hopalong Cassidy. Boyd had a good career as a motion picture headliner in the 1920s, starring in such non-Westerns as Cecil B.

DeMille's *The Volga Boatmen* (1926), and with Lupe Velez in D. W. Griffith's *Lady of the Pavements* (1929); off-screen he was notorious in the movie colony as a roguish party animal who drank, dated, and stayed up all night having fun. He was on top of the world, but in 1931 a strange twist of fate changed his life: a different, older actor, also named William Boyd, was arrested by Hollywood police on a morals charge. Newspapermen who knew the young William Boyd's wild ways simply assumed that it was he who had been pinched, and they ran his picture, by mistake, with arrest reports in the papers. Young Boyd's reputation was ruined, and he turned to the bottle to drown his sorrow. He became even more notorious as a drunkard and his career went to pot; no one would hire him. In 1934 he sobered up enough to land the role of Hopalong Cassidy, which turned out to be such a hit that he played Hoppy for the rest of his life. He also quit drinking; he quit smoking; he stopped going to wild parties; and he is reported to have stayed faithful to his wife until the day he died, in 1972. William Boyd had been transformed into a genuine good guy by his role as white-hatted Hoppy.

William S. Hart, the star who did the most to establish the image of Hollywood's cowboy as a strict enforcer of virtue in movies he made during the 'teens, fell out of fashion in the Jazz Age. Hart's vision of the West had been severe, and he had been a stickler for realism in the way towns looked (dusty, gray, windswept) and the way he, the hero, dressed (in rugged, practical cattle hand's clothes). Westerns remained fundamentally moral tales even in the libertine 1920s, but they developed a new sense of style. Celluloid cowboys soon supplemented their moral purity with another trait for which actual cowpunchers hadn't exactly been famous: they were incredible fashion plates. Tom Mix was the first saddle dandy, who so loved the trappings of his role that he sometimes rode to the premieres of his movies on top of a custom Cadillac that Harley Earl had designed for him with a saddle built into the roof. His full-bore buckaroo attire set a standard that movie cowboys would emulate for years. Bearing only a symbolic connection to the tough, leathery clothing real ranch hands wore, his outfits were more like regal vestments suited to a potentate. He delighted in solid white pearl-button shirts and matching riding britches; he sported an immaculate white, high-peaked ten-gallon hat and a horsehair belt with diamond buckle and the inscription TOM MIX, AMERICA'S CHAMPION COWBOY. Mix, who had actually served as a U.S. deputy marshal in Oklahoma, learned showmanship while working with the 101 Ranch Show; and it was mostly because of his success as one of the 1920s biggest superstars that the realistic, near-documentary look of early cowboy movies gave way to a more flamboyant sense of Western high style.

Tom Mix was abetted in his quest for finery and fringe by the greatest parade saddlemaker of all time, Edward Bohlin. Bohlin, a young Swedish immigrant, came to visit Hollywood in the 1920s from Cody, Wyoming, where he had set up a leather shop. When Tom Mix saw the fancy alligator-skin boots and calfskin coat Bohlin wore to a show one night, he literally bought them off his feet and back and encouraged Bohlin to set up shop in Hollywood. Soon known as "the Michelangelo of saddlecraft," Bohlin crafted silver-encrusted, elaborately tooled parade saddles, bridles, gunbelts, and boots the likes of which the world had never seen. All of the movies' best-dressed cowboy horses wore Bohlin attire. To this day, Roy Rogers wears a hand-tooled belt and saddle-shaped ring his good friend Ed Bohlin crafted for him; and the finest saddles in his collection are all Bohlin originals.

Well before Roy Rogers acted in his first movie, the public's image of the cowboy had become more show business than cow business. Even in the early days of the Sons of the Pioneers, Roy recalls adding silver conchas and fringe to their stage outfits to give them a more resplendent Western look. By the early 1930s, deluxe ranch wear was in vogue, and not only among cowboy movie stars. Dude ranches had become a passion among Americans who could afford to visit them; the Santa Fe railroad lured thousands to visit the Southwest (and come home wearing Indian jewelry and cowboy hats), and championship rodeo had become a glittering annual event in New York, Boston, and Chicago as well as in more traditional cowboy capitals such as Cheyenne and Pendleton.

In 1930 a tailor named Rodeo Ben opened a shop in Philadelphia known as "The East's Most Western Store." Ben set the sartorial standards for movie cowboys as Ed Bohlin did for their horses; Tom Mix became his best customer, and after Tom, it was de rigueur for any serious sagebrush celebrity to outfit himself with tasseled, embroidered, brightly colored outfits made by Ben. Ben later went on to market his marvels to the public at large, inventing snap-button shirts (in 1933, when he saw a cowboy on a bucking horse get hung up by his button-front shirt on the saddle horn) and Wranglers, the first zip-fly jeans. Western clothing authority Tyler Beard reports that Ben had a deal with Roy Rogers and Gene Autry that he would never make a similar outfit for both of them.

Curiously, Western movies had been considered an endangered form in the 1920s. Cowboys were, after all, relics of the nineteenth century; and after Charles Lindbergh became the nation's darling by flying solo over the Atlantic, how could a mere hero on horseback command respect? The Jazz Age loved anything modern, which cowboys most certainly were not, and in an era that was learning to find its thrills in action-packed gangster melodramas and sophisticated bedroom comedies, some critics came to see Westerns as a mere vestige of movies' early days. Furthermore, the coming of sound to motion pictures seemed to make horse operas ob-solete because they told their stories via action rather than dialogue. Who'd want to sit in a theater and listen to a couple of tobacco-chewing cowboys have a conversation about oats and hay and horseshoes?

On the other hand, a clean-cut singing cowboy proved to be something else! About the time Roy Rogers and the Sons of the Pioneers were making a name for themselves around Los Angeles performing the kind of rich-harmony, *modern* cowboy music that would eventually be called Western swing, a former telegraph operator from Oklahoma named Gene Autry was making a splash as a performer on the "National Barn Dance" radio show in Chicago. Gene Autry appeared in the Ken Maynard Western, *In Old Santa Fe,* to sing a few cowboy songs as a kind of novelty act. What was curious about this movie was that it wasn't set in *old* Sante Fe. It took place in the twentieth century, on a dude ranch, and its bad guys were gangsters with Tommy guns. The picture was a hit, Gene became a star, and the up-to-date setting established a pattern for all of his early pictures, as well as for many of the Westerns Roy Rogers later made: the juxtaposition of contemporary life and cowboy values. Billed as "The Singing Cowboy," Gene Autry revived Westerns by making them look—and sound—modern.

As it turned out, the old-fashioned good guy wasn't nearly as dead as he had seemed in 1929 when *Photoplay* magazine declared that the new age of airplane travel had put "the cowboy into discard as a type of national hero [who has] slunk away into the brush, never to return." The overwhelming national anxiety generated by the Great Depression in the 1930s caused many Americans to reconsider the high-riding buckaroo and his "old-fashioned" values. Culturally speaking, you could say that the Roaring Twenties had left the nation with a hangover, the kind of ache that makes you promise to be good and pure of heart and never sin again. In that frame of mind, the clear-eyed, strong, steady cowboy that the movies had polished to a fare-thee-well was a timely hero. Goodness was his middle name.

When war began to loom in Europe and twentieth-century wickedness took on a distinctly foreign face, there was something especially reassuring about America's indigenous good guy, the cowboy. His down-home skills, his confidence, his unalterable sense of right and wrong, and the fact that he always got his man made him the perfect defender of the American way of life. The 1930s were the golden age for B-Westerns, series pictures produced quickly and cheaply for an audience that included (but wasn't limited to) children. Roy Rogers and Gene Autry were the top stars of these pictures, each of which contained a clear moral point in its adventure. Like often-told folktales, the plots and characters of Roy's and Gene's pictures were familiar, and their lessons were always reassuring. Even if Nazis or foreign agents weren't the bad guys, the message was still the same inspiring one: good old cowboy values—American values—were certain to prevail.

For Roy Rogers, playing an all-American good guy was no stretch. He grew up in the hollers of Duck Run, Ohio, believing in cowboy values long before he ever dreamed he would be the movie's greatest symbol of them.

—J. & M. S.

CHAPTER 5

Roy's Story

Seventy-five dollars a week, each and every week! That's what Republic agreed to pay me for the next seven years. I was sitting on top of the world.

Before I signed, I had to wangle my way *out* of the contract the Sons of the Pioneers had only recently signed with Columbia Pictures. Actually, that was easy. Harry Cohn, the studio boss, was happy to release me so long as I promised to find someone to replace me in the group. His decision made my move to Republic possible, and also underscored why I wanted to be at Republic rather than Columbia. I would have been just another cowboy singer at Gower Gulch—easily replaceable—rather than a potential leading man the way they were talking at Republic. Besides, Republic made the best, most action-packed Westerns in those days.

My place in the Sons of the Pioneers was taken by Robert Ellsworth O'Brady, a fine bass fiddle player who had also learned comedy from his parents, who were vaudevillians. Everyone called him Pat Brady, and I liked him a lot. He was originally an Ohio boy himself, and would later become one of my best pals, then a good sidekick in movies and on television. He was a real mugger when he got up stage—made faces of all kinds, cracked up the audience; but you know something funny? Offstage, he was more shy than me. Why, he'd paw the floor and look at his shoes whenever he had to talk to someone new.

All the high spirits I felt after my screen test and getting the contract with Republic were soon replaced with the harsher realities of finding myself described as "raw talent" that needed to be made into a marketable commodity. My singing voice, yodeling talents, and acceptable screen presence were just the beginning of the package Republic wanted to put together. They decided to use studio machinery to rework me into something that the moviegoing public would like.

The first problem they wanted to solve was my eyes. The studio felt that a movie star should have big, soft, limpid ones like Clark Gable's. Mine were squinty, just like Pop's—I guess because of our Choctaw blood. They put me on a routine of prescription eyedrops that were supposed to relax my eye muscles and dilate my pupils. Fortunately, this lasted only a short while. After I appeared as a bit player and sang a solo in *Wild Horse Rodeo* (one of a series of "Three Mesquiteer" Westerns that were popular in the 1930s), the studio got a good handful of letters from folks who had liked my face the way it had been. "What did you do to his eyes?" they wanted to know. After that, I quit using the eyedrops, and once I got popular these squinty eyes of mine pretty much became a trademark.

Next, my body was examined and it was decided that my upper chest and shoulders were too puny. I was instructed to do a hundred handstands a day and walk around on my hands as long as I could. I actually got pretty good at it, and could walk around on my hands nearly as comfortably as on my feet. I wonder if my Pop's talents as an acrobat might have been passed down to me along with his eyes. Anyway, this hand-walking came in handy as a way to pass the time during my first few months at the studio. I showed up for work every day, but most days I had absolutely nothing to do. So I whittled some, shot the breeze with other bit players between takes, and walked from set to set and around the lot on my hands.

At the time, I was calling myself Dick Weston. I had traded in Leonard Slye for the new name when I first started getting small roles in movies because I believed it sounded more rugged. But the studio people didn't like it—thought it was too bland. One day I was called into the office of Herbert Yates, the head of the studio. Sol and Moe Siegel were there, too. They all kind of ganged up and told me that if they were going to make anything of me, the first thing they had to do was give me a new name. Because Will Rogers had been a wonderful man and was loved by all America, one of them suggested the last name "Rogers." I liked that because he was one of my heroes, too, so I said okay. Then one of those fellas said he thought Leroy would go pretty good with it. I said a loud NO. You see, I had known a kid named Leroy back in Ohio when I was young, and I didn't like him one bit. I sure didn't want his name stuck to me for all the world to know. But then I shortened it to Roy, which sounded pretty good. Mr. Yates approved. He said it flowed off the tongue. "I like it," he declared. "It's alliterative."

Sol Siegel pointed out with great delight that in French, Roy means "king."

So it was that early in 1938 I became Roy Rogers. As a matter of fact, I didn't legally change my name from Leonard Slye to Roy Rogers until 1942; I reckon I wasn't quite certain until then that my work as an actor was for real. Before I even got comfortable with my new name, I was sued by a vaudevillian named Roy Rogers. He felt that there wasn't room for two of us in show business. Republic made a deal with him, giving him some money and the right to use his name on stage but keeping the rights to the name Roy Rogers for motion pictures. I'm not sure exactly what they paid the other Roy Rogers, but he walked away a happy man; and I walked away with a whole new identity.

The new and improved Roy Rogers was supposed to be a man who had a much more interesting life than I ever did. Studio publicists decided that to go with my name, they'd brew up a tale or two about where I came from. I guess they figured the saga of poor ol' Len Slye from Duck Run, Ohio, wasn't romantic and heroic enough. So they came up with a biography for me that they started sending out in press releases even before I had a featured role in a movie. Republic's "newest Western star," Roy Rogers, had been born in Cody, Wyoming, and grew up on a vast cattle ranch, where he picked up horseback riding skills before he learned to walk. He was a rodeo star at a tender age, and a top hand with a gun and a rope. He left home (on horseback) for New Mexico, where he worked as a cowpuncher before galloping West and tying up his trusty mount at Republic Studio's hitching post.

The studio was so danged busy fussing around with my name, my looks, and whoppers about my background that they pretty much forgot to put me in any pictures. Other than my small roles in *Wild Horse Rodeo* and Gene Autry's *The Old Barn Dance,* I had way more time than I wanted to perfect my hand-walking skills. Don't get me wrong. After pickin' peaches and working in the shoe factory I was as happy as a plump pig in the sunshine to be in the movies and taking home a weekly paycheck. Arlene and I had a roof over our heads, and I was confident that my big break would come along any day.

It happened when Gene Autry did what he had been threatening to do: up and quit. He and Mr. Yates came to loggerheads over the fact that the studio was getting a nickel for every dime he made, no matter how he made it—not just movies, but radio, personal appearances, and endorsements. Another problem was that Gene didn't like the way Republic was selling his pictures—as part of a package, forcing exhibitors to take a bunch of movies they might not want in order to get one of his. He was one of the most popular movie stars in the country at the time, but the only person more stubborn than ol' Gene was Mr. Yates, who refused to alter the contract. On the first scheduled day of shooting a picture to be called *Washington Cowboy,* Gene sent word to the studio that he wasn't going to show up. In retaliation, Mr. Yates suspended him, then sued to prevent him from performing in any venue or using his name for any purpose until he fulfilled his obligations to Republic.

I was called into the offices of Republic and offered the leading role in *Washington Cowboy.* This was what I had been shooting for, although it sure as heck wasn't how I wanted to get my first big part. At the time, I didn't know Gene Autry all that well—he was a big star and I was pretty much a nobody—but I liked him. I've always liked him. Ever since the beginning, though, a lot of studio p.r. people have tried to create a rivalry between us, and the fact that I replaced him when he walked out made it easy to imagine we saw each other as enemies. With all the write-ups, you'd think we hated each other. But believe me, that's just Hollywood malarkey. Problem was, that when you were under contract to a studio, you didn't have much control over what they said about you or even over the words they'd put in your mouth. There were plenty of times they'd give something to a writer that Gene supposedly said about me, or I about him—something mean and ugly—and it would go into print. Whenever that happened, he'd call me or I'd call him and say, "Listen, Gene, you know I said nothing like this whatsoever." We've gotten along just fine over the years. We're different sorts of people, that's for sure—I like the outdoors, hunting, and such; he was always more of a businessman—but we're two human beings, and we respect each other. Always have, no matter what words they've put in our mouths.

I liked the story of *Washington Cowboy.* It was about a buckaroo who goes to Congress to save poor starving farmers and ranchers during the Depression. Well, I knew a little something about those hard times myself, and the idea of at last being the good guy really appealed to me. The leading lady was Carol Hughes; my sidekick was Smiley Burnette, along with his horse, Ring-Eye Nellie; and my horse was a newcomer to pictures, a big golden palomino named Trigger.

A few days before shooting began, several different stables brought horses around for me to try. After all, you can't be a movie cowboy without one! Each outfit was eager for me to pick their horse because if I did, it meant that they would likely be able to supply all the posse horses for the picture. There were six or seven good—I mean really good—mounts to try. They were handsome, well-trained, and fast. But the minute I got on this palomino stallion brought over by the Hudkins Stables, I didn't even consider any of the others. He was beautiful with his flaxen mane and tail and proud arched neck. As I hit an easy lope, then a fast gallop, I could feel that this boy was an athlete with power to spare and fine balance that would set him in good stead for chases over rocky grades and down steep mountain slopes. His sire had been a racehorse; his mother was a cold-blooded palomino; he took his power from Dad and his good looks and easygoing personality from Mom. Named Golden Cloud, he was four years old at the time and had already appeared in one other movie—as Olivia De Havilland's horse in *The Adventures of Robin Hood*. His name got changed when Smiley Burnette and I were hanging around the set one day and I was practicing my quick-draw. Smiley said, "Roy, as quick as that horse of yours is, you ought to call him Trigger."

Washington Cowboy was renamed *Under Western Stars*. Republic put everything they had behind making and promoting it. In April 1938, they sent me, Smiley, and the Sons of the Pioneers down to the premiere in Dallas, where we performed live to a full house and were given the key to the city. Critics liked it, and I got reviews that made my head swell. *Variety* called me "a cinch B.O.'er"; the *New York Times* said I was "a new Playboy of the Western World ... who has a drawl like Gary Cooper [and] a smile like Shirley Temple." Republic was known for producing B-Westerns, but *Under Western Stars* made its way to first-run houses such as the Criterion Theater in New York City. Audiences in cities and small towns liked it as much as the critics did; but no long lines of people waiting to see my first picture thrilled me quite as much as my own mom and pop's reaction. They drove their old jalopy to the theater it was playing in and watched it over and over again, night after night. A few years later I had the studio make them their very own print.

During the three months after the picture was released, I toured the country and promoted it in every big and little city you can think of. Wherever I went and listened to people tell me how much they enjoyed *Under Western Stars,* I heard how much they liked not only my performance but also Trigger's. Trigger was still owned by the Hudkins Stables, which meant that I couldn't take him out on a personal appearance tour if I wanted to; it also meant that they could lease him to another cowboy actor if they wanted to. When I returned from the publicity tour I went out to see Clyde Hudkins. I found him in the barn. "Sell the palomino to me," I said, "and if I hit the jackpot, I'll make sure Hudkins horses are on the set."

Mr. Hudkins considered my proposition as he watched me rub the nose of the golden stallion, who had stuck his head out of his stall when he heard my voice. Then he named his price: $2,500. Remember, I was earning seventy-five dollars a week. Twenty-five hundred dollars was like Sutter's gold. Still, I took a deep breath and held out my hand to shake. It was a deal. Mr. Hudkins agreed to take care of ol' Trig until I came up with the money. I paid him off on time, just like you would a bedroom set. It seemed like a lot of money back then, but I can tell you for sure and certain that it was the best $2,500 I ever spent.

Exactly what it meant to be a star didn't hit me till I came home from that first publicity tour and walked into the mailroom of Republic Studios. There I came face to face with a Mount Everest of fan mail. The next day Arlene went over with me to try to sort it all out, and piece by piece, we answered letters and signed photographs and handaddressed every one. By the end of the day, the pile of new letters that had come in was twice the size of the ones we had answered.

I may have been a star to the public, but you sure wouldn't have known it by the way I was treated at the studio. Why, Arlene and I spent half our time running back and forth to the post office all day long and buying stamps with money from our own pockets. I was actually spending more in postage than my salary. When I asked for a secretary to help answer all the letters, Mr. Yates refused. He suggested doing what some other movie stars did—throwing the fan mail in the garbage.

I didn't like that idea at all. It went against my nature. It was rude, and Mom and Pop didn't bring me up to be rude to people who were nice enough to take the time to sit down and write me a letter. Anyway, all the people who wrote those letters were the same ones who stood in line to buy movie tickets. It seemed like a sensible exchange to me: spend a few pennies for a stamp to mail them back on autograph in return for them spending a dime to buy a movie ticket. The more I traveled around the country to do personal appearances and met the people who were writing these fan letters, the angrier I got at Republic for disrespecting them.

I returned to Hollywood from a long road trip with a full head of steam about this matter, and decided to put my old skills as a truck driver to use. I rented a five-ton dump truck and drove it over to the studio. I pulled it up to the loading dock at the mailroom and filled it full of Roy Rogers fan mail waiting to be answered. I backed the truck up in front of Herb

Yates's office, opened the back gate, and hoisted the bed. Out tumbled a cascade of letters forming a huge pile in front of his picture window. He came running out screaming and yelling and demanding to know what I was doing. I told him that this was the mail that I alone was supposed to handle and that I would appreciate it if the studio gave me a hand in writing back to the fans. The Old Man was red in the face with anger as I climbed back into the cab of the truck. "Rogers, take this away," he screamed as I waved sweetly back at him and drove off.

"Nope," I called back. "I'm going to leave it here on your lawn." As I drove away, I saw him in the rearview mirror, jumping up and down next to that mountain of letters.

It would be great if I could tell you that the next day I had a squadron of secretaries at my disposal, but Yates was as stubborn with me as he had been with Gene Autry. I received a twenty-five-dollar-a-week raise (I suppose to help with the price of stamps). I, Arlene, my mom, and my sisters still spent a whole lot of free time slogging through the 20,000 pieces of fan mail that came in each week for me.

Mr. Yates kept me plenty busy after the success of *Under Western Stars*. I made thirty-six pictures between 1938 and 1942. Each was about an hour long. Gene Autry had ironed out his contract dispute and come back to the studio, so we were working there at the same time; but our movies were generally pretty different. Gene always played himself, and his movies were all set in modern times with cars and radios and bad guys in business suits. Most of my early pictures after *Under Western Stars* were set in the past, and I played someone else, not Roy Rogers. I was Billy the Kid, Wild Bill Hickock, or Buffalo Bill; and we tried to give each picture an historical flavor. I always seemed to be wearing some sort of costume from the Civil War or the old days, and I didn't always play the good guy either. In *Billy the Kid Returns*, I played two roles—one as Billy the Kid and another as a good guy who looks like him and gets accused of killing some-body. I sang about a half-dozen songs in each picture, and even though I started out thinking of myself as more a singer than an actor, I eventually learned acting pretty much the way I learned music—by ear. I would read a script and I'd hear it a certain way in my head, and that's the way I did it. If I was a bad guy, I didn't smile; if I was a good guy, I had plenty of pleasant personality and a lot of smiles. That was about it: I never tried any fancy trick acting on screen. I was just me. The Roy Rogers way back then was the same as the one sittin' here today. As Popeye used to say, "I yam what I yam."

I did argue with Mr. Yates when he tried to cast me as a real heel in a non-Western movie about a newspaper called *The Front Page.* I was supposed to be a cigarette-smoking, hard-drinking reporter. I knew for sure that my fans wouldn't like it at all if I played that part, but when I said no, the Old Man started yelling and reminding me I was under contract to the studio. To get me in line, he threatened to take away my upcoming cowboy roles as well, and to put a point on his threat, he said he would replace me with another actor who could ride Trigger in my place. The horse would make a star of anyone who rode him, he argued. "Trigger is the one who's earning the paycheck, not you, Rogers," he said. It sure was fun to tell Mr. Yates that there wasn't going to be any other cowboy riding Trigger, because I owned him. As angry as he was, he wasn't fool enough to press his hand. Trigger was pulling in hundreds of fan letters a week in his own right, and if Yates insisted on having me play the role of a drunk he was going to lose two stars for his Western movies, not one. He backed off and let me have my way. Lloyd Nolan played the part of the newspaper reporter in *The Front Page.*

Herb Yates never entirely dropped the issue of trying to get me to play more than just cowboy roles. Sometimes he won, and the result was worthwhile. In 1940 I was cast in *Dark*

Command along with John Wayne, Walter Pidgeon, and Marjorie Main, a group of actors anyone would be proud to work with. The picture got good reviews, but I was much more comfortable playing a good guy cowboy in "oaters" by the dozen.

I was becoming part of an ensemble that would stay with me most of my professional life. Trigger was always by my side, soon getting second billing on posters and marquees as "The Smartest Horse in the Movies." When Gene Autry came back to Republic, Smiley Burnette returned as his sidekick, which meant I needed one. Gabby Hayes, who had developed his role as a crazy old codger playing Windy Halliday, sidekick to Hopalong Cassidy, filled the bill perfectly starting with *Southward Ho* in 1939. Gabby became a good friend as well as movie sidekick—a brother, father, and buddy all in one. You know, the funny thing about Gabby is that his old-coot character was all an act. He was a fine actor, and one of the best-dressed men in Hollywood, someone you couldn't imagine rambling on about "them dag-nabbed persnickety women" like he did in all those movies we made. I called him Pappy, and we confided in each other. One time between pictures he called me in a panic, moaning, "Roy, I'm in big trouble! I shaved off my beard. When I looked in the mirror, I almost died. I forgot how ugly I am!" We talked about it awhile, and after I reassured him the beard would grow back, he calmed down. "You won't see me for a while, though," he warned me. "I'm not even going to stick my head out the door until the dang thing's grown back and I look myself again."

Starting with my second picture, *Billy the Kid Returns* in 1938, I was teamed up with Mary Hart, who was added to give the stories some romance. We never kissed or anything; but she balanced all the action with a nice, soft touch and gave the movie someone I could sing to. Studio publicists labeled us "Sweethearts of the West." After we did six pictures together, Mary decided she had had her fill of sage-brush romance, quit the series, and took back her original name, which was Lynn Roberts. You see, when she started making Westerns Mr. Yates made her change her name to Mary Hart just so he could bill us as "Republic's own Rogers and Hart," like the successful Broadway musical writing team.

I was a star, at least judging by the amounts of mail I got. But believe me when I tell you I sure wasn't rich. Arlene and I lived in a small frame house, and we were always cooking up schemes to try and bring in enough money so we didn't have to live from paycheck to paycheck. We opened a Western-wear store in Studio City called Roy's Hitching Post, but dust gathered on the shelves and our bankbook stayed flat.

My fortunes began to change when I got a call from an agent, Art Rush, who asked me to have lunch with him at Eaton's, a restaurant across the street from Republic Studios. I didn't have much use for agents at that time, but I was still enough of a hungry country boy at heart to agree to meet him when he said he'd pick up the check. I was skeptical; I knew Art Rush represented some pretty heavy-duty talent, including MGM's Nelson Eddy and the Sportsmen Quartet, who were regulars on Jack Benny's radio show. Before striking out on his own, he had been a well-known boy wonder on the Hollywood music scene, producing records for RCA by such artists as Benny Goodman, Tommy Dorsey, and Artur Rubinstein when he was only in his twenties. I couldn't imagine why he would want to do business with a Republic Studios singing cowboy earning $150 per week.

The William Morris Agency had been interested in me, but after that lunch, I knew Art was the agent for me. My decision was based less on any particular deals he outlined and more on the way I felt about him. He seemed like such a decent and honorable man, plus he had grown up in Ohio.

What more could I ask? We shook hands at the end of that lunch, and neither of us ever felt the need to put it in writing. Art remained my agent for forty-eight years on the strength of that handshake, with never a written contract between us. Nowadays, no one does business like that; but, then, Art Rush was one of a kind.

Art got me work doing some radio shows and public appearances to supplement my income. I came to learn much later that he was so worried about the state of my finances that he never drew his commission until two years after he started working on my behalf. For a while I starred in a syndicated dramatic radio show called "Manhattan Cowboy," which added a hundred extra dollars a month to my income. It was Art's idea for me to make appearances at rodeos all around the country, including the big one at Madison Square Garden in New York, and he made it so the studio didn't get a cut. I think if Mr. Yates knew how much I was making on the side, he would have busted a gut. Once those personal appearances began, I was earning ten times what my acting job at Republic paid.

"Roy, I think you and Arlene can start looking for a nicer house," Art called to tell me one day. He knew we were eager to move. "I think you can afford one that costs $10,000."

I jumped for joy. The next day, Arlene and I went out house-hunting. But the place we found wasn't for us. We now knew we'd get that soon enough. What we found instead was a home for my folks: a white bungalow on a little chicken ranch in the San Fernando Valley. "Welcome home!" I said to Pop as I handed him the key. The place had cost a little under $9,000, so I took the money left over from my ten and hid it in a dozen sugar bowls in the pantry where I knew my mom would find it.

Arlene had a lovely singing voice and could play the piano well, but she did not share my interest in show business. She was a homebody who wanted children more than anything.

I was pretty eager for some little ones myself. It hurts when the thing you want the most doesn't come your way, and this was the case with us having babies. We simply couldn't conceive a child. As time went by, we started to think of other ways to have a family. Right from the beginning of my career I had always played charity events, and I could never turn down a request to perform at an orphanage or children's hospital. Those little faces looking up at me made my heart ache; and now that I was married and had enough money to be a good daddy, it became all the more difficult to walk out the door of a place filled with babies who needed homes.

There was one orphanage I visited in St. Louis more than fifty years ago that I remember like it was yesterday. A little girl with coal black hair and bright blue eyes ran up to me and hugged me tight, begging me to take her home. She just grabbed me and refused to let go. I sang a couple of songs to her, and it near killed my heart the way she held on. When it was over and I had to leave, the staff pried her little hands from my arms. I can still feel them, and I can still see that lonesome girl as though she's standing right here now.

Adopting was never far from my mind, and I could see the need for a baby in Arlene's eyes, too. In 1942 I traveled to Dallas, Texas, to meet with two men who were releasing my pictures. When we got through talking business, I said, "By the way, you guys wouldn't know where a fella could adopt a child?" They grinned, looked knowingly at each other, and then back at me. "Roy," they said "it just so happens that we're on the board of directors for Hope Cottage." Hope Cottage was a home for orphaned, abandoned, and neglected children. We went right over and met the matron, Mrs. Carson, who showed me around.

There were forty-two little cribs in one big room, each one occupied by a baby that needed a home. Some were just weeks old, and I was told that they couldn't be adopted until they had reached four months. I started through, looking into each crib, and when I got to the seventh one, this little blond head just popped up and looked straight at me with her big brown eyes. I don't think I ever saw a baby look so hard. At that moment, I knew God had given us a child. Her name was Cheryl Darlene. I told Mrs. Carson I wanted her. When I called Arlene and told her what I had done, she wept with joy.

Mrs. Carson, head of Hope Cottage, came to stay with me and Arlene for two weeks to make sure we were not "Hollywood types" and that we would make good parents. She watched every move we made and asked questions day and night: "What time do you go to bed on Friday night? . . . How often does the milkman deliver eggs? . . . What sort of music do you listen to on the radio?" The questions weren't so bad, but the wait for our baby to turn four months seemed like forever. We passed the inspection, and when Cheryl Darlene was old enough we drove to Dallas to claim her as our own. Our friends and family were thrilled that at last we were a family. The only bitter note was the disdain shown by some Hollywood columnists who apparently hadn't known that Roy Rogers was a married man. It was standard procedure in those days for leading men to be single and available, so publicity sent out by the studio didn't mention anything about a Mrs. Roy Rogers. To the surprise of some folks in Hollywood, I now not only had a wife, but a baby, too; and the gossip columnists wrote that my image as a heart throb was tarnished. It didn't bother me a whit. I was too happy being a new daddy to concern myself with the bitter words of a few reporters. When Cheryl Darlene batted her brown eyes and smiled in my direction, nothing else mattered very much.

Things got better every day. Arlene and I moved to our own bigger home—a six-acre spread in the San Fernando Valley. I decided my career was going well enough that it would finally be all right to change my name legally to Roy Rogers (although to my mother I would always be Leonard).

One day I came home from work with real exciting news. The city of New York had asked me to ride Trigger in a grand parade to benefit the war effort. They were dropping a long-standing no-horses regulation for the occasion, and I was thrilled at the thought of taking my golden palomino up Fifth Avenue alongside the governor's and mayor's cars. Arlene seemed delighted to hear about it, too. But then she asked me to sit down. She sat next to me, on the arm of the chair, put her hands on my shoulders, looked me in the eyes, and topped my news by a mile.

Arlene said, "Roy, I'm pregnant." There and then, I was certain that the world had stopped spinning. After waiting so long, Arlene and I finally made a baby together. Linda Lou Rogers was born April 18, 1943. The Rogers family was now three girls and me.

That year it was like my career had been hitched to a shooting star. Gene Autry left Republic to join the Army Air Corps, and Mr. Yates, who had always had a fondness for pictures with the word "King" in the title, decided that with Gene gone it would be the proper time to crown me once and for all as King of the Cowboys. It turned out to be the right time to make that move, because that year the theater owners elected me the number-one Western star. Cowboy pictures, which had once been the staple of Saturday matinees and second-string theaters, were popular among all kinds of folks, not just the kids. Partly, it was because of the success of John Ford's *Stagecoach* in 1939, which showed that cowboy movies could be more than shoot-'em-ups. I reckon maybe it also had something to do with the war: at times like that, when people feel insecure and threatened, it's good to have a hero who knows just what to do when he's faced with trouble. Whatever the reasons, it seemed that all over America the cowboy had become everybody's favorite kind of movie star.

To prove my royal status, Republic starred me in a movie called *King of the Cowboys,* set in modern times, in which I foil a band of Nazi saboteurs. During brief lulls in the action, I get together with the Sons of the Pioneers to sing "A Gay Ranchero," "I'm an Old Cowhand," "Red River Valley," "Ride 'em Cowboy," and a few other numbers. The studio initiated a nationwide billboard campaign to promote me. They had used billboards in the past to promote a movie, but this time it was for me, King of the Cowboys. By July 1, there were 192 roadside billboards; Republic was buying spots on the radio and big advertisements in all the newspapers. The cost for all this was supposedly half a million dollars, which in 1943 was a plentiful amount of money to spend on any movie or movie star. Westerns were suddenly no longer relegated to second-run theaters and Saturdays matinees. *Variety* wrote about "the return of the cowpokes," commenting, "Republic's Roy Rogers saddlers are galloping into high-admission houses that once refused to recognize Gene Autry." *King of the Cowboys* played on 7,500 screens when it was released, including the prestigious Loews chain.

The corker for all this came in July, when *Life* magazine put me on its cover. I guess you could say that in the 1940s *Life* was the ultimate test of stardom, sort of what *People* is today, but maybe even more so. The cover showed me waving on ol' Trigger, who was rearing up with the city of Los Angeles in the background. The story that went with it was kinda silly, written by the humorist H. Allen Smith. Mr. Smith, who as a journalist was very aware of Republic's publicity campaign for me, was tickled by all my fancy clothes and the big studio buildup, describing me as a "manufactured personality." He didn't believe I was for real, so he had some fun with my image as a hero:

> He is the protagonist in the American morality play. He is purity rampant—never drinks, never smokes, never shoots pool, never spits, and the roughest oath at his command is "shucks!" He never needs a shave, and when it comes to fist-fighting, he seldom takes on a single opponent: he beats their

brains out in a group. He always wins the girl though he doesn't kiss her. He kisses his horse. His immense public would have him no other way.

Franklin D. Roosevelt invited me to the White House for a March of Dimes Ball held on his sixty-first birthday. I brought him a pair of silver spurs engraved "To FDR from Roy Rogers." There were other Hollywood celebrities there, too, including James Cagney, Loretta Young, and Edgar Bergen, but while they were dining off fine china in the formal room, Mrs. Roosevelt came along, tapped me on the shoulder, and invited me back to the kitchen. To be honest, I was a lot more comfortable there; and you know something funny? So was she. She asked the chef to make us some hamburgers, which we ate with our hands, and we gabbed all night about one of my favorite subjects, and hers: Trigger!

After Mary Hart left the series of Westerns, I had a string of leading ladies, including Sally Payne, Gale Storm, Peggy Moran, Ruth Terry, and Linda Hayes. None of them lasted long for the simple reason that playing opposite me wasn't much of a plum part. Trigger was my costar, and Gabby Hayes got all the funny lines; the girl was lucky if she appeared in three good scenes. Gabby was always arguing for better women's roles in the movies. "Half the people who come to see our pictures are girls," he reasoned. "I betcha they'd like to see ladies in the story, maybe even see Roy give one a kiss." In 1944, I did get my first screen kiss, with Jean Porter, in *San Fernando Valley*. It was in a dream sequence, but even so, I am told that a lot of my loyal audience—the young boys—moaned and groaned and squirmed in their seats when they saw it.

In 1944 I got a new costar, who was hired to play in a picture called *The Cowboy and the Señorita*. Her name was Dale Evans and, like me, she had started out as a singer. In fact, I had met her a few years earlier when we were both entertaining the soldiers at Edwards Air Force Base in 1941. I appeared with the Sons of the Pioneers, and I was dancing with Claire Trevor when Art Rush introduced us. I was too bashful to do much other than say "Howdy," but I thought she seemed like an awfully nice girl.

When we started to work together, I got to like Dale right away. She was a person who always looked like she had just stepped out of the shower—real fresh and clean; and she was a good sport, too, carrying her weight in each and every scene and never complaining when we had to work long hours and do stunts that wore us out. I knew that being the girl lead in a cowboy movie wasn't her greatest dream in life, but she never gave it less than her all. When we weren't rehearsing or filming a scene she made me feel comfortable because she was so easy to talk to. When my daughters visited the set it seemed they always liked to pay a visit to Dale's dressing room. She had a way about her that made people feel good. The only thing I found hard to believe was that she had been raised in Texas, because she sure didn't know one end of a horse from another.

I had lots of fans who were girls and grown women, and at least half the fan mail I got came from them. Oh, I'd get ten or twenty proposals of marriage every week! Dale was brought in to make my pictures a little more romantic for their sakes; but we had to watch ourselves. If we got too romantic onscreen, we knew we would hear from those boys out there who were allergic to "mushy stuff." Dale was a more sophisticated leading lady than I had had before. Her parts were often written to contrast her city ways to my country ways; she would play a reporter or a rich smart aleck who'd have to learn her lesson the hard way. In *Song of Nevada,* she plays an uppity gal who lives back East and has an obnoxious rich boyfriend named Rollo Bingham. She comes out West to sell the ranch of her dead father, but it turns out that her father's only playing dead: he fakes it to lure her back out West, where I'm supposed to win her back to good old Western ways. It takes some convincing, and some singing (including "A Cowboy Has to Yodel in the Morning" and "The Harum Scarum Baron of the Harmonium"), but in the end she falls in love with the West, and with me. It turned out to be a good contrast: her sass and my patience. We made a good team. On screen, of course.

Miraculously, Arlene and I were able to conceive another baby, and I was beside myself with joy when it turned out to be a boy. On October 28, 1946, Roy Rogers, Jr. (we called him Dusty), was born. The press went wild with the news. One headline proclaimed, THE KING HAS A PRINCE. Wire services spread the story all over the globe, and telegrams and presents poured in. I was so tickled by Dusty's birth that I stopped production on the movie I was shooting to take a few weeks off; there was no way I could remember dialogue while I was thinking about the new little fella. I wanted to concentrate on nothing but my wife and my baby boy.

In the days after he was born, I spent nearly all my time at the hospital visiting them. One day Art Rush suggested a game of golf just to ease me back to earth a little, and I thought it sounded like fun. Before I left the house to go meet him, my telephone rang. I stood pinned to the floor as I heard a doctor from the hospital give me the news. Arlene had suffered a massive brain embolism from a blood clot. They wanted me to come at once. I hardly remember the trip there; but I do remember that when I reached Arlene's room, she was in a jungle of tubes and wires and beeping machinery. The doctors looked grim. All their attempts to revive her had failed. I stood by the side of the bed dumb with pain. All the good fortune that I had worked so hard to achieve—to share with her, to build a family with her—was fading as surely as the life in her pale body. I couldn't think straight, I couldn't make sense of what was happening. How could life be so good one minute, then be all over? I stood beside my wife until the last breath left her. I laid my hand on her forehead and whispered good-bye. The nurse pulled a sheet over her face.

I stumbled to a phone and called Art Rush. When his wife answered, I gasped for breath, unable to say the words, finally croaking out, "Arlene's dead." Art got on the phone and told me not to move; he'd be right down to the hospital. I was frantic. I needed to get out, get some air. I went down in the elevator and outside into the parking lot. Shaking so hard with grief I could hardly stand up, I leaned against my car as the world around me spun. I stood there rocking back and forth, weeping. Some children noticed me. Gradually they approached. Too shy to speak, or maybe frightened by the way I was behaving, they nonetheless recognized me as their hero, the King of the Cowboys. They handed me scraps of paper for autographs. I stood there red-eyed and dizzy with grief, looking down into the little faces of my fans. I tried my best to scribble my name and whisper the words "Happy trails" before I sent them on their way, one by one.

CHAPTER 6
Dale's Story

I liked Roy Rogers. It was hard not to like the guy. On the movie set, he was as comfortable as an old shoe to be around. His star was up there when we were teamed together. Another actor in his place might have let success go to his head. Roy was a different sort of man. There wasn't anything phony about him; there was no hungry ego and he had nothing to prove. He had a job to do and he did it, sitting easy in the saddle; and what's more, he enjoyed doing the work so much that his attitude was contagious. He reminded me of home, of Texas when I was young: a breath of clean country air, a boy next door. In short order we made twenty pictures together.

In those days, when you made a Western you made it fast and you worked long hours: up at 4:30 in the morning, home after sunset. So we were close, and I do mean *close.* Roy and I and Gabby Hayes and Pat Brady and the Sons of the Pioneers spent nearly all our waking hours together, week after week, in the studio and on location. With that kind of hectic schedule, there was no way any one of us could put on a false front; we saw the best and worst in one another, in and out of makeup, when we were grumpy, upset, or dog-tired. We became like a family. Roy was the acknowledged head of the family, and I felt as snug around him as I did with my own kin.

My father, back in Texas, got nervous when he saw I was

being teamed with Roy on a regular basis. He wanted to know what kind of man this Hollywood movie star was. I wrote him a letter in which I told him that Roy made me think of my brother Hillman. "No matter what comes up," I wrote, "he seems forever to be on the side of the underdog." I assured him, "You don't have to worry. He's a fine person and a good friend. I guess the best way to describe Roy Rogers is that he rings true."

Good old Gabby Hayes became a dear, dear friend, too. He was such a gentleman, nothing like his screen image as a cantankerous old coot. A former Shakespearean actor, he drove a stylish black Continental convertible, wore fine English tweeds, smoked a pipe, and spoke eloquently when he wasn't on camera with his teeth out of his mouth. He had so much experience on stage in serious plays that he was able to help me with the craft of acting more than I can measure. "Get your face in there," he'd always say if he saw someone upstaging me. Of course *he* was the scene-stealer to top them all.

"Blast you," I said one day after we had done some dialogue together in which he walked away with the scene. "You will chew up and swallow a scene with anybody. You know what I'm going to do one day?" I threatened. "I am going to raise my dress up to here." I hiked my hem above the knee to demonstrate how I would take people's attention away from his mugging.

"Jes' try it," he said, plunging full bore into his most curmudgeonly character, rubbing his hand against his whiskers with conspiratorial glee. "I'll do the dangdest take you've ever seen in your life!"

Of all the studios in Hollywood, Republic was a special place. It was a homey lot—not so big you got lost on it; there were lawns and flowers that were so pretty. After a while, you got to know nearly everybody there. It was a good place to work. Still, that old searing flame of ambition began to lick at my insides. Much as I enjoyed being with Roy and all the gang, it wasn't doing enough for my career to please me. In Westerns, it was always the handsome cowboy and his horse who got the spotlight, not his leading lady. I wasn't even second banana on posters and marquees. Trigger got that honor! Then came Gabby Hayes, and, finally, me. In fact, sometime later I wrote a song called "Don't Ever Fall in Love with a Cowboy (Because He'll Love His Horse the Best)," with a lyric in there that went "We're just as happy as can be/I love him and he loves me/And Trigger makes three." Of course, when we first started working together, falling in love was not an issue. It was work, good hard work. Now, when I think back on it, I believe it was the best way to get to know somebody—better than a date where you're all prettied up and overly polite and pretending to be more glamorous than you are; but at the time, as I said, I was unhappy. I craved a starring role in a sophisticated picture. I didn't want to be part of a team in a Western. And I sure didn't like being "teamed" with Roy Rogers or anybody else.

Mr. Yates, the head of the studio, turned a cold shoulder to my request for something else. He said that exhibitors liked Roy and me as a team; we sold tickets. If I wanted to avoid suspension (and the fines that went with it), I would stay in the saddle. Danny Winkler managed to get me a regular spot on Jimmy Durante's radio show singing and doing comedy bits for a while, but that wasn't sufficient. My ego had become a monster, demanding I think only of my career. I have always been an aggressive kind of person who needed to feel in control of things. What I didn't know then was that I was completely out of control; I was at the mercy of this crazy lust for success.

I did feel pangs of guilt about the way I had brought up Tom—about how little time I was able to devote to him. So I decided to make an effort to have some heart-to-heart talks with him when I came home from work. What I discovered amazed me; I saw a spiritual side of my son that had been

missing in me for such a long time. Tom had become a fine
Christian, thanks to my mother's influence; he was worried
for me; he prayed for me. *My boy prayed for me.* When I realized this, I vowed on all that was high and holy that I would
make up for the time that had been lost between us. I would
be the kind of mother a fine, good boy like that deserved . . .
just as soon as I made it to the top.

Every day when shooting was done, I went to the screening
room to watch the rushes. I studied my gestures and expres-
sions, I listened to the way I delivered each line. I figured out
how to cheat in two-shots so the camera got my face in three-
quarter angle rather than a flat profile. All the way home, I'd
replay mistakes in my head, thinking of ways I could look
better in front of the camera. At night, when I went to bed,
my thoughts were of camera angles and lines of dialogue;
and I sprang up each morning eager to prove myself on the
set. I remember one time Roy and I were doing a two-shot,
standing close to each other supposedly having an intimate
conversation. I wanted my three-quarter view, so when they
called "Roll 'em," I started talking to a tree about a hundred
yards over Roy's left shoulder. In retaliation, he delivered his
dialogue past my left ear.

"For the love of Mike," the director shouted, "who are you
two talking to?"

"When she looks at me, I'll look at her," Roy said. It was a
standoff, which ended when we both broke into a good laugh.
For the retake, we looked into each other's eyes.

I still treasure the time I spent on the set during those early
pictures listening to Roy talk about his family. He loved kids
so much; he liked nothing better than sitting around talking
about them. How I admired him for that! I think it was the
first real spark between us. I had always wanted lots of kids
myself, but of course I had been too busy with my career to
do anything about it, too busy even to dote on my own boy.
And too busy for my second marriage, which ended in divorce.

I told Roy I had a son, but the front office at Republic knew nothing about Tom; he had been a secret ever since that first screen test. One day Dorothy Blair from the publicity department came rushing onto the set, white as a ghost. She pushed me into a private corner somewhere and breathed out the words, "Do you have a son?" A columnist had called, reporting that the army induction center was saying that a recruit named Tom Fox claimed Dale Evans as his mother. My head spun, but to tell the truth, I was never so relieved! "Yes," I said. "Yes! Tom is my son." It felt so good to say it after all those years.

"Keep quiet," Dorothy snapped at me. "Keep quiet. We'll bury the story." And she glided off the set. After that, if ever anyone asked her about it, she told them that stories about Dale Evans's son were just crazy rumors. Tom went off to play in an army band and I went back to my deception, sadder but not a bit wiser. Later on, Louella Parsons finally broke the story to the public, revealing that Joan Bennett had had a child very early in life, too. And finally, when it was all out in the open, I was grateful to her for forcing me to be honest. I hated the lie. And I was so proud of Tom.

Roy and his wife, Arlene, had two children: Cheryl Darlene, whom they adopted at Hope Cottage in Dallas, and their natural daughter, Linda Lou. Linda was a lot like Roy—the quiet type, who let her sparkling eyes do the talking for her. Cheryl was older; she used to come around the movie set quite often, and enjoyed being photographed with her dad when the fan magazines came around. With her honey-colored hair and bright brown eyes, she was as pretty as Shirley Temple, and every bit as extroverted. She could talk the ears off a billy goat: a true Texas gal, like me! I often used to gaze at her and think wistfully, "She is so much like me. She could have been my child."

When Roy wasn't talking about his own children, he was talking about other kids. He especially worried about sick and handicapped ones, and spent a lot of time visiting them in hospitals and shelters. There was magic in the air when Roy Rogers came to visit those kids; their eyes lit up with joy. And when that happened, Roy's eyes sparkled, too. There was no show about it; it was a picture of real love. Oh, how his heart ached for the sick ones, the lonely ones, the frail ones! As I watched the handsome cowboy climb down from the saddle and put his strong hands on the shoulders of a weak little boy or girl, I too fell under his magic spell. This guy was no Hollywood ham. This was a real man!

In 1946 I up and quit Republic Studios. Mr. Yates kept promising that he would put me in a musical comedy after I did just one more Roy Rogers Western, but the part I wanted always went to someone else. So when my contract came up for renewal, I walked out. I didn't think it was fair to be teamed with Roy—not for me, and not for him, either. He was way up there, after all; he didn't need me at all. At the time RKO was planning a lavish picture starring Eddie Cantor and Joan Davis, and they wanted me for the ingenue part. Ironically, it was called *Show Business Out West,* but it was no Saturday sagebrush serial. It had a sophisticated script: at last, my chance to break into real musical comedy! With regrets, I said good-bye to Roy and waited for production to begin at RKO. And waited. *Show Business Out West* never got off the ground. I was left high and dry. Oh, I felt sorry for myself.

Tragedy certainly has a way of putting life in perspective. Roy and his wife, Arlene, were expecting a third child. Roy was certain it was going to be a boy, and he was right. On October 28, 1946, Roy Rogers, Jr., was born. Eight days after the cesarean delivery, Arlene died of an embolism. Suddenly, my woes seemed mighty puny when I looked into Roy's face, stricken with grief over the death of his wife. He was alone with three babies to care for, and he was distraught. Arlene had always managed the house, and suddenly everything was his responsibility. He hired a series of nurses and housekeepers and companions to help with the kids, but none of them could alleviate the sense of loss he felt. It was hard for him in a material way, too. Roy was a top box-office star by this time, but his salary was pitifully low, and he was responsible for so much of his own publicity and wardrobe, even hiring people to answer the thousands of fan letters he got each week. All that plus the cost of all the help he needed at home became a real financial strain. So Roy had to keep working, almost constantly.

After that musical comedy of mine fizzled, Republic offered me a good contract and promised that if I came back I wouldn't make only Westerns. In *The Trespasser,* which was released in 1947, I got my first on-the-lips screen kiss from my costar, Doug Fowley. The kiss, a moment I had dreamt of since I was a little girl, turned out to be a big, fat nothing. No emotion at all, just a job. Reviewers thought the picture was a big, fat nothing, too, so I headed off on a singing tour in hopes the studio could find me something better. While performing at the Steel Pier in Atlantic City I looked out into the audience and spotted Art Rush and Roy Rogers, whom I hadn't seen in months. Old friends! How good it was to see them! After the show we sat together. Roy told me how his kids were doing. I told him Tom had enlisted in the army. We talked long into the night.

The next evening Roy and I had dinner together alone. We began to remember some of the fun we had making Westerns. Roy relished our reminiscing, and as we talked, I saw him brighten with an idea. "Dale," he said, "those movies we did together were good. An awful lot of people liked us as a team. Come on back, won't you?"

"Thank you, Mr. Rogers, but no thank you!" I said, putting my hand on his to let him know it was nothing personal. After all, I had a serious acting career I was just beginning; cowboy movies were not part of the program. Roy didn't press the issue; but he turned his hand up and held mine. It was a friendly gesture.

125

My next picture was *Slippy McGee*. If such a thing is possible, it was a bigger stinkeroo than *The Trespasser*. As I licked my wounds, I remembered Roy's invitation. I went to Herb Yates and said, "Mr. Yates, I would like to ride the range again."

Once more, Roy and I were together most of our waking hours. The schedule was unbelievable: when we weren't making pictures, we were on personal-appearance tours that took us to rodeos, state fairs, auto races, and grand openings in a different town every night.

Often, at the end of a long day we had dinner together. It wasn't like a date, not at first. There was none of that tension or expectation. It was just two tired friends—people who work together—enjoying each other's company, sharing thoughts and feelings. In so many ways, we were opposites, at least in temperament. Roy is steady and dependable; I am hasty and impulsive. He is such a quiet fellow, and he has a way of taking life as it comes; no one has ever accused me of being shy or easygoing. But the differences between us were all to the good; we each had strengths that were good for the other one. When we were together, I felt balanced.

One time I asked Roy if he believed in Jesus Christ. I was shocked by his answer: "No." He said he didn't take his children to Sunday school and he didn't much go to church. "I've performed in too many children's hospitals," he said. "If there is a God, I cannot understand how an innocent child can be born with a bad heart or crippled legs. I cannot understand the meaning of all those faces I see in orphanages. How can God let it happen? If you can tell me why He lets children suffer, I'll go to church." He then told me about traveling evangelists who used to preach in the country church in Ohio when he was growing up. They would preach up a storm; townsfolk would mend their ways. But after the preacher moved on, all those saved souls went right back to where they had always been. "It doesn't make sense," he declared. I wanted to tell him otherwise, but I kept my mouth shut. I didn't have the ammunition—the faith—to counter his doubts.

We were King of the Cowboys and Queen of the West when we appeared in arenas, often as part of a rodeo. The show began with the house lights going down to total darkness. They announced Roy Rogers and Trigger, and he came barreling out at full gallop. The spotlight followed him; he was wearing flamboyant rhinestones and fringe so even the kids in the top row could see him clearly. The effect was like a bolt of fast-moving lightning. He'd rear Trigger up a few times, waving to the crowd, then introduce me. I came galloping out at top speed in my rhinestone outfit—something that complemented Roy's, but in a feminine way—and we began the show on horseback, singing a duet of "The Star Spangled Banner."

Some of the rodeo cowboys resented Roy and me. All those glittery clothes didn't sit right with them; they used to make fun of the way I wore my hat—tilted back, so my face wasn't lost in shadows. And I guess they might have been a little jealous of the crowd's reaction when we rode out. There was one time at Madison Square Garden—this was back when that was the premier rodeo in the country—when some old boy decided he would embarrass us. Roy galloped out, reared Trigger, then introduced me. The big drum roll sounded. My horse, naturally, was on edge, waiting to burst into a run. The time came and I spurred him in the flanks; and just as I was clearing the chute, one of the rodeo cowboys stuck his foot in our path. The horse shied to one side, smashing my leg onto the cement of the chute, and he careened into the arena out of control. I hunkered down and stayed on him—I am talking about a *deep seat*—but my leg was skinned top to toe, and bleeding. The horse settled down and I remember feeling the blood trickle into my boot as we sang "The Star Spangled Banner." When our part of the show was over, Roy stormed back into the chutes, fists swinging, shouting words I never heard him say. "Where's that so-and-so chicken!" he called out. "I'm going to wring his neck!" We never found who did it, but after the way Roy reacted, let me tell you, whoever it was never tried it again.

Six months after Arlene died, Roy bought a ranch called Sky Haven. It was at the top of a mountain near Lake Hughes, in Lancaster, California. One bright Sunday morning, we drove there together—along a winding, unpaved mountain road that seemed to go up, up, up nearly to the clear blue. It wasn't anything grand—just a little house surrounded by flowering almond trees, alongside a smooth lake where ducks paddled around. I watched his daughters, Cheryl and Linda, greet him with big hugs; and I saw joy in the face of baby Dusty (Roy, Jr.) when his daddy bent down to hold him. The happiness they shared was so plain, I ached. And strangely—wonderfully—I felt completely at home. I *was* home.

In the fall of 1947, we were booked at the rodeo in Chicago. We were on our horses, in the chutes, waiting to be introduced, when Roy said, "Dale, what are you doing New Year's Eve?"

New Year's Eve was still months away. I had no plans.

Roy's face crinkled into that overpowering smile of his. His eyes sparkled. He reached into his pocket and pulled out a small box. Inside it was a gold ring set with a ruby. He reached down for my hand and slipped the ring on my finger. "Well, then," he said. "Why don't we get married?"

The drum roll sounded, the lights dimmed, Trigger reared up, and Roy Rogers galloped into the arena to the thunder of applause. I followed, on cue, and our horses took their position side by side in the spotlight in front of thousands of people. Before lifting the microphone to sing the National Anthem, I turned to look at Roy. He looked back at me, beaming with delight. The din of cheers made it impossible to speak. I formed the word "Yes" with my lips. He nodded, and we began to sing.

Me at age four.

Mom and Pop Slye.

School photo, Duck Run, Ohio. That's me on the far right.

The Slye family home in Duck Run.

Portsmouth, Ohio. Here I am with my three sisters—Mary, Kathleen, and Cleda.

I picked fruit in California during the Depression. This is me and my brother-in-law Josie.

My wife Arlene's parents are on the left. My mom and pop are on the right.

My start in show business—the Rocky Mountaineers.

January 1933: the International Cowboys. I am second from right.

In 1936 we called ourselves the Gold Star Rangers for the radio. I am on the far right.

The original Sons of the Pioneers. I am at the top left. Bob Nolan, who wrote "Tumbling Tumbleweeds," is at the top right.

The Sons of the Pioneers, 1943, in my movie *Idaho*.

Dale on her way to Hollywood.

This is a Republic Studios publicity shot of Dale.

These are the boys from the 77th Pursuant Squad at Glendale, where they made Dale a captain. This picture was snapped at lunch in the Fox cafeteria.

Dale Evans, Queen of the West.

I married Arlene Wilkins in Roswell, New Mexico, on June 14, 1936.

To my mother, I was never Roy Rogers—always Len.

Arlene and I with our daughters, Cheryl and Linda Lou.

This is the picture *Life* magazine put on its cover in 1943.

My pal
Trigger.

Horsin'
around.

Trigger could turn on a dime and give you nine cents change.

Trigger was a ham and loved the crowds.

When sugar was rationed during World War II, Trigger did his patriotic duty.

Bullet, the Wonder Dog, was also our family pet.

From the movie *My Pal Trigger*, 1946.

I still miss my sidekick and dear friend, Gabby Hayes.

Me, Dale, and Pat Brady, my TV show sidekick.

Dale and I have never regretted a minute spent with children.

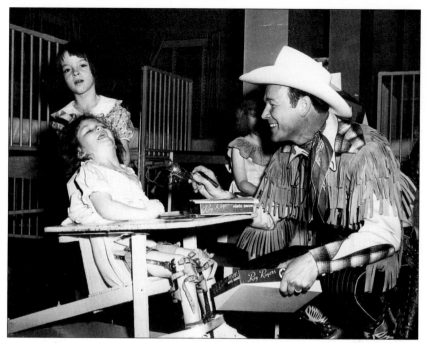

The best and most heartbreaking part of my job: visiting sick children.

Trigger often joined me in children's wards.

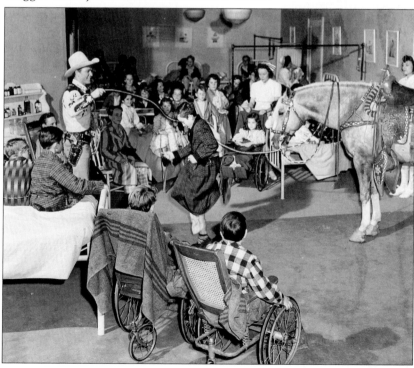

Test shots in search of the right cowboy hat.

The studio
originally
thought my
eyes were too
squinty for a
leading man.

One week's worth of fan mail.

It seems every little boy dreamed of being a cowboy.

After every show, I tried to shake as many little hands as I could.

Trigger gives New York's Mayor La Guardia an invitation to the rodeo at Madison Square Garden.

The Roy Rogers Riders Club taught kids to obey their parents and go to church.

I catch forty winks in my dressing room between performances.

The King of the Cowboys lassos his Queen of the West.

I proposed to my leading lady, Dale Evans, while riding Trigger.

Our wedding day, December 31, 1947. Don't we look like scared rabbits?

Roy Rogers, Jr. (Dusty), meets his sisters, Cheryl and Linda Lou, and my mom and pop.

Sandy, our adopted son.

My son Dusty test-markets a Roy Rogers comic book.

Shortly after Dale and I were married, her son Tom (far left) was married himself. His wife, Barbara, is standing next to me.

Dusty, on the right, was waiting at the airport when we brought his new brother, Sandy, home from the orphanage.

Debbie and Dodie were always Daddy's girls.

The Rogers family on tour. Clockwise from upper left: Linda, Cheryl, Marian, Dale, Sandy, Dodie, Debbie, Dusty, Roy.

Our angel, Robin Elizabeth.

Our baby Robin helped show us the true meaning of love and faith.

My last movie—*Mackintosh and T. J.* (1976).

We've been partners for half a century.

It wasn't easy, getting married. Sleet and snow and fire conspired against us. And at the last minute, I got cold feet. I was in the bedroom putting on my wedding dress—I wore powder blue, Roy's favorite color. Suddenly I felt all alone. What was I getting into? Roy had a family; marrying him meant I would become part of that family. I worried about his children. Would they accept me? Could I discipline them? I thought of what I had put Tom through. I didn't want Roy's children to suffer that. And I thought about my conspicuous lack of success as a wife, with two divorces to my name. I went into the closet and closed the door. I got down on my knees and I prayed to God. I said, "I promise You there will never, never, never be another divorce, under any circumstances." I promised, and I have never forgotten that promise. (Sometimes, I'll admit, I think of what Billy Graham's wife said when someone asked her if she ever considered divorce: "Divorce, never. Murder, maybe.") I asked God to help me raise Roy's children, because I knew I needed His help. I heard no bells and saw no heavenly lights, but I did feel a deep, reassuring calm well up in my heart. At that moment on my knees in the closet, I was close to something that had been missing from my life for such a long time. When I stepped out into the room again, I heard "Here Comes the Bride" begin. My time had come.

We had decided to be married in Oklahoma, in the den of Bill and Alice Likens's Flying L Ranch. Bill and Alice were old friends; we had spent time with them two years before while filming *The Man from Oklahoma*. The Flying L is a beautiful place, far from Hollywood. We figured it would protect us from the spectacle atmosphere bound to surround a ceremony in Los Angeles, and it was closer for my Texas relatives. The problem was that on New Year's Eve in Oklahoma, 1947, it snowed like crazy. Most of the guests managed to fight their way through, but Bill Alexander, the pastor of the First Christian Church of Oklahoma City and the man supposed to marry us, got stuck in the storm. The roads were closed, so to get to the ranch, he had to come by horseback. Two hours late, he blew through the front door dressed in frock coat and string tie; he had dressed for a real old-frontier wedding!

I walked down the aisle and waited for Roy and his best man, Art Rush. The guests waited. The pastor waited. Heads turned toward the door in anticipation. Minutes ticked by. Where was the groom? When I was nearly ready to give up hope and run out the door, Roy and Art came rushing into the room, smoothing down their clothes and trying to comb their hair with their fingers. They were out of breath and sweaty; Roy smelled like smoke. I looked daggers at him, and all he could do was roll his eyes heavenward. The ceremony proceeded, we were wed, and as soon as my husband kissed me, Art Rush burst out, "What a way to start a wedding!" They had been late, he explained, because just when they were about to come downstairs they smelled smoke. Someone had tossed a smoldering cigarette into a trash basket in a bedroom. The paper in the basket had caught fire, and the curtains above it were in flames. Roy and Art had run in, yanked down the curtains, and stomped out the flames. They then threw the smoldering curtains in the bathtub and started the water running. Satisfied the ranch wouldn't burn down, they ran downstairs and into the den for the ceremony as the tubs upstairs overflowed with water.

We stayed at the ranch that night, and in the morning Roy turned to me and said, "Honey, we've made a mistake."

"What!?"

"We made a mistake. We've been married a year already. It's 1948."

I pretended to pound his chest with my fist. He was counting the age of our marriage in horse years. No matter what day a horse is born, it always gets a year older on January 1. Roy Rogers *would* think of something like that.

The second night of our honeymoon, he had a suggestion of how we might spend our evening together: coon-hunting! Oh, brother! "For better or for worse," I had promised, so I agreed to join Roy and the other Oklahoma hunting men on a coon hunt. I never imagined I would spend my honeymoon tramping through the cold and dark, stumbling over rocks and tree stumps, and sloshing into mud holes trying to follow a pack of yelping hounds. We were "lucky," and the hounds managed to tree a pair of raccoons. What followed was the most sickening fight imaginable between them. When I saw it, my stomach turned, and I thought to myself, "What have I done?! I am no sportswoman. I should have married a college professor." Roy patiently explained that coons were actually very destructive creatures, and it was a fair fight, but I wasn't even interested in listening. I put my hands on my hips and lectured him and his friends about how cruel they were. They stared at me in slack-jawed disbelief. Roy took my arm and walked me away from the scene on the crime. "Maw," he said, "I'm afraid you'll never be a hunter." Amen to that!

Republic decided that our wedding meant the end of my career. The studio reasoned that the public would not be interested in seeing a married couple teamed together. Roy got a series of new leading ladies and I embarked upon a new job: mother to three youngsters. At the time, Cheryl was seven. Linda was four. Dusty was just fifteen months. I had my hands full.

Roy's daughters resented my stepping into their lives, as I feared they would. Cheryl was angry; Linda brooded; thankfully, Dusty was still too young to know about jealousy and resentment. Roy and I found a beautiful two-story Spanish home originally built by Noah Beery at the top of Vine Street; we filled it with furniture from his ranch at Lake Hughes and my house in North Hollywood. Early on, when I was arranging the couch and chairs in the living room, Linda Lou

131

stepped up to me with a great frown on her face and declared, "This isn't yours. This is Mommy's." My instinct was to scold her; but I knew better. As gently as I knew how, I said, "Honey, your mommy has gone to heaven, where she doesn't need this furniture. Your daddy and I will have to use it now." Being their stepmother was no picnic in those early years. Roy was working long hours at the studio; I felt alone—frightened, on edge, at a loss for how to handle it.

My son Tom suggested that I might find the answer in church. To this day he denies it, but I believe that he and the minister conspired one Sunday night to reach me. Dr. Jack MacArthur's sermon topic this evening was "The House That Is Built on the Rock." He told the congregation that a home built on the rock of faith can take anything that comes against it and survive. I felt certain he was speaking directly to me, and when he finished his sermon and invited listeners to step forward and accept Christ, I yearned to go to that altar. But I did not. I fought the feeling. I was afraid of confessing my sins. "Why don't you go?" Tom said, seeing the conflict in my eyes. "Give Him your life and let Him give you the peace you've sought for so long."

"Tom, I *am* a Christian," I argued. "I've been since I was ten. Isn't that enough?" My defense sounded hollow even as I spoke the words. I simply didn't have the courage to go down that aisle. "Give me until next Sunday," I said to Tom, stalling for time. "I need to think." My son's eyes filled with tears of pity for me. He turned away.

I went home and felt more alone than ever. Roy was away on a hunting trip. That night, I fell to my knees at the bed and cried as I had never cried in my life. As I cried, a dam broke; out poured a long, stammering confession. All the years of my life flooded past my eyes, and I shuddered at the sins I saw. I had let so much slip away; I had been so blind to all the things that really mattered; I had wanted to use Christ only as an ace up my sleeve against the possibility of future punishment and damnation. "Forgive me, Lord God!" I cried. "Let me live until next Sunday, and I will go down that aisle."

I did live, and when the time came, I fairly bounced from my pew so I could come clean with God. I didn't shout out all my life's misdeeds. I simply remembered them before Him. I asked Him to come into my heart, to take my life and use it for His glory. As I got up from my knees that day, I felt as though a crushing burden had been lifted from my back and shoulders. When I left church, the sky was brighter blue than it had ever been; flowers were bursting with colors I had never seen. Every tree along the road home sang to me; branches waved with glee; I was ecstatic.

Roy was home when I got there and I bubbled over with my newfound joy, telling him I had just made the greatest decision of my life. "I'm glad for you, Mama, if it makes you happy," he said. "But be careful, won't you? Don't go overboard."

I promised I wouldn't pressure him to make the same decision I had made. Nevertheless, I had changed. And the Christian life I was leading turned out to be contagious. I never pushed him, but example is always better than nagging; and Roy could see how much happier I was. One Saturday night we had a huge fight, one of the biggest in our marriage. It happened during a party in our den. There were a lot of show folk there, drinking and smoking, and it started to bother me. I was explaining to a friend that I wasn't much interested in whooping it up now that I had three small children to take care of. Roy overheard, and misunderstood; he thought I was complaining and passing judgment on the others in the room. I retreated to the bedroom in tears.

The next morning, neither of us spoke about the fight. But a strange thing happened: Roy announced he was going to church with me and the kids. During the sermon, I noticed his eyes were closed. I assumed he was sleeping—the party had finally broken up very, very late—and I got mad, thinking his trip to church was nothing but a gesture to appease me. To my amazement, when the invitation was given at the end of the sermon, he opened his eyes, sat up straight, squeezed my hand, and said, "I'm going down there." It was his own decision, with no pressure from me, and I was never happier in my life. That Palm Sunday, he and Cheryl were baptized together. The spiritual bond that connected Roy and me that day can never be broken.

It was a year of joy and goodness. My son Tom was married; I wept a bucket of tears at the sight of him and his bride, Barbara, standing side by side at Fountain Avenue Baptist Church. And in December, I learned I was pregnant. When Roy and I were married two years before, my gynecologist had told me I would never again have a child unless I underwent extensive surgery. Besides, I had a boy in college; I was thirty-seven, which in those days was considered pretty near the upper limit for giving birth. When the doctor called me to confirm that a baby was on the way, I laughed—long and loud—first in disbelief, then in joyous thanks for the miracle about to be visited on Roy and me.

PART IV

Roy and Dale: Happiness, but Not Without Pain

ON APRIL 21, 1949, Roy Rogers and Trigger were granted an entitlement that marked the pinnacle of success in old Hollywood: they put their boot and hoof prints into wet cement in the courtyard of Grauman's Chinese Theater. Roy reigned across the land, breaking box office records when he appeared at rodeos and on theater stages, turning out six moneymaking pictures every year. Each monthly issue of his comic book sold 1.3 million copies; he was voted the most popular movie star in England; and in America he remained unchallenged as the top moneymaking Western star for twelve years, from 1943 to 1954.

Some film historians like to characterize the postwar era by the appearance of "adult" Westerns that began to deconstruct the conventions of the genre: *The Outlaw,* featuring Jane Russell's big breasts; *High Noon,* an allegory about McCarthyism; *Shane,* a self-conscious Western about cowboy mythology. But such apparently important movies were anomalies. For the late 1940s were also the time when A-budget pictures directed by John Ford and Howard Hawks, such as *She Wore a Yellow Ribbon* and *Red River,* elevated the Western genre to a grand and classical dimension. At the same time, lower-budget B-Westerns, with their cheery song interludes, familiar plots, and rudimentary characters, remained immensely popular, especially among their prime audience—children.

Cowboy movies every Saturday afternoon were the favorite entertainment of millions of American kids, but these sixty-minute oaters, starring Roy Rogers or Gene Autry or Charles Starrett or Bill Elliott or Tex Ritter or Lash Larue or any one of a dozen other incredibly good guys, offered their audience of little buckaroos something more than just fun. They provided young baby boomers with unconfusing heroes and a clear sense of right and wrong—a lesson in how to behave each and every week. To grow up with Roy Rogers as your mentor in the postwar years was to have a role model who was kind and decent and immensely capable, and who taught you that life rewarded courtesy, bravery, and hard work. In the world of his movies, goodness always prevailed.

"He has survived other wars and he will survive this one," *Life* magazine wrote about America's cowboy hero in 1943. Survive he did: and thrive! Despite atomic-era anxieties lurking in the shadows, popular culture of the late 1940s and early 1950s was a mighty happy trail for silver-screen cowboys who fought for truth and justice. After all, their message was that good guys win—which is exactly what had seemed to happen in World War II. America felt mighty proud of itself. Goodness had indeed prevailed.

If we as a nation could do great things overseas, we could do them at home as well; and after wartime years of deprivation and sacrifice, America was a country that felt ready and raring to build things (highways, suburbs) and buy things (cars with tail fins, dinettes of boomerang Formica, TV sets for one and all). As a new, optimistic generation was born, children and parents alike learned that it was good—in fact, it was downright patriotic—to be extravagant consumers. The postwar years were a golden age of modernistic product design, exorbitant advertising, and unblushing celebrity endorsements. Cowboy movie stars pitched products almost from the beginning (Tom Mix was the spokesman for Gold Medal flour); but the coming of television gave them heretofore unimaginable powers of salesmanship.

The movie cowboys' switch to television from the big screen ultimately did spell the end of B-Westerns in theaters by the mid-1950s, but for those who made the move, it meant a whole new magnitude of popularity, prosperity, and power. The first cowboy to learn what TV could do was Hopalong Cassidy (William Boyd), who by 1948 had been pretty much forgotten as a cowboy movie star. Television made him a national idol of a proportion no mere movie star had ever known. It started in 1948 when a Los Angeles TV station began running some of his old features to fill up its schedule. The next year, NBC put them in prime time. Clean, pure, black-and-white Hoppy—whose forte was close-up dialogue scenes rather than panoramic action shots—was a perfect fit for the new small screen. William Boyd, who had secured the broadcast rights to his films, edited them down to thirty- and sixty-minute programs, and shot another fifty-two, especially for TV (with Edgar Buchanan as his sidekick, Red Connors). Right up there with Howdy Doody and pro wrestler Gorgeous George, he became one of America's first TV stars, and in 1950 both *Life* and *Time* featured him in cover stories about Hoppymania. *Time* called the phenomenon "one of the most amazing jackpots in the history of the entertainment business," spinning off into radio shows, a newspaper comic strip, and 108 licensed manufacturers selling $70 million worth of Hoppy products to TV viewers that the magazine labeled his "electronic slaves."

"The Lone Ranger" went from radio to television in 1948; Gene Autry began producing "The Gene Autry Show"; and in 1951, Roy Rogers and Dale Evans finally moved to television. The small screen proved to be a comfortable medium for Roy and Dale's kind of Western stories, which had always depended less on scenery than on dialogue, songs, and character. Broadcast at 6:30 p.m. on Sundays, their show became one of television's first successful "family" programs, with musical numbers, action, and philosophizing aimed at young and old alike. An MGM Western street served as the series' town, Mineral City; Iverson's movie ranch provided location scenery; and movie bad guy Jack Ingram's ranch in the Santa Monica Mountains served as Roy's Double R Bar Ranch. The show began each week with a shot of Roy on Trigger, racing along a trail with the rest of the cast close behind as an announcer intoned, "Post Cereals—Post-marked, yes, *Post-marked* for happy eating—presents 'The Roy Rogers Show' with Roy Rogers, King of the Cowboys; Trigger, his golden palomino; and Dale Evans, Queen of the West; with Pat Brady, their comical sidekick; and Roy's wonder dog, Bullet."

Soon after the show went on the air, Roy's likeness began appearing on Post cereal boxes, advertising such prizes as cardboard reproductions of the Double-R Bar and lapel pins with portraits of Trigger and Buttermilk. Roy Rogers had begun seriously endorsing products the year he became King of the Cowboys, in 1943. Within a short while, the only celebrity name on more things than Roy's was Walt Disney's. He lent his imprimatur to every kind of child's toy imaginable, including cap guns and quick-draw holsters, child-size guitars, "branding iron" rings to fit little fingers, badges, lassos, and musical hobby horses. There were whole suites of Roy Rogers clothes, too: Comfort-A-Foot moccasins, Roy or Trigger bandannas, Trigger-themed cowboy boots, and "Ranchjamas" (known among dudes and grown-ups as pajamas). In addition to kids' stuff, Roy lent his name to many adult products, too, including Magic Chef stoves, Friskies dog food, and Kodak film. The Sears catalogue of 1955, issued at the peak of his TV show's success, had more than a dozen pages of Roy Rogers things for sale. Among them were a rodeo hat with Roy's name on its rayon band, matching Roy and Dale ten-piece "Palomino Sets" that included chaps, belts, holsters, pistols, bandanna, and lariat—everything but hat and boots—and specially made Roy Rogers "Chap-Pants" with scarlet corduroy fronts and black suede trim. Sears also offered denim pants and jackets "specially designed for the 'King of the Cowboys'" and Roy Rogers flashlights with a four-color picture of Roy and Trigger on the side, suitable for use to signal danger. (The flashlight alone cost a dollar. For $1.39, you got it with a holster and a Roy Rogers Morse Code guide.)

For those of us who grew up with Roy and Trigger and Dale and Buttermilk as our ultimate heroes, there was one souvenir that definitely took the cake as the most coveted ever. In 1955 Post sponsored a "Name the Pony" contest. "Boys! Girls! Give me a name for this pony," Roy said in advertisements. "Names like Beauty, Dandy, and Flash are all good, but you can do better. So get going, buckaroos! Send in your names today!" Each entry had to be accompanied by a Post Cereal boxtop. For those who came up with the best names, there were 5,000 pairs of roller skates (fourth prize), 500 paperboard bunkhouses (third prize), 100 Dougboy Family-Size Swimming Pools (second prize), and twenty-five first prizes—YOUR VERY OWN PONY! Complete with "genuine Roy Rogers saddle and bridle," the child-size first-prize horse looked just like a miniature Trigger. Magazine advertisements showed the little palomino rearing high up on his hind legs as the happiest boy in the world sat astride his back, waving his ten-gallon hat in the air and preparing to gallop through his backyard and neighborhood on an adventure that was the dream of millions of American boys and girls.

—J. & M. S.

CHAPTER 7
Roy's Story

With Dale by my side, life's colors grew bright again. I think one of the things I loved most about her as our marriage began was the way she worked to become my kids' new Maw. It required some gumption for her to take on the family of little ones that came along with me, but she did it. Sometimes they were a handful, I suppose because they just couldn't understand why Arlene had to die. But whatever it was that troubled them, Dale was right there to roll up her sleeves and help. She is a woman who faces up to whatever comes her way, and that has always been something I've admired about her. Believe me, she had her hands full! When she married me, she didn't only get a singing cowboy and three young children. There was one other part of that bargain Dale had to learn to love: my horse. Maybe it sounds odd that I proposed marriage to her on horseback—not too romantic, you might think. But Trigger wasn't just some horse. He was my partner and my pal, and part of nearly everything I did.

Trig and I made 88 movies together and 104 TV shows, and he never once fell or let me down. He was so sharp, so eager. There wasn't anything I asked of him he wouldn't do: running mounts and dismounts, jumping over rolling barrels (that's a lot harder than going over a fence!), storming full tilt

alongside speeding trains, or walking gently through the corridor of a children's hospital—whatever was required.

When I bought Trigger from the Hudkins Stables, I was
twenty-six and just starting out in the movie business. He
was a looker, that's for sure. His mane and tail were full,
flaxen white, and his palomino coat shone like a newly
minted gold coin. He was 15.3 hands tall, which is about
average height, but he was extremely strong and could turn
on a dime and give you nine cents change. How that boy
loved to run! All I had to do was shift my weight forward and
he was off like a streak of lightning. Sit deep in the saddle
and he'd shutter right down like the best roping horse there
ever was. Most cow ponies that you see in movies are geld-
ings because a gelding is usually calmer to work around,
especially with other horses. But Trigger was a stallion, and
you could tell. You could see it in the proud arch of his neck
and the way he carried himself. A lot of stallions are too wild
to be handled easily, but Trigger was always a gentleman. I
used to put all my kids on him at one time, sitting from his
ear clear back to his tail, and he was just as sweet as a lamb.
There never was another horse like him. I insisted he get star
billing in all my pictures. After all, what's a cowboy without
a horse?

I was King of the Cowboys, Dale was Queen of the West,
and Trigger got himself a title, too: the Smartest Horse in the
Movies. He knew close to a hundred tricks, and he was a
natural ham who loved to show off in front of people. After
I bought him, I got in touch with Glenn Randall, a horse
trainer out in Hollywood; and by the time Glenn and I were
through, there wasn't any spot on that horse you could tap or
touch that wouldn't cue him to bow, shake his head to say
"yes" or "no," smile, kiss someone, do a little jig, look left or
right . . . you name it! Why, there was one time when we
were in New York for the rodeo in Madison Square Garden
that we put specially cushioned rubber shoes on Trig so he

could walk right into the lobby of the Hotel Dixie on Forty-third Street in Times Square. When he got to the front desk, he sniffed around, found a pencil, grabbed it in his lips, and signed his name—actually, just a big *X*—on the guest register. Flashbulbs were flashing and reporters cheered! That trick was kinda silly, but I'll tell you one thing he learned that came in right handy—and that was to never go to the bathroom indoors. Whenever we were about to go on stage or into a children's hospital or ballroom or TV set, I took ol' Trig outside, cued him to take care of business, and he did, you bet. I could depend on him.

One of the fancy routines Glenn worked out for me and Trigger began the way most of our traveling shows began, with us galloping out into the arena at top speed, rearing up a few times and waving. Then an announcer started to tell the audience a story about the old days of the West when wandering cowboys were often shot by outlaws. A gunshot then rang out and I slumped over in the saddle. A second shot followed, and Trigger shook like he was hit. He began to limp worse and worse, like he was about to die. Growing weaker with each step, he gradually went down, falling to his side, motionless, with me lying there next to him, also dead. The two of us lay there on the arena floor; the lights dimmed; "Taps" played over the loudspeaker. Let me tell you, I could hear the sniffles from the little ones, and they'd cry, "Get up, Trigger! Please!" We'd lie there till the last note of "Taps," then I'd sneak Trigger a cue, at which point he leapt to his feet and shook himself back to life. I swung into the saddle and we loped around the arena, waving to everyone, and galloped out of there. The one problem with that little performance was that Trigger was too smart, and too eager to run. He listened to "Taps" being played, knowing that when the last note sounded he was going to get his cue to jump to his feet; so gradually, he began to get up too soon. It got to be a real wrasslin' match between us—me trying to

keep him still and down until the exact moment the music
was over and him tensing up and rarin' to go before the final
notes. What I did was slowly sneak my leg over the saddle
and get a foot in the stirrup while he was still down there to
make sure I was on him when he sprang back to life. One
night at the rodeo in Baltimore, Trigger pulled himself up so
fast that he started cantering around the arena before I could
swing my other leg over the saddle. I was half on him, flap-
ping along the side like Old Glory as he broke into a run that
could have licked Secretariat in the final stretch of the Kentucky Derby. The fans applauded wildly for that; I suppose
they thought I had planned to ride away hanging upside
down from Trigger's side.

Because Trigger was smart, he figured out some pretty darn
good kinds of mischief. Just about his favorite stunt was to
wait until I was in costume making a personal appearance
before thousands of fans. He'd do everything he was supposed to do, and stand there patiently when I dismounted
and went to the microphone to sing a religious hymn. The
house lights lowered, and a single spotlight shone on me,
with Trig in the background. I raised my eyes to heaven and
began to sing, and just then, he crept up behind and grabbed
a piece of my good satin shirt in his mouth, along with plenty
of skin from my shoulder or back. He bit and held on, hard
enough to leave a big bruise afterwards. To the audience it
looked like he was giving me an affectionate little nuzzle, but
it hurt like heck; and that ol' horse was smart enough to
know that I couldn't scream with pain in the middle of
"Peace in the Valley"; and I sure as shootin' couldn't turn
around and whale him. The reason I know he had this figured out is that he would never, ever pull this stunt during
rehearsal, or when it was just the two of us alone, away from
the safety of a crowd of adoring fans. At one point, I finally
decided I had had enough of these shenanigans. I was going
through fancy costume shirts like they were disposable nap-

kins, plus I had bite marks all over my back. When the performance was over and the crowd had exited the stadium, I left Trigger alone to contemplate his crimes while I went off looking for a quirt. When he saw me approaching with the whip, his eyes widened. Without any cues from me, he started to go through every trick he knew: bowing, walking on his hind legs, counting, nodding his head, and blowing kisses, the whole shebang. It was so funny I started laughing and threw the whip on the ground. He had won again.

There was one time Trig misbehaved that I really couldn't get mad at him. It was when we went to Hawaii to do a series of shows. We flew over, and Trigger came later, by boat. As he walked off the ramp onto shore, he got a real Polynesian welcome. There were photographers everywhere and someone had made a gigantic flowered lei to put around his neck. Trigger was pleased as punch to be back on solid ground, and apparently he had grown mighty hungry on the voyage over, because as soon as the hula girls started swaying to greet him, he ambled over and started munching on their grass skirts!

One kind of trouble he used to get into all the time was on movie sets. He had a way of maneuvering around and turning up where he wasn't supposed to be. Usually to keep a horse in one place you use hobbles, which are sort of like loose handcuffs that go around his legs to keep him in one spot. When we were shooting a scene in a movie that didn't require the pleasure of Trigger's company, we would hobble him far away from the action. But being a sociable fellow, he grew bored, and before long he figured out that if he couldn't get from one place to another by walking, he would teach himself to hop. Sure enough, even wearing hobbles, he developed a way of making tiny little jumps so no matter where we parked him, you could bet he'd show up where he wasn't supposed to be.

I don't think there ever was a horse who was better for

running mounts and dismounts. These require some pretty close timing, and are difficult for both the horse and the rider. For a running dismount, he knew exactly what to do so I could rise up to a particular spot, leap off him and hit the ground as he came to a neat, sliding stop behind me. Running mounts can be even trickier, and you need a horse you really trust. To do it right, you have to hit the left stirrup with your left foot at the exact moment he takes off, then sail into the saddle as he's plunging into a full gallop. When he did it right, it looked good! But there were times, I've got to tell you, when he was feeling a little ornery and he made a fool of me. He knew that all he had to do was shift his weight just the tiniest bit at the exact moment my feet left the ground; if he did, my left foot missed the stirrup and I hit the saddle like a sack of potatoes instead of like a hero off to rescue someone in distress.

When he wasn't playing around, Trigger was not a horse to be trifled with. One of my fondest memories was when I was doing a personal appearance at a movie set in Palm Desert. Some local cowboys were hanging around and started to rag me about Trigger not being much of a horse—just being a pretty boy, a coddled movie star, you know. Trigger was up in years at this point, in his twenties I'd say, but those Yahoos were really getting my goat. Finally I decided I had to call their bluff. I said, "Okay, boys, let's race." I put a wad of bills on the table. They matched my bet and four of them mounted their ponies. We lined up, someone dropped a flag, and the horses took off. Fifty yards after the start, Trigger was nosing out in front, and a few hundred yards after that, the other horses were eating his dust. I'll tell you, the money I picked up from the table that day wasn't anywhere as satisfying as seeing the look of respect for the palomino on those men's faces after the race.

That wasn't the first time ol' Trig had raced and won. Once we were shooting *My Pal Trigger* at the Santa Anita racetrack in Pasadena and the scene called for him to come out of the gate with the other racehorses, but then stop so they could substitute a double for him going around the track. They wanted to make sure that Trigger, the star of the picture, didn't get injured and didn't strain himself. When the bell at the starting gate sounded and the chutes opened, the horses shot out. But Trigger had no intention of stooping to allow a stunt horse to finish his race. He had always been at the head of any pack of horses he ran with, and much to the jockeys' surprise, Trigger flew right past them and straight into the lead.

Trigger was always the center of attention when we made personal appearances, and on occasion someone would try to pluck a hair from his mane or tail for a souvenir. There was one time Glenn Randall was transporting him to Hereford Heaven, Oklahoma, where we went to make some scenes for the movie *Home in Oklahoma.* Glenn parked the open horse trailer in front of a small-town café and went in to get a sandwich and a cup of coffee. While he was inside, some crazy fan walked up to the trailer, took a pocket knife, and hacked off a big hunk of Trigger's tail! When he was unloaded from the trailer, I couldn't believe my eyes: there was nothing but a straggly stump where Trigger's flowing white tail used to be. Oh, I was steamed! Fortunately, every movie set has a talented hairdresser, and in this case he got to work fast, outfitting Trigger with an artificial tail wig for the filming. His tail took almost two full years to grow back; and from then on Trigger rarely made appearances without a backup tail or two just in case.

Boys and girls like Trigger so much that I tried to station him and his fancy trailer outside each auditorium for a few hours before a performance. I figured that this was a way for those who didn't have enough money for a ticket to get a chance to see him. During the show, one thing we always did was to go all the way around the arena with him kinda prancing slowly sideways, facing them. I could reach down and shake hands with all the little ones in the front rows, and a lot of them got a chance to rub ol' Trig's nose or pet his neck. Dale did a sidepass all around, too, right alongside me on her horse, so the kids could shake her hand as well. It took awhile to get all the way around an arena that way, especially if it was a big one; and there were times when the rodeo promoters tried to tell us to go just a little ways around because they thought the sidepass took too long. They wanted to get on with the show—"time is money," and all that. Well, we put our foot down. They had no idea how much it meant to those boys and girls to get a chance to shake hands and see us and our horses. We'd often hear from someone who said, "Oh, I missed your hand and I cried for a week!" We got letters from their mothers and fathers asking when we'd be back in town so they could be sure to get seats up front the next time. The officials up in the offices didn't have any idea how important it was to the kids, and they'd always tell us to go just a little ways. But we always went all around; we took our time. We shook hands with everyone we could.

I'll tell you about one time we nearly got into a real war with the promoters: at the World Championship Rodeo at Madison Square Garden in 1952. During the first rehearsal I started to practice "How Great Thou Art," a religious song that I wanted to make the centerpiece of our musical act. There's a line in that song that goes "Then sings my soul, my Savior God to Thee . . ." Someone in the front office heard the rehearsal and came to me that night to tell me I wasn't allowed to mention Christ at the rodeo. "It might work for kids in Houston, Texas," he told me, "but this is New York. You can't preach to kids here." I told him I wasn't preaching, but that the Savior was part of the song, and I fully intended to sing that song in New York or anywhere else we performed. They suggested I could change the words to the song so it didn't mention Him. I'm not one for grandstand plays, but I told those fellas that if I couldn't sing "How Great Thou Art" just as it was written, Dale and I would pack up and leave town. The song stayed in the show. That year we did forty-three performances over twenty-six days and broke all Madison Square Garden attendance records.

When I think back to the late 1940s and early 1950s and the kind of schedule Dale and I kept, I get tuckered out just remembering it all. Being King of the Cowboys and Queen of the West required a morning-to-night timetable that hardly left us a minute to catch our breath. Nowadays you hear about stars having contracts that call for someone to pick all the green M&Ms out of the candy bowl or only have a certain kind of yellow rose in their hotel suites, but that sure wasn't the way it was for us. Nobody carried us around on velvet cushions; in fact, if we could find time to grab a sandwich between performances we considered it an easy day.

I figure I started living on the front burner even before they made me King of the Cowboys. After my very first picture came out, I lit off on a road trip during which I did 135 shows in twenty days through Georgia, Alabama, Louisiana, Mississippi, Virginia, West Virginia, North and South Carolina, all the mountain states, and the Southeast. It was just me and a couple of musicians. We played every little theater in every little town. They charged eight or ten cents admission in those days. We did a show, they ran the movie, then ushered the crowd out. Another audience came in and we did the show all over again. It was like that all day long. If we made a hundred and fifty dollars in a day, we were doing well. Once Art Rush became my agent, he made sure that when I wasn't filming a picture or promoting one, I was out doing personal appearances—in theaters, at rodeos, state fairs, auto races, grand openings, and parades.

I'll never forget the first time we appeared at R. H. Macy's in New York, in 1943. We weren't quite sure how we'd be received there, but when we arrived, there was a line of parents and their kids that stretched clear around the block, calling out for me and Trigger. There were so many of them there that day that we hadn't even gotten to putting on a show when it turned into a near riot. Parents started putting their kids on top of the glass display cases inside the store to give them a better view, and pretty soon glass started to shatter everywhere. Then people pushed each other out of the way, trampling one another to get to us or to get out. Macy's sent for extra police, who just cleared everyone out of there to avoid a real disaster.

That fall when we were in New York for the rodeo, I managed to get an afternoon off to see a World Series game between the Yanks and the St. Louis Cardinals. Ned Irish, president of Madison Square Garden, invited us to join him in his box, but as soon as I arrived, I realized it wasn't going to be easy to relax and watch the game. People started coming from all around to get my autograph. That was all right with me, but I felt kinda bad about the spectators around us who weren't going to be able to see the game if there was a crowd at our box. One old boy, I remember, wanted to get to us so bad that he just ignored the steps and aisles and climbed over seats, stepping on heads and hats and shoulders, calling, "Roy! Roy! Roy!" Trying to keep his balance, he mashed a hand down on the homburg hat of a gent in the next box who, I only then noticed, happened to be former President Herbert Hoover. I started to stammer an apology, but Mr. Hoover just rearranged his hat, took a long puff on his cigar, and said, "That's all right. I'm a Roy Rogers fan myself."

Much as I appreciate people wanting to shake my hand, I've got to admit that sometimes being famous can feel suffocating, and I never have felt very comfortable among strangers. For me, being with my family was like heaven because it was private. And I think one of the reasons I have always loved the woods where I went hunting was that camera lenses didn't follow. There have been a few times when Dale and I were on the road that I felt I needed a break so bad that I actually resorted to disguises. In Toronto there was a big exposition of firefighting equipment that I wanted to see, but I knew that if I went there I would spend all my time talking to fans. So I spoke to some of the firefighters, who were good enough to find a fireman's uniform in my size. I put it on, hat and all, and joined the rest of the squad; but don't you know, it took someone about two minutes to figure out it was me, then the jig was up. Another time in Ohio we were playing the state fair and I had the makeup man fit me with thick glasses and a black mustache so I could go and enjoy some of the livestock exhibitions, but again people spotted me almost at once. When I asked them how they knew it was me, they all said that my eyes and my voice gave me away.

There was one time I *wasn't* recognized that was one of the few occasions I lost my temper with a stranger. I'm usually polite, but this lady really got me going. I had just performed a full show with the band, and during the intermission Dale and I got out of our costumes and into casual clothes so we could stroll over to the concession stand and pick up some chicken to eat. As we walked along two women who fell in step behind us were talking loud enough for us to overhear. "Roy Rogers wears a hairpiece!" one said. Her friend disagreed. But the first lady said that she had it on good authority that Mr. Rogers was bald as a cue ball and always wore a rug. I guess my pride took over, so I spun around in front of her, took off my hat, lowered my head, and said, "Pull it! Pull my hair! You'll see it's real." Dale started laughing her head off, and the two old biddies ran way, red in the face.

I was just about the worst kind of celebrity when it came to Hollywood parties and that kind of thing. My idea of fun is to wear an old flannel shirt and shoot the breeze with some buddies. I've always been more of an outdoor guy, and have a whole lot more to say about what kind of lure a fellow ought to use if he's going for trout than about some big deal an agent is making at a studio. The truth is that when I'm at a Hollywood party I feel like the backward kid from Duck Run all over again, and usually about all I can do is stare at my feet and mumble. I just can't think of anything to say. Still, the folks at Republic used to try to get me to go to those parties because they thought it was good for their actors to hobnob with members of the press and "the right people" in the movie business. After I refused so many times I couldn't rightly say no again, I figured out a way to do what they wanted. I invited a couple of my hunting buddies to come along with me. It was great: we could hole up on a couch somewhere and talk about our coon hounds. I don't think that's what the p.r. people had in mind. After a while they got the message and pretty much gave up trying to make me into a social butterfly.

It's a funny thing: even though I wasn't much of a Hollywood type, one of my biggest supporters in town was Louella Parsons, the gossip columnist. She said she liked me because I was polite, but someone once wrote that when I walked past her into the premiere of one of my pictures, she said, "There goes the best behind in show business"!

I didn't pal around with a lot of the stars, but I can tell you one good story about Clark Gable. I got my favorite shotgun from him. He and some other guys from Hollywood came out to the skeet-shooting range we had at Chatsworth. Well, old Clark had this new gun, a beautiful Winchester with a hand-carved stock. I think he shot only eleven out of twenty-five that day, and he was really mad about it. He came off the field muttering about how bad he shot, just getting angrier and angrier. As we walked back to the clubhouse together, he called out, "Does anybody want to buy this so-and-so gun?" Well, I thought it was mighty pretty, so I said I'd buy it from him. And the next day I went out and shot my first twenty-five straight. A few months later I went to the Grand, which is the big trap and skeet match, in Ohio, and shot 199 out of 200 with that same gun!

I guess the biggest celebrity I ever met was Queen Elizabeth. When she came to America one time, she visited Hollywood, and since our pictures had always done well in England, we were invited to a dinner party that 20th Century–Fox gave for her and some movie stars. I was worried that I wouldn't have much to say to the Queen, although I had heard she was a pretty fair shot with a rifle herself, and knew her way around horses, too. We never did get to talk about hunting or horses, though. We ate papaya with bay shrimp, chicken pot pie, spinach with bacon, and a toasted coconut snowball for dessert. I concentrated on that coconut snowball and the evening sailed by just fine. It was a lot more fun for me to meet the Crown Prince of Indonesia, because he was ten years old. I'm always more comfortable around kids than adults. He came to visit us at the ranch in Chatsworth, and I think it was the thrill of his young life when I lifted him up into the saddle, and cued Trigger to prance around in a circle with him.

I've met nearly all the Presidents since FDR, and Dale and I were invited to the White House for the birthday party of Ike's grandson, David, in 1956. We sang some Western songs for the children (who were all wearing cowboy hats) and I gave little David a nice three-foot model of the President's fishing boat. But I have to admit that my favorite presidential memory has to do with something that happened to Ronald Reagan. We knew him from his days as an actor, of course, but after he became President he used to tell a story about the time he first decided to run for national office. He had already been governor of California, so he was going house-to-house to shake hands and get people to vote for him. He knocked on this one old-timer's door, but the man was a little hard of hearing and didn't recognize him. Reagan said, "I'm running for President, and I'd like your support." The old man squinted, trying to place him, and cupped a hand to his ear to try and hear. "I said, *I'm running for President!*" Reagan repeated. "Surely, you know me. The initials are R.R."

"Well, I'll be darned!" the man said with a big smile, turning back into the house and shouting, "Honey, you'll never guess who's here. It's Roy Rogers, and he's running for President!"

One of our closest friends in Hollywood was Gabby Hayes, who played my sidekick in more than forty pictures. I've already told you what an elegant guy he really was, sitting like an English lord behind the wheel of his Continental when he cruised into the studio every morning. His wife was a refined person, too. She was a former Ziegfeld girl, tall and willowy, who used to work at a Lerner dress shop when Gabby wasn't earning enough to make ends meet. He absolutely adored her. Gabby didn't care what critics thought of him in movies and he didn't care what the director said, or even Mr. Yates. If Gabby's wife liked his performance, he was overjoyed. If she had the slightest criticism about the way he handled a role, it ruined his day. I remember we were doing a live radio show for NBC that was sponsored by Alka-Seltzer. During a break, he called her from backstage to find out if she liked what she was hearing. She must have had something bad to say because I watched him collapse onto the steps near the pay phone, grabbing his heart like someone had plunged a knife into it.

When Gabby's career began to blossom, his wife quit her job at the dress shop. He bought her a nice condo in Palm Desert, and furs and jewelry and everything. And then she got cancer and died. The two of them had never had any children, and I remember one time after she was gone when he was visiting us at our ranch in Chatsworth. He used to come to the house regularly. He wrestled with our sons, and teased Dale all the time, calling out to her, "Come on, butter-butt, give us a hug!" One night at supper, he looked around that big round table of ours with all the kids causing a commotion and fighting over the mashed potatoes, and tears started to roll down his face. Dale got up and put her arm on his shoulder.

"You okay, Pappy?" I asked.

Gabby said, "Roy, you don't realize how lucky you are." It almost broke our hearts. He lived to be eighty-three, but he was never the same after his wife died. The spark went out of him, and he seemed so lonely. Not a day goes by when I don't think of ol' Gabby. He was a real friend.

There was one fellow I'm proud to say was a pal, even though he made me madder than almost anyone I've ever known. Alfie, we called him; everybody knew him as Alfalfa, from the Little Rascals, though his real name was Carl Switzer. Alfie was like my son, we had so much fun together. He was cute as can be, real nice, and very big-hearted, but he could also be troublesome as a swarm of bees on a summer afternoon. He would do anything to get a laugh out of someone; he would tease you until you screamed; he concocted practical jokes that would make a preacher want to curse. He was always gettin' into trouble somehow, and it seems like I was always figuring ways to bail him out. He was about sixteen when we first met, so it was long past his days as a Rascal, and like a lot of former child stars, he was having a hard time making a go of things. But he sure did like to hunt; in fact, for many years Alfie was my best hunting partner. It seemed like the only time he was happy was when we were out in the woods trailing hounds.

The problem was that he just couldn't resist pulling tricks on people—especially me! There was one time when I had just bought a brand-new red pickup truck and he stopped by the house to visit. I knew he'd like it, so I invited him to come outside and have a look. We walked over to the garage, and as soon as I opened the door of the vehicle, smoke started pouring out. I thought the truck was going to blow up, so I screamed for Alfie to duck and made a dive for cover myself. Alfie stood there laughing and jumping up and down with glee. It turns out he had sneaked over an hour before and planted a smoke bomb on the front seat. When I figured that out, I chased him all the way down the street.

He just loved seeing people be the victim of his jokes; but on occasion, somebody would turn the tables and get him back good. Lee Greenway, our movie makeup man, had suffered one too many times at Alfie's hands. So one day, in seemingly casual conversation, Lee got to talking with Alfie about hunting, which he knew was a favorite subject. He asked Alfie if he had ever trapped a willow bird. "Oh, they're very rare," he said, "very hard to trap." As he spoke, he drew a detailed picture of this fabulous big black bird with sparkling eyes. He explained to Alfie that the only way to nab one was to sneak up to it when it was on the ground and throw a hat over it. Once the hat was in place, all the hunter had to do was slip his hand under the hat and grab hold of the bird. The next day, one of the horses on the set let drop a big, steaming manure pile and Lee placed a ten-gallon hat on top of it. He called for Alfie, who came running over with great excitement. Thinking a willow bird was waiting to be caught, he slipped his hand under the hat and grabbed a mess of horse plop instead. He was so mad he was livid, and he lit out after Lee and chased him near to the horizon.

In truth, Alfie wasn't the easiest guy to be friends with. One time when I was making a movie he asked if he could borrow my hunting dogs. He said a big group of hunters was willing to pay him a lot of money to lead an expedition, and all he needed was the dogs. I wanted to help him out, so I agreed, suggesting he take my Jeep, too. A week or so later, I came home to discover that Alfie had fallen in love with a woman somewhere along the trail, abandoned his hunting party, and sold my Jeep and my best dog so he would wine and dine his new sweetheart. I just couldn't believe it; he was like my own son.

Sometime in 1959 Alfie borrowed another friend's dogs to go hunting, and this time he lost them on the hunt. It wound up costing Alfie thirty dollars to get them back. He went to get the thirty dollars from the friend who had lent him the dogs. The two of them got into a fight, and during the fight, Alfie was fatally shot. He had told me he didn't have a nickel to his name at the end of his career. When he turned twenty-one, he found that all the money he had made as a child star was gone. He was broke, and had to struggle. You can see why they've passed laws to protect kids like that.

Pat Brady, my sidekick after Gabby Hayes, was another dear, close friend; in fact we made him and his wife, Fayetta, our daughter Dodie's godparents. How they liked to spoil that girl! Pat was a practical joker, too, but the kind of guy you just couldn't get mad at. He'd make me laugh no matter what kind of mood I was in. His rubber face was enough to get me going, but he would also do some of the dangdest things just to see me react. Part of our act on the road was target shooting: Pat tossed clay pigeons in the air and I shot them. One time he managed to stuff a clay pigeon with a pair of pantyhose, so after I shot it the stockings came drifting down from the sky. I couldn't help but laugh over that one myself. Another time, he put a miniature parachute inside and all the kids in the audience cheered when it came floating down. Once he really got me good when he substituted an aluminum pigeon for the clay one, so no matter how accurate my aim, the blasted thing wouldn't break. The audience groaned with disappointment when I missed, but when I went over to examine the pigeon, I discovered what he had done and started chasing him around. He was making faces and I was hollering, and I'll tell you, the kids liked that a whole lot more than my marksmanship. In fact, we kept it in the act for a while.

Pat met a sad end too, after he lost Fayetta after being married to her for thirty-five good years. He married a much younger woman, and they had a baby, but something was wrong with the child. It just tore him up emotionally, and he was so upset that he had a serious car wreck while he was driving somewhere in Colorado. They sent him to the hospital and it looked like he might make it, but in the morning he was dead. We still miss him so much.

One other old boy I used to enjoy going hunting with was Nudie Cohn, better known as Nudie of Hollywood. Nudie got famous for outfitting all the movies' rhinestone cowboys; he even made Elvis Presley's gold suit in 1956. Back when I met him in 1940, though, he had just set up a little tailor shop in Hollywood. He had come West after failing in his career as a flyweight prizefighter known as "Battling Nudie Cohn" of Brooklyn. I liked the kind of clothes he was making so much I helped bankroll that tailor shop. I think maybe Gene Autry and I might've been his first customers.

I had always liked to wear stage clothes that set us apart. Even in the early days of the Sons of the Pioneers, I used to make leather vests for us to wear with fringe along the sleeves and a "Sons of the Pioneers" brand on the back. When Dale and I started working together in the 1940s, she sketched ideas for a lot of the clothes we wore and gave her pictures to Nudie, who went wild with them. He made shirts with embroidered Trigger heads on them and pictures of Bullet the Wonder Dog, cactuses, Indian heads, horseshoes, stars, and fringe and sparkles galore. Dale has always said I was the original rhinestone cowboy. Those loud outfits were designed more for personal appearances than for movies. When we rode into the arena, we looked like glittering flags, which made it easy for kids in the last row of the balcony to see the show.

I always wore a white Stetson hat, but back in the 1940s I changed from a high crown and pitched crease to a special kind of "horseshoe" crease that I kinda invented. The way I like it, my hat is peaked high in the front and slopes easy down toward the back. At the top, I put a kind of double crease all around. I guess a hatmaker could do it, but I like to take my own hat into the shower, get it good and steamy, and shape it myself.

I was known for wearing cowboy boots with a spread-eagle design on them, most made by Nudie and by the Hyer Boot Company in Kansas, but I think just about every bootmaker in America sent me free pairs to wear back then. I would hate for you to see some of those nice boots, because if a pair I had didn't fit just right, I used to take out my pocket knife and cut a big hole on the right side to give my toes a little air. I used to nag Nudie and other bootmakers about making them wider at the toe, but they almost always sent them back to me the way the most cowboys like them—too tight. I limped around all summer while my feet swelled and my boots shrank. One time I went into a boot store and got the widest pair of boots they had on the shelf and I was fine. Actually it was better than buying custom boots for hundreds of dollars and then making them look like Swiss cheese. Another thing that I would gladly have taken a knife to were those dang woolen cowboy shirts I used to wear. They were hot as an oven and liked to itch me to death but they didn't get wrinkled and always looked nice.

Dale and I dressed pretty fancy, but our outfits were nothing compared to what Trigger wore. Trig's best saddles were made by Edward H. Bohlin, whom people used to call the Michelangelo of saddlecraft. He had started in the business out here making tack for Tom Mix's horse, Tony. Eddie Bohlin's saddles were covered with the most intricate silver and gold work and some of them weighed up to a hundred and fifty pounds each. He also made gun belts, holsters, belt buckles, chaps, and spurs, and he did some of the most beautiful gun engraving you ever saw. To this day, I still like to

161

wear my Bohlin belt buckles, and a nice ring he made for me shaped just like a little Western saddle. But I'll tell you one thing he made I don't wear much: the silver-trimmed *buscadero* gunbelt and twin holsters that used to be part of my King of the Cowboys outfit. For fun recently, I strapped that big rig on, and I couldn't believe how much it weighs! I swear I can hardly stand up in it, much less do a running leap onto Trigger.

Gene and Hoppy and I were known for wearing some pretty fancy duds, and I guess it was only natural that a lot of little partners would want to imitate us. Nowadays, some of those old movie-cowboy souvenirs are worth near as much as the real silver saddles Eddie Bohlin used to make! There were Roy Rogers gun belts, sweaters, boots, galoshes, hats, pants, shirts, sweaters, wristwatches, and just about everything else you could think of wearing or playing with or using to decorate a little buckaroo's bedroom. You could even buy Roy and Dale lookalike masks! There were altogether nearly four hundred different products with our names on them, and not only stuff for kids. We had full-size adult stoves, dog food, and car parts, too. That kind of merchandising is pretty common in movies today, but back when we were doing it in the 1940s and 1950s, it hadn't really been done much before. A lot of what we sold went right through the Sears catalogue, which was a family market that suited us just fine.

All those commercial tie-ins came about in a funny way. Nowadays, studio bosses are plenty savvy about how much money a star's name can mean, and contracts all have lots of clauses about royalties from souvenirs with a character's name or picture on them. But when I started out in the business, that kind of thing wasn't done much. Early on, when I had gone to Herb Yates at Republic to beg for a raise, he put his foot down, as usual. As we talked about it, I mentioned to him that I had a chance to do some commercial tie-ins for products using my name. He said, "Fine, do all the endorsements and products you want; just don't ask me for any money." When I walked out of his office that day, he was happy because he didn't have to pay me any more than the $150 a week I was already getting. I had really wanted a raise, and I was feeling kind of bad that all I got was the right to use my name and likeness for products. I thought I had lost the fight with Mr. Yates. As it turned out, the "Roy Rogers" label he let me keep was worth a whole lot more than any raise he would have given me. We learned that the hard way: when I had to sue Republic Pictures for the right to use my own name.

In happened in May 1951, when my second seven-year contract expired. In talking with Mr. Yates about another contract, Art Rush insisted that the studio grant me the right to do some television shows. Yates refused. William Boyd, who played Hopalong Cassidy, had been smart enough to get the rights to all the pictures he made in the 1930s. When he sold them to television, he became a bigger star than he had ever been. Gene Autry was going into television, too. About the time my contract expired, Mr. Yates instructed his people at the studio to start trimming all my old pictures to fifty-three minutes so they would fit an hour-long TV slot. Well, that got my back up! He didn't want me to do television because he was planning to sell all my old pictures to TV himself! But thanks to that clause in my contract, giving me the right to use my name and likeness, I was able to get a court order that stopped the studio from selling my pictures. That was good for me, but of course it meant the end of my job at Republic. Suddenly there I was in 1951, a movie cowboy without a movie contract—after being chosen as the exhibitors' favorite Western star every year since 1943!

Television was new, but we were certain it was the way to go. Along with Dale and Pat Brady and a small group of the fellas from the old Republic crew, we made a thirty-minute movie, what you'd call a TV pilot today, called "Presenting Roy Rogers—King of the Cowboys." In the fall of 1951, after the courts stopped Republic from selling my old pictures to TV, General Foods' Post Cereals agreed to sponsor our show. On December 30, "The Roy Rogers Show" went on the NBC network. The premiere was a grand affair broadcast from the El Capitan Theater, starting with a live half hour featuring songs by Dale and the Whippoorwills, a novelty music act by Pat Brady, and Bob Hope promoting a picture we had just made together, called *Son of Paleface*. We did a sketch in which Bob, I, and Trigger were all supposed to be playing poker together. When Trigger spots Bob trying to pull an ace from his sleeve, he knocks over the table with his nose and pushes him offstage. After that, we showed our movie, which established the setting and the characters for the TV series.

"The Roy Rogers Show" took place in Mineral City, located in Paradise Valley. It wasn't the old West—we had cars and telephones—but most of the action was on horseback. I owned the Double R Bar Ranch; Dale ran the Eureka Cafe; and just like in our movies, there wasn't a whole lot of mushy stuff between us—more like good friendship. The plot of the first show had to do with Dale helping a falsely accused man escape from jail. Pat Brady played my sidekick, along with the stubborn old army Jeep that he called Nellybelle. Of course, Trigger was part of the series. We got Dale a spirited buckskin quarterhorse named Buttermilk because Pal, the palomino she used to ride in movies and live shows, looked too much like Trigger on the little television screen. Our German shepherd, Bullet ("the Wonder Dog"), was always part of the action, too. The show originally ran on NBC at 6:30 p.m. on Sundays. We made a hundred episodes through 1957, then went into syndication and over to CBS for four years.

We heard from people of all ages who liked that program. When it was broadcast on Sunday nights, whole families used to sit around and watch it together. I guess the thing that tickled us most about going to television was how much closer kids felt to us. TV made us more like their pals, people they really knew rather than someone in a movie. I know this from the way audiences at rodeos and live shows reacted to us in the 1950s. "Roy! Dale!" boys and girls cried out, like they had been our friends forever.

I also know how strong the effect of TV was from all the kids who started showing up on our doorstep asking us to take them in after that show went on the air. Each one would put on a big, sad face and tell us how their mean ol' ma and pa made them do awful things like take out the garbage and clean their room and wash their hands before supper. From seeing Dale and me on TV, they figured that being the child of the King of the Cowboys and the Queen of the West had no such hardships. They believed that our life was nothing but happy songs, fast horses, and exciting adventures—a child's dream come true.

CHAPTER 8
Dale's Story

When we learned I was pregnant, Roy wanted a boy for Dusty and I wanted a girl. But neither of us was fussy. We were thrilled to be having a baby of either sex—just so long as he or she was healthy.

The second month of my pregnancy I came down with German measles. It was not a bad case; I wasn't too sick, and as far as anyone then knew, it had no implications for the baby. Twice after that, though, doctors ordered me to bed to prevent a miscarriage. Once, I developed laryngitis so severe that I sounded like Louis Armstrong. When I was seven months pregnant, my doctor did a blood count and told me I was close to anemic. Worse than that, he also informed me that I had Rh-negative blood; Roy was Rh-positive. Our blood types could mean some difficulty for the baby, he said, but in all likelihood any problem could be taken care of.

Shortly after midnight on August 26, 1950, Robin Elizabeth Rogers was born—seven and a half pounds and pretty as an angel. "She's beautiful," Roy declared. He kissed me and said, "Honey, she has little ears like yours!" I looked at Robin and saw almond-shaped eyes, just like her daddy's. Later that same day Roy rode as grand marshal of the Sheriff's Rodeo, during which he boasted to an audience of ninety thousand people in the grandstands that he was the father of a baby girl. In the hospital, I rested in a roomful of flowers. We were ecstatic.

The next day I began to think that the nurses weren't bringing me my baby nearly as often as they brought other babies to their mothers. When they did bring her, she was sleeping so soundly I couldn't wake her up. The doctors assured me that all was well; they said only that little Robin needed her rest. Whenever I boasted to one of them about how pretty I thought she was or what a fine, healthy child she seemed to be, they changed the subject. On the third day, when I was scheduled to go home, a nurse slipped and said, "Are they going to let you take her home with you?"

"Of course I will take her home with me," I said. I was confused. "Is there any reason why I shouldn't?"

Realizing she had spilled the beans, the nurse turned to leave the room. But she stopped at the door, spun around, and walked back to face me. She lowered her voice and, woman-to-woman, said, "Tell your doctor to tell you the truth." Then she was gone.

My heart began to pound. In desperation I rang for help—nurses, doctors, someone, anyone! I picked up the phone and called Roy at home.

"I've just found out myself," Roy said in a melancholy voice. "I'll be right there, Maw." Art Rush had come to the house to break the news to him: For three days specialists had conducted tests on Robin Elizabeth Rogers. They determined she was suffering from what was then known as Mongolism—Down syndrome. Her muscle tone was poor, she had problems swallowing, she would be mentally retarded, and her heart was defective. For the first few days, they gave her oxygen to keep her going. She had responded poorly to all their tests. The prognosis was grave.

At the hospital the pediatrician explained the physical characteristics of Mongolism: square little hands full of creases, tiny ears, an undeveloped nose bridge, slanting eyes.

Once, the first day, I had held Robin up to the light and thought she looked faintly Oriental. But when they told me of her condition, I indignantly told the doctor that her daddy had slanted eyes, too; so did his daddy; they were part Choctaw Indian, and so was Robin: she had Rogers eyes, that was all! I told them what a sleepy baby I had been, and I had turned out all right, hadn't I? It felt as though the doctors were indicting my child, so I fought them every step of the way, trying to rationalize their diagnosis.

"Institutionalize her," they advised. "Put her away before you become too attached to her." They said that if we took her home our life would soon revolve around her—to the exclusion of everything else, even of our other children. They explained that there weren't many institutions that accepted Down syndrome children, and that the few state homes and hospitals that were equipped for them were so overcrowded they wouldn't even consider a child until it was four years old. But because we were Roy Rogers and Dale Evans they might be able to pull some strings and find a place to put her away.

"No," Roy said. "We are going home." And that was that. When we got her home, I called the other children into the living room. They were fascinated by their new sister; Dusty said he thought she looked like a Kewpie doll with pixie ears. He asked to hold her. Although he had begged for a brother, I could see him melt with delight as he held this little shining star in his arms. We put her in her rattan bassinet and I sat on the sofa, patting the cushions for the little ones to come sit by me. I told them, "Robin is a very special baby. She's not very strong and she's going to be slower than other babies are." I told them she might never do the things they could do. "We have to take care of her just as though she were a delicate little flower," I said. "Your daddy and I need you to help us protect her. Will you do that? Do you understand?" Perhaps they didn't precisely understand Robin's medical condition, but those children knew, as all children know, how to be kind to a little being that needs loving care. Robin was fascinated by music, so Cheryl used to hold her up to the piano and let her pound away at the keys. Dusty, who so craved a brother for rough-and-tumble boys' games, was as gentle as a lamb. He spent hours hiding under Robin's bed, playing peek-a-boo and making her laugh.

We were perpetually on the alert for signs from Robin, some indication that she really wasn't as bad off as they said. When she seemed to wiggle with glee, we lit up. When she smiled, we jumped for joy, for the doctors had told us that the severest Down syndrome children never smile. At night, when she sang herself to sleep, as normal babies sometimes do, I thought, *How could anything be wrong?*

We consulted the head pediatrician at the Mayo Clinic in the hope that he would have a cure. It was he who helped us get over seeing Robin as a problem to be solved and realize she was a child to be treasured. "There is nothing I can do," he said about her physical condition. "There is no help." But I will always remember his advice: "Love her. Love will help her more than all the hospitals and medical science in the world." Then I remembered that years ago, in Kentucky, I had promised God that if he would save my son Tom from polio, I would put my life in his hands. Now, He had sent us Robin.

Why did this happen to us? That question haunted me. I thought Robin's affliction might be punishment for my sins— for my pride, my ambition, my failures as a mother. Then I thought it might be God's way of speaking to Roy, Roy who always cared so deeply about children. Harley Wright Smith, pastor of St. Nicolas Episcopal Church in Encino, told me that he believed Robin came to us with a purpose. "You will learn wonderful lessons from her," he said. "God will guide you." He was right. That little baby gave us a perspective we might never have found without her. We needed her, more than we ever knew when she was with us. She brought a wonderful peace to our lives. How well I remember the times Roy and I came home after a long, hard day and went straight in to see her. We played with her. She smiled. Our troubles fell away. She taught us patience and humility; and in the end, she showed us how to be of use to God. The Lord has many ways of refining people; usually His crucible is fashioned from whatever we hold most dear. In this case, it was our child. Roy, who was once so plagued by the sight of handicapped children in the hospitals he visited that he had questioned God's plan, learned to overcome his skepticism. I learned more than ever to trust His will: what other choice did I have?

Robin had a terrible time eating. Her tongue was thick and she could not hold food in her mouth. She was too weak to grip a milk bottle, so we sterilized a perfume bottle and filled it with milk, topped with a tiny nipple. She drained it dry. It was hard for her to hold her head up or focus her eyes and attention; so often she had a distracted look, like she was seeing things faraway. At her first Christmas, we had a small party for her. She was all dressed up, with a bow in her fine, blond hair, and she seemed to want to reach out from her little crib. I bent down and took each of her tiny hands in mine and tried to help her raise herself up. She tried, oh, she struggled to come toward me. But she couldn't make it. Her face turned blue from the effort; she gasped for breath and began to perspire. Roy and I stood over our child with tears in our eyes. It was a sad Christmas.

The Hollywood Hills where we lived were damp and smoggy. Robin needed clean air, so we moved to the San Fernando Valley, to a lovely, rambling Spanish ranch in Encino. Roy named it the Double R Bar. There Roy's father and uncle built a separate little bungalow for Robin and a nurse. She needed privacy; she was so fragile that the commotion of a household agitated her nerves. And the doctors were worried that with her constitution any childhood illnesses that Cheryl, Linda, or Dusty might contract could prove deadly.

The Double R Bar was a home with plenty of room for the children. There were fields where cattle grazed and horses basked in the sun. We had orange, plum, and apricot trees; I put up my first jams and jellies that summer. There was a swimming pool, too, and we soon discovered that Robin loved to splash and kick in the water when Roy or I held her there. "She looks like an angel and swims like a frog!" Roy used to say. I think now that she loved the water so much because she felt nearly weightless in it; she had some strength; she could make her arms and legs do what she wanted them to do.

Robin seemed to thrive at the ranch. She discovered our Weimeraner dog, Lana; and at the same time Lana discovered her; from that point on, the two were nearly inseparable. Lana tagged along whenever we wheeled Robin anywhere. There were times when Robin was so fretful and nervous that any human company upset her; then Lana would nuzzle close, pressing her cold nose into the baby's face. Robin stroked the dog's sleek, dove-gray fur and ran her delicate hands along Lana's floppy ears, and as Lana settled in to nap by her side, the baby breathed easy once again.

There was an immense, ivy-covered oak tree that grew right up through the middle of the patio of our home—so old that the Encino Chamber of Commerce declared it a monument. Town fathers worried that the ivy would damage the venerable tree and asked us to remove the vines. When Roy and the kids took the ivy down they discovered a nest of baby squirrels. Evidently we had frightened the mother away. Linda Lou, who was eight at the time, worried terribly about them. "What will happen to the babies without their mother?" she demanded to know. Roy fixed a spot in a little cupboard where the children could watch over the babies. He showed them how to give the orphans milk with an eyedropper. How they cared for those little animals! When two died, Linda lined a shoe box with soft cloth and buried them in the backyard with a bouquet of geraniums atop their grave. The children were so distraught at the loss: they couldn't understand why the little creatures had to die, or why their mother hadn't taken care of them

Two of those squirrels grew strong and healthy; soon they were so plump and sassy that they were biting holes in the nipples of milk bottles that the children brought them. Dusty used to take them over to Robin, who would reach out and pet them. When she felt the softness of the little animals' fur, she giggled with delight.

The older children knew Roy and I were troubled by all of Robin's frailties and handicaps, so they did what they could to make us feel better. Whatever resentments they felt toward me for marrying their dad fell away as they joined in concern for their baby sister. I hardly realized it at the time, but Robin's presence was helping us grow close as a family. Dusty colored a picture of Pal, the palomino horse I rode in parades and rodeos, and left it on my dressing table inscribed, "To my mother." Linda outlined her hand on a piece of cardboard and sprayed it silver as a gift to me. For Mother's Day, Cheryl—our oldest—wrote a card that said,

> . . . You came to live with us at rather a bad time, with Daddy so sad, and two little girls who were naughty, and a little boy who needed a mother's love that he had never known, and that the youngest of those girls had had for only three years. The older girl, when she was smaller, always kept her sorrows and problems in her, and even when you had problems of your own you were always there by our sides and you helped make our Daddy a Christian. I can't find anything fancy to say, but thanks from all of us and we really, really love you.

Robin came to us at a tumultuous time in our career. Before I discovered I was pregnant, I had gone back to work. I managed to buy my contract back from Danny Winkler, which meant Art Rush could be agent for both Roy and me once again. Republic determined that a married couple would not necessarily be box-office poison, so we resumed making Westerns together. We began a weekly "Roy Rogers Radio Show" for the Mutual network; we recorded songs for RCA, including some of my own compositions like "Hazy Mountain" and "Aha, San Antone." It was a tremendously productive period for us—exhausting, but exhilarating. Roy was the number-one Western box-office draw and had been ever since *Life* magazine surveyed children to find out which man they most wanted to be like. The result had been a three-way tie between Franklin D. Roosevelt, Abraham Lincoln, and Roy Rogers. We were on the road almost constantly, doing our show at rodeos and in city and small-town theaters and riding in parades.

Strenuous as our schedule was, Roy never lost his passion for needy children. I remember one night in the midst of a long and tiring tour we returned to the hotel and fell into bed, looking forward to sleeping late the next morning. When I woke up, though, Roy was gone. The day wore on, and I began to worry. That afternoon, before our first performance, he returned. I wanted to be angry with him ... until he explained where he had been. There was a five-year-old girl out in the countryside who had been in an explosion and lost all her limbs. Her fondest wish was to see one of our shows. That morning Roy had driven two hundred miles to her house to issue a personal invitation and let her parents know that they had three reserved seats for the evening performance. Both parents sat beaming in the front row, their daughter in the chair between them. They had brought the little girl in a wicker laundry basket, and her smiles that night filled up the auditorium.

When I became pregnant, I had to quit touring and making pictures—in those days, pregnancy was something to be hidden from the public. But Robin's birth did not mean the end of my career. In some ways, she was an inspiration. Just days after we brought her home from the hospital, I got to thinking about the music on the "Roy Rogers Show" on the radio. Roy had a cute theme song at the time called "Smiles Are Made Out of the Sunshine." It was popular, but I felt it wasn't Western enough, and it didn't say enough about what it means to be a cowboy—especially when the trails you ride *aren't* always sunny ones. A cowboy has to ride no matter what the weather. For years, Roy had signed autographs with *"Many Happy Trails"* or *"Trails of Happiness,"* and I thought, that's what he needs—a trail song. I was sitting at home with Robin and I started to remember way back to a trip my mother had taken down into the Grand Canyon, a trail ride. I had always loved "The Grand Canyon Suite," which has a trombone slide in it that made me think of someone saying "Happy trails" in a deep canyon, with a kind of echo effect: "Happy trails to yooo . . ." Once I thought of that, I wrote the song in three hours. At the time, I never suspected it would become our theme song; nor did I realize just how much the words would mirror our lives:

> *Some trails are happy ones, others are blue.*
> *It's the way you ride the trail that counts;*
> *Here's a happy one for you.*
> *Happy trails to you until we meet again.*
> *Happy trails to you, keep smilin' until then.*
> *Who cares about the clouds when we're together?*
> *Just sing a song and bring the sunny weather.*
> *Happy trails to you until we meet again.*

We took the song to the Mutual network, taught it to the group singers, and closed our show with it, as a duet. When it became a hit, nobody was more surprised than I.

By her first birthday, Robin could nearly stand up when

she was held in someone's lap. I often held her like that, listening to religious programs on the radio, believing that somehow she would understand. Roy sat her up in the middle of a big play table, where she learned to throw bright balls—"like a big-league pitcher," he used to boast. She could turn over in her bed, get on her hands and knees, and chew "cack-cack," which is what she called crackers. The clean air and good life in the San Fernando Valley had done wonders for her. One thing she used to love to do from the time she was six months old was to lift her legs straight up over her head and throw them sideways. "Look, Maw, she's doing the splits!" Roy said with glee.

I read in a medical magazine about a doctor in San Francisco who was helping children with Down syndrome, so I took Robin on the train north. (After her birth, I had been afraid to fly. If a plane I was on crashed, she would be motherless. The thought haunted me from the time we knew she was special: *What if I die first?*) The doctor made no promises, but he suggested we try powdered extract from the pituitary gland of a young calf to improve Robin's muscle tone. When we returned two months later, the doctor noted that her arms and legs had indeed improved. That was fine, but then he spoke about her heart. It was enlarged and worsening, and he expected that within half a year it would be critical. The end was near.

When we started the trip back to Los Angeles, I was lost in a dark cloud of despair. Robin had been overstimulated by the sights and sounds of the city. She began to cry frantically and developed a case of violent diarrhea. In desperation, I lay down beside her in the train's sleeping compartment and began to pray. I focused on an overhead light and noticed, to my sudden amazement, that there was a blue haze around it. The haze spread fast and filled the whole room, enveloping me on the floor. I threw open the door to see if something was leaking in from the aisle, but the aisle was clear. Then I knew what the blue haze was. The Holy Spirit had boarded the train to comfort me. I was lifted up and strengthened by His warmth.

One day I came home from work and found doctors at the house. Robin had suffered a series of convulsions, weakening her tremendously. Her legs could not support her any longer. She would never again stand in my lap, and she was too weak now to sit in her stroller and watch the other children play. It became more difficult to wake her up from afternoon naps, and her weight evened out at seventeen pounds—never more than that. The doctors warned us that in her newly impaired condition, she might dislocate her hips when she swung her legs up. That would be extremely painful. So they gave us a brace to keep locked between her feet, holding her legs safely down. She cried when we put it on her. That Christmas, her second, we gave her a bright red toy piano. It was Dusty's suggestion; he thought she would like playing with it in her crib. Cheryl asked to write Robin's letter to Santa.

Before we left for the Houston rodeo in the early spring, Robin was christened, wearing a white organdy dress with a pink sash and a blue ribbon in her light blond hair. At the rodeo, Roy rode out on Trigger, alone in the darkened auditorium, illuminated by spotlights that formed a huge cross, and sang "Peace in the Valley."

Late in August, Robin came down with the mumps. The mumps became encephalitis and the doctors said that if she survived she would no doubt be afflicted by severe brain damage. On Saturday, her temperature rose to 108. She cried constantly from the pain in her head. We dipped her in ice water to cool her down and gave her coffee enemas for inner stimulation.

I managed to fall asleep Saturday evening, but was awakened at midnight by a blood-curdling cry somewhere just outside the house. I threw on a robe and rushed into the darkness. The cry continued—a long, deep, primeval moan. It was our dog Lana, scratching at the door of Robin's room. Lana wailed and howled and paced through the night as Robin weakened and slipped into unconsciousness.

Many months before, an elaborate press party for us had been scheduled at the Brown Derby Sunday afternoon. Originally, it had been set for August 26, but because that was Robin's birthday, we moved it to the twenty-fourth. Now it was too late to call it off. Neither Roy nor I wanted to leave Robin, but I finally persuaded him to put in an appearance. I will never forget how he looked on the way to the luncheon, outfitted in his white hat, embroidered shirt, silver-trimmed gunbelt, and spread-eagle boots—the King of the Cowboys!— standing over our little girl with tears in his eyes.

Sunday evening, Robin's heart gave out. Her room was filled with gifts and new toys waiting to be played with. But there would be no party on August 26. Robin's second birthday would be the day we put her in the ground.

When the nurse came out of Robin's door to whisper, "She's gone," Roy and I stood in the carport, not knowing where to go or what to do. We held onto each other and cried for what seemed like an eternity. The birds had stopped singing in the trees; Lana yelped mournfully outside Robin's door.

I could not bear to look at her in death. With our friend Reverend Leonard Eiters, Roy went into her room and stood by her side until they came to take her body away. Later he and Art Rush made arrangements for her funeral at Forest Lawn. Roy took her christening dress and a blue ribbon for her hair and selected a child's blue casket. Monday, the day before the funeral, he asked me to come look at her in the funeral home. I could not. I was afraid I would fall apart, or try to pick her up and carry her away with me. Again alone, Roy went to see her in her coffin. "That's the hardest thing I ever did, but I'm glad I did it," he told me. "She looks like a small-size sleeping angel." Even at the funeral, I could not look at her. Roy made sure the casket was closed during the service and opened for the congregation only after I was out of the room. What a coward I was! How often I have regretted not looking at her one last time.

Just hours after Robin's funeral we rehearsed songs with the Sons of the Pioneers for the rodeo at Madison Square Garden. The rehearsal had been scheduled months before, and they were leaving for New York the next day, so it had to be done. I was racked by the worst pain I have ever known and felt on the ragged edge of a nervous breakdown. But that night I realized something: life must go on, however deep the sorrow. We do what we must do. The Roy Rogers Show had been booked into Madison Square Garden for a year, and there were too many people counting on us to let our sorrow get in the way. On the way to the train for New York, we drove past Forest Lawn. There was an illuminated cross on top of the mausoleum where Robin had been laid to rest. I thought of her little body in there and a great sense of guilt welled up in me: I had let her down by refusing to look at her before the funeral.

When we boarded the train, I wept for an hour. "Maybe we'd better adopt another baby right now," Roy suggested.

"I just want Robin!" I cried. The pain was a great boulder crushing my heart.

The train took us to Dallas, where I visited my father, who was recovering from a stroke. While in Dallas, Roy insisted we go to Hope Cottage, where he and Arlene had found Cheryl. "Seeing babies might help both of us," he said. There was a little girl there named Mary Doe, whom I had met two months earlier when I had come to town. She was of Choctaw Indian descent and her appearance was the opposite of Robin's: she had enormous deep brown eyes, long black hair, and olive skin; and she was as vigorous as a jumping bean. She had reminded me of a happy little fawn. I asked if Mary Doe was still there.

"Yes, she is," said Mrs. Carson, the matron of Hope Cottage. "She has finished her medical tests and she is ready for adoption."

When I saw Mary I swept her into my arms and hugged her fiercely. Her arms locked around my neck like she never wanted to let go.

"This is *our* child," I blurted out to Roy. "I want her!"

"Are you sure?" he asked.

I was never so sure of anything in my life: wildly, happily, brokenheartedly sure.

"It's all right with me," he said with a grin.

Mrs. Carson promised to let us know about little Mary Doe as soon as possible. That wasn't nearly soon enough to suit me. After walking out of Hope Cottage without her, I kept feeling we had left something terribly important behind.

We boarded a plane for New York. When we got there I had to let Roy do most of the talking at our press conferences. I wasn't making much sense when I spoke; and when people spoke to me, it was hard to understand their words. I was so busy asking God to give me strength that I hardly knew where I was. In the hotel at night, I awoke in a cold sweat. I saw Robin in my dreams. I saw her lying in her casket, dead. She rose up and looked at me. Her eyes were open and full of questions. I tried to pray for answers, but my nerves were shattered.

Roy and I always ended our Madison Square Garden performance with a sidepass all the way around the arena—we walked our horses sideways so we could lean forward and shake hands with all the children reaching out or being held on the shoulders of their mommies and daddies. That year, as we circled around each performance, I saw a thousand two-year-olds reaching toward me. So many little ones, their strong, able hands grabbing mine, their smiles gleaming in the lights of the arena: they were so alive, so alive and healthy and happy, with wonderful futures ahead of them. We rode among them and the air boomed with deafening cheers, laughter, and applause; we reached out and they shouted with glee; again I thought of a small blue casket with a child in it and the deathly hush of a mausoleum.

A short while after Robin died we were shooting a scene on location. I was supposed to take off my cowboy hat. After the first rehearsal, the cameraman took me aside and said, "Dale, I have a problem with the lights. I can't light your hair anymore." I hadn't noticed—at this point I wasn't noticing anything; I was just trying to get through the day as best I could—but in the time since the funeral the crown of my hair had turned white. "You've got a halo," the cameraman said. "You look like the Pope."

In my unending grief over Robin, something Roy had said kept running through my mind: "She looks like a small-size sleeping angel." I recalled a verse from the thirteenth chapter of Hebrews: "Be not forgetful to entertain strangers: for thereby some have entertained angels unawares." Like sunlight breaking through clouds after a storm of darkness, it all became clear to me. I knew what Robin's life meant and I saw what I had to do. She had come to us from God—an angel—with all her handicaps and frailties to make us aware that His strength is found in weakness. In the two years she had been among us we had grown close as a family and we had learned how deeply we needed to depend on God. My job was to help deliver that message that had been given us by an angel.

I grabbed a pen and began to write. I wrote until my hand cramped and could write no more. I looked at the pile of paper on my desk. It was my handwriting, but somehow the words didn't feel like *mine.* I picked up the pen again and tried to write more, but nothing happened. After that initial burst of inspiration, a curtain seemed to fall across my mind and, try as I might, I could not force myself to conjure up the words.

I was obsessed with getting Robin's message onto paper, but didn't know how to do it. One evening during a radio

broadcast when I had time away from the microphone, I
closed my eyes and sought guidance. In that moment, I knew
what the problem was. I was in the way! I was trying so hard
to put her message into my words that I was blocking hers. It
was so simple! All I had to do was stand aside and let Robin
speak for herself. I was not the messenger; I was merely the
instrument. From that moment on, the words—*her words*—
flowed onto paper. For weeks, my hand felt guided as her
story flew from my pen. I wrote it on the backs of envelopes,
script pages, the margins of newspapers, whatever was
handy. It turned out to be a short book—sixty-three pages in
all—but the message was a simple one that didn't need
windy elaboration. The story was Robin's—and God's—not
mine, and it was for parents and children who needed to
understand, so I decided to donate all the royalties to the
National Association for Retarded Children. In an introduction to the book that I wrote (in my words), I told readers,
"This is what I, her mother, believe she told our Heavenly
Father shortly after eight p.m. on August 24, 1952." Her story
began:

> Oh, Father, it's good to be home again. I thought sometimes
> that You had forgotten me, Down There. Two years Up Here
> doesn't seem like much, but on earth it can be a long, long
> time—and it was long, and often hard, for all of us.
> When You lifted me up from the earth, just a few minutes
> ago, it was Sunday, and my Mommy and Daddy were crying,
> and everything seemed so dark and sad and confused. And all
> of a sudden it was bright and clear and happy, and I was in
> Your arms. Was it the same way for them Down There, Father?
> You can put me down, now; I'm perfectly all right, now that
> I'm rid of that lump of hindering clay . . .

Robin's story concluded with these words:

> They're a lot stronger, since they got Our message. There's a
> new glory inside them and on everything all around them, and

they've made up their minds to give it to everybody they meet. The sun's a lot brighter in Encino, since we stopped off there for a while.

And now, Father, please . . . could I just go out and try my wings?

I called the manuscript *Angel Unaware.* I soon learned that the publishing business could be as tough as show business. The first publisher who read it said they already had a book about a handicapped child, and didn't want two. Besides, they informed me, the reading public does not want to cry. More rejections followed. My faith began to slip. Why had I been guided to write the book if no one cared to read it?

We were in New York. I went to Central Park and sat alone on a bench trying to figure out what to do. I wanted a sign from God, so I bowed my head to pray. "Please give me a word," I begged Him. "Is it Your will that I seek a publisher for Robin's book?"

I looked up from my prayer and saw a little girl standing in the grass looking at me. She was about six years old. She had slanted eyes, tiny ears, little square hands, and a thick tongue that caused her to drool. She was a Down syndrome child, tethered to a middle-aged woman whose face was furrowed deeply with the scars of mental anguish. There were hundreds of office workers strolling in the park at that moment, but I saw only the mother and child. The little one tried to look at me, tried hard to focus her weak eyes just as Robin had done so many times, then walked on. *Oh, thank you, Lord!* I thought. That girl in the park was the word I had needed. Now I knew I could persevere until I found a publisher for Robin's book. I had to let other mothers of Down syndrome children know they were not alone. I had to let them know how Robin had blessed our lives.

That afternoon I got a call from Dr. Frank Mead of the Fleming H. Revell Company. He said he wanted to publish

Angel Unaware. The book would be released Easter week, 1953. It became a best-seller and has gone through twenty-nine printings altogether, but I never enjoyed its success as much as I did that autumn at the rodeo in Madison Square Garden.

When Roy and I rode out into the arena, the stands were filled with children, as they always were for our shows. But this year, after the publication of *Angel Unaware,* the audience was different. Among the cheering youngsters were hundreds of retarded boys and girls—Down syndrome kids, all kinds of kids with disabilities and handicaps—who had been brought to the show by their mothers and fathers. We had never seen them before; in those days parents seldom brought children like that out in public; they kept them in back rooms and closets, as though they weren't human beings. But Robin's book helped change that. Mothers and fathers had come to the rodeo because they wanted us to see their children, and they wanted their children to see us. They told the little ones that Roy and I were their friends. As we circled around, parents proudly held their fragile children in the air so they could wave to us and reach out with their little hands when we passed. The children smiled and laughed when we came close in our glittering cowboy clothes on our prancing horses. Down syndrome children all share certain features, so I saw Robin's face shining in every one of them. She filled the arena and her love filled my heart. I was blessed.

PART V

Roy and Dale: A Large and Loving Family

Ｊ N 1949 ROY ROGERS thanked readers of *Modern Screen* magazine for all the letters they had written to Republic Studios insisting that he and Dale be reunited as an on-screen team. "The plan Dale and I made when we married was centered around our home," he wrote. "We decided we'd guide our careers so we could spend as much time as possible together—as a family." It had hurt, Roy said, when the studio separated them as a screen couple, and now he was pleased as punch that they had next-door dressing rooms on location, with a hitching post for Trigger right outside.

In movies, on the radio, and in personal appearances, Roy and Dale had turned into an inseparable team by the late 1940s. Dozens of stories in fan magazines showed them at home with Cheryl, Linda, and little Dusty; and when they moved to television in 1951, they had become America's best-known and best-liked couple, seldom photographed by the press without their passel of kids, who often dressed in matching Western outfits. Children had become an essential part of Roy and Dale's public image. They seemed to draw their energy and inspiration from their own growing family as well as from the worldwide family of millions of little buckaroos who adored them.

Their unabashed devotion to children made their personal tragedies all the more poignant. When Robin was born in 1950, it wasn't only doctors that suggested the little girl with Down syndrome be institutionalized. Studio publicists, who felt that it was their duty to present stars as flawless, suggested that it would be a bad idea for fans to see the King of the Cowboys and the Queen of the West with anything other than a "normal" child. But for Roy and Dale it was impossible to exclude one of their little ones from their life—public *or* private—and so Robin was often part of family photo sessions, the one proviso being that her parents could select the pictures so that she always looked good. When Robin was alive, many magazine editors asked Dale to write about the experience of having a Down syndrome child; but she refused to turn Robin into a story, telling them the tale would be told when the time was right. When finally Dale wrote *Angel Unaware,* she was able to complete the book only when she came to think of it as Robin's, not hers.

For Hollywood celebrities, Roy Rogers and Dale Evans were not only unusually family-oriented; they were also startlingly personal. They told us fans all about themselves, and they seemed to want to know about us, too, as if they really cared if we were happy. To kids in the audience of the rodeo, or those who only watched them on TV, it actually seemed that Roy and Dale worried about our well-being—about our safety, our fun, and our souls. By the mid-1950s, when their arena shows always included Roy singing "Peace in the Valley" as Trigger knelt alongside him in prayer, Roy and Dale frequently told little buckaroos in the audience about their own kids at home, and in the summers when school was out, the Rogers kids came onstage right along with them. Like a kindly older brother, Roy told his partners in the audience that they ought not to think of Sunday school as sissy stuff, and that it would be a good thing if they honored their parents and helped people less fortunate than they were. To all members of the Roy Rogers Club he issued this prayer, which was supposed to be read at the beginning of each meeting:

> *Oh Lord, I reckon I'm not much just by myself.*
> *I fail to do a lot of things I ought to do.*
> *But Lord, when trails are steep and passes high,*
> *Help me to ride it straight the whole way through.*
> *And when in the falling dusk I get the final call,*
> *I do not care how many flowers they send—*

Above all else the happiest trail would be
For You to say to me, "Let's ride, My friend."
Amen

Dale followed up *Angel Unaware* with a book about her own journey into faith called *My Spiritual Diary,* and to date she has written twenty books using her own travails and those of Roy and her children as a way of reaching out to readers and helping them get along. *Time Out, Ladies!,* which was published in 1966, began, "I write as a mother who has been through the mill, for those now going through it. . . . This is what I've found and experienced in the daily living of one wife and mother, and what God and the Bible have done to help me with it all. I hope it may help you, a little. Anyway, thanks for listening!" It has always seemed important to Dale and to Roy to make that connection with their audience. In 1979, in the introduction to *Happy Trails,* the story of their lives they wrote together, Roy explained that his and Dale's autobiography was "the story of a family which . . . had the good fortune to have been adopted by millions of people who were interested in who we are and what we do."

Roy couldn't have been more right in his assessment of the way people feel about him and Dale. When we wrote a profile about them in *The Atlantic Monthly* in 1993, we got stacks of mail from readers who were delighted to find out how they were doing and what they were up to these days. In almost every case, the person who wrote expressed some deeply personal feelings about the couple and many asked us to pass on their thanks to Roy and Dale for having been so inspirational. We have never known any stars about whom devotees are so openly fond—in the caring, trusting way most of us reserve for feelings about close family. Perhaps our favorite letter came from Joe Silva, National Foreman of the Buck Jones Western Corral #1, a movie cowboy fan club headquartered in Oregon. Mr. Silva wrote:

I have always been a fan of Roy Rogers and Dale Evans. Their genuine concern for FAMILY and children is more of what we need in our society today. And this in spite of the heartaches that they have experienced with their own personal problems. They "bounce back" and continue with their good work by immersing themselves in charitable work that involves children because they believe in what they are doing.

I have always remembered Roy and Dale on the silver screen riding for justice, but their BIGGER calling is demonstrated in the simple life that they live. I have tremendous respect for them on and off the screen because in the final analysis their reward will be on judgement day. They will both claim their Oscar in heaven, and justly deserved.

—J & M. S.

CHAPTER 9

Roy's Story

While we were in New York performing at the rodeo in the days after little Robin passed away we got the call we had been waiting for from Miss Carson, the matron at Hope Cottage. She said that Mary Doe was ours if we wanted her. We arranged to pick her up on our way home to California. That was just grand, and Dale and I were tickled to death, but I got to thinking that one more little girl—"Dodie" we started to call her even before we picked her up—would bring the total of females in the Rogers house to four. Dusty and I were the only boys around, seeing as how Dale's Tommy was all grown up and married. I felt pretty strong about wanting Dusty to have a brother, and told Dale I'd like to adopt a son, too. She agreed, and we came across a brochure from an organization that rescued needy Jewish orphans in Europe. I called them and asked if they might help us find a boy, but they said that Jewish children were not adoptable in Christian homes. This made Dale plenty mad, and she wondered out loud what Jesus, with his Jewish background, would have thought of their rules! But we had to accept their wishes; and when we left New York, we still hadn't found a boy.

We did a series of one-night performances before we went to Dallas to bring Dodie home. The last of them was in Cincinnati. The morning before the show, while browsing through a stack of mail, I found a note from a woman in Covington, Kentucky, just across the river from Cincinnati, who ran a private home for handicapped children. They had nineteen boys and girls there and the woman wanted to know if there would be some way to introduce one of those children—her own daughter, Penny—to Roy Rogers and Trigger if she came to the show that night. I called her and said I'd be happy to meet her and Penny. While we were talking on the phone, a notion popped into my head. "Say," I said to the woman, "you don't happen to have a little boy about five or six years old who's adoptable, do you?" I told her my boy Dusty was nearly six, and that I was looking for someone to bring home for him, to be his brother. She said there was a boy I might like to meet. She would bring him to the show, too.

Backstage that evening, I was dressed in my full Roy Rogers getup, with hat and guns and boots. I saw the woman pushing a wheelchair with a pathetically twisted little girl with cerebral palsy in it. Beside them walked a five-year-old boy in a yellow corduroy suit and short billed cap. He was tiny; he had blond hair and big blue eyes. I walked over to them, tipped my hat to the lady and said hello to her girl, then knelt down to the boy's level. Cautiously, I extended my hand. His eyes grew wide. He seemed timid and fearful, but he overcame his fright and boldly stuck out his hand to shake. He was weak, but I could tell he was giving that handshake everything he had. As his little hand tried to get a grip on mine, he mustered a surprisingly loud voice to say, "Howdy, pardner!"

I held the boy's hand in mine and looked at him hard. I could tell that his eyes had seen a lot of things that scared him; they looked like they held secrets too dreadful for any little boy to know. But whatever the tragedies were that brought him to the orphanage, they had not extinguished a spark of life that was still shining in him bright as Northern Lights. I picked him up and hugged him, then put him on my shoulder and walked over to Trigger, who was outfitted for the show. I lifted him from my shoulder and swung him into the silver saddle on ol' Trig's back. The boy grinned ear to ear; he just glowed. At that moment, I knew he was the one for me. He was my son.

As the little boy sat on Trigger's back, I asked one of our crew to watch him so the lady from Covington could take us aside and tell us about him. He had been born in Kentucky and was found abandoned in the motel where his parents had lived. They had been alcoholics, and so cruel that their other children had been taken away from them. Either because of birth defects or brain damage suffered at their parents' hands, the other children had been diagnosed as mentally retarded and institutionalized. This little boy had not walked until he was two years old, had suffered the effects of serious and prolonged malnutrition, and showed the scars of regular beatings. After he was rescued he had spent eight months with his legs in braces to correct the ravages of starvation in his infancy. As I heard this story and watched the boy, happy as a lark in Trigger's saddle, my stomach turned. It was almost too frightening to think about what he had been through. Dale and I looked at each other nervously, wondering if we were up for the challenge of being his parents. We told the lady from the orphanage that we had to think about it.

That night, we didn't sleep. Over and over, we said to each other how much easier it would be to adopt a healthy, happy child. But every time I started thinking about all the plump, pink-cheeked youngsters out there in the world, the needy eyes of that skinny five-year-old came back to haunt me. "Mother," I said to Dale, "anyone can adopt a strong, healthy kid who has everything going for him. But what happens to a little guy like this?" Dale slowly shook her head back and forth, knowing what I was about to say, and she began to beam with the most loving smile. "Let's take him," I blurted out.

"Yes!" Dale agreed.

At three in the morning we called the lady in Covington, and at nine we were in a cab crossing the Ohio River, which runs between Ohio and Kentucky. A judge was waiting for us at the other end with the papers to be signed. An hour later, the little boy we called John David Rogers—Sandy for Short—jumped into my arms and said, "Hi, Daddy!"

He left the orphanage with nothing more than the clothes on his back and a rumpled paper sack. We carried him aboard our traveling bus and introduced him to the whole crew. He had never been surrounded by so many people being nice to him, and it didn't take long for his shyness to evaporate and a big, happy smile to appear on his face as band members let him strum a guitar or try their harmonicas. He was having a jolly time, and so was everyone else, when someone on the bus asked little Sandy what he had in the sack he was clutching in one hand. He seemed reluctant to open it. "Aw, come on, show us what you've got, little fella," one person said again. Sandy was a trusting sort, so he peeled back the top and reached in, pulling out the contents. It was a small, torn sweater. It was the only thing he owned. The jokes and chatter on the bus trailed off. He looked so small there, standing among us proudly holding up his possession to admire. I reached down and swept him into my arms, hugging him to my chest.

The bus took me, Dale, and Sandy to the airport. On the way, we stopped so I could buy him a pair of cowboy boots. He was ecstatic, and that night in the hotel room in Dallas, where we were scheduled to pick up Dodie the next day, he made me promise that he could sleep in his boots. The one thing that was even more exciting to him than his new cowboy boots was food. This child had never had enough to eat, and I remember how Dale and I sat in absolute shock during our first meal as we watched him. He devoured everything on his plate, and then proceeded to eat everything on both of ours. I told him that there was plenty more food around and that he should slow down and take it easy, but he pretty well inhaled everything he could see. That's one thing that never changed about that boy: he could eat any man under the table.

The next day when we drove to Hope Cottage to pick up Dodie, Sandy was terrified. He knew an orphanage when he saw one, and he sure didn't want to go inside with us. But he was even more scared of being left behind, so we went in with him walking right between us, clinging ferociously to my pants leg with one hand and to Dale's skirt with the other. I think he held his breath the whole time, because you've never heard a little fella burst out with a longer, louder sigh of relief than he did when we walked out of there.

On October 28, 1952, two months after Robin died, we returned home to Los Angeles with two new children. Baby Dodie took the flight in stride; she ate and laughed all the way. Sandy grew deathly quiet, and by the time we arrived on the West Coast, he was drenched in sweat. Dale said she thought that all the excitement had knocked him for a loop. We soon found out that Sandy's nerves and sweat were symptoms of some serious ailments.

October 28 was Dusty's sixth birthday, and although we had told him about Dodie, Sandy was a surprise. Looking back on it now, I realize we should have prepared Dusty. There we were—his parents—coming off the plane with a strange little boy clinging to us, calling us Mommy and Daddy. The look of suspicion and distrust when Dusty met us at the airport with the rest of the family told the story: he was none too pleased. In fact, he looked like he was about to bolt. Ginny, his nurse, grabbed him and pushed him toward

Sandy. He stood there glowering and looking the little guy up and down. He was a head taller than his new brother and twice his size, even though they were practically the same age. Sandy grinned and stuck out his hand to shake, but Dusty ignored it. Sandy lifted up the cuff of his jeans to show off his new cowboy boots. Dusty didn't crack a smile.

I saw that it would take some doing for these two to become friends. You know what? I enjoyed thinking up a way to get them acting like brothers. My plan was a simple one. I would do with them what I like doing best in the whole world: spend some time outdoors. We loaded up the car with fishing gear, sleeping bags, a tent, and a handful of matches in a waterproof box, and the three of us took off for a camping trip in the woods of Marysville in Northern California. We didn't take any food, because I figured it would be a fine thing for those two to learn to live off the land. And that is exactly what we did. Boy, did we have some fun! I taught Dusty and Sandy how to bait hooks using balls of cheese. I stuck on the bait and they pulled in so many bluegills that we had to give them away to other campers nearby. I shot rabbits just like I had done when I was a little boy back in Duck Run; then I showed the boys how to skin them and clean them and check them for warbles (you don't want to eat a rabbit with warble fly larva in it); then we cooked them over a campfire. Dusty was an old hand at camping already, but given Sandy's childhood, I wondered how he would adjust to all these new experiences. I needn't have worried. He liked it all. That fella wasn't afraid of anything so long as I was around, and he wasn't the least bit squeamish, especially about eating things. We cooked frog legs over the open fire and we gobbled them off wooden sticks. Good old Sandy was delighted to eat anything we cooked, picked, hooked, or caught. He was a bottomless pit of hunger that never filled up.

At night, we all got in our sleeping bags, gazed up at the

stars, and let the owls hoot and crickets chirp us to sleep. Oh, we were feasts for the mosquitoes, but we didn't mind one bit. I had planned that trip to get those boys together, but by golly, I don't think I've ever had so much fun myself as I did that week with my two sons. By the time it was over, I had a grizzly beard and the boys were fussing and feuding and laughing and poking each other just like they had always been brothers. At Dale's request, I shaved the beard off straightaway, but the friendship that had grown between Sandy and Dusty was forever.

We didn't put Sandy in school immediately. We wanted to keep him home awhile so he could adjust, and so we could figure out exactly what his handicaps were. It was hard, so hard, to watch all the difficulties he suffered just getting through the day. We bought him a tricycle, but he couldn't figure out how to coordinate his legs to make it work. His balance was so bad he couldn't stand on a chair without shaking and lurching forward. Heights frightened him. The pediatrician said that his head was enlarged, his bones were soft, his muscle tone was terrible, and his spine was bent. Brain-wave tests revealed an abnormality. He had trouble breathing because the bridge over his nose had been smashed, probably by someone's fist. Maybe worse than all his physical problems was Sandy's emotional frailty. The smallest correction to his behavior sent him into a frenzy. He would vomit, sweat, and shake—sometimes all night long. Nights when he was calm, he sometimes woke up a dozen times to come in our bedroom and make sure we were still there.

Eventually he started to tell me and Dale about his life; and as he spoke about it, he cried and shook. We wanted to cry, too; but instead, we did the best we could to let him know he was finally safe. He told us about one time he was beaten with a baseball bat because he dropped a milk bottle. At the orphanage, he said, he was responsible for changing all the babies' diapers, and it had been his job to care for Penny, the girl in the wheelchair. If ever this five-year-old boy neglected his responsibilities, the matron told him he was bad and made him sleep in a chair outdoors. Sometimes, he woke up covered with snow.

We had reconstructive surgery performed on his nose so he could breathe normally, but he was so weak and uncoordinated that everything regular kids do was a challenge for him and required great effort. Hard as it was for him to just play, or run, or jump, he never gave up. When he was in a game he knew he would lose, he kept playing, right to the end. He wrestled with Dusty all the time, even though he knew he didn't have a chance. He ran alongside the other children as long as he could, then when he fell behind, he ran some more. And I'll tell you this about him, too: he was every bit as mischievous as any untroubled little boy! He delighted in teasing Dusty and the other kids, and sometimes he drove me and Dale to distraction making silly faces and stirring up a ruckus at the dinner table. Dale always said that Sandy fought with the broken sword of the handicapped. The point is, *he fought:* he was one brave little guy.

I think maybe the most important thing Dale and I have in common, along with our faith, is our love for children. Both of us wanted a big family; and our roles in cowboy movies made other kids, as well as our own, an endless part of our lives. We were put in a position to be role models for many American boys and girls, and believe me, we have taken that job seriously. We have always been careful to act the way we feel children ought to see their heroes behave on screen as well as off. In our TV show, we made Dale's place the Eureka Cafe, not some saloon where drinks were served. And even off-camera, we've tried to portray a good image. I always used to like to have a beer or two when I was off on a hunting or fishing trip, but there came a time when I realized that drinking even beer didn't fit the kind of person Roy Rogers was supposed to be. I thought about how bad it would look if someone took a picture of me with a drink in my hand, so I gave it up altogether. I've always told my kids that their image is important. That's what you've got in life: your handshake and the image you portray.

When I'm talking about my image, I don't mean there's anything about it that isn't really me. It's just that I always try to be the best me I can. I believe children should have heroes, not antiheroes. I think they need people to look up to. That's why there was one reporter back in the 1950s that got my dander up worse than anybody ever has. If someone criticized my singing, my acting, my looks, anything about me, I didn't mind so much; it was no big deal. But this one time some fella wrote a newspaper article saying that Dale and I adopted our kids just because it would get us some publicity. Honestly, I have never been so mad at anyone or anything in my life. It was all I could do not to locate this man and break his face into a million pieces. I wondered what would happen if one day our babies saw this article: what would they think? We had a long talk with the kids about adoption that night. Dale said, "Some people don't understand it. They don't know how happy a home is when there are lots of children in it, and sometimes, when they don't understand, they say mean things about us. When they do, we have to forgive them." She was right, and I have tried to find it in my heart to forgive, but you'd better believe that it's a good thing I have never met that reporter in person. Forty years later, I am furious about it. And if the year 2000 rolls around and I see that man, if I have to get out of a wheelchair to go get him, I will. Oh, you'll see a real boxing match then!

Dale and I have always held strong beliefs on how to raise children, and we believe that they need guidelines and rules in order to learn how to live correctly. Like the time Dusty and Sandy dared each other to steal a cap gun, a toy submarine, and some other toys from a local pharmacy. They were caught and the pharmacist called me to come pick them up. I drove them home and took them out to the back porch at Chatsworth, where I sat the both of them down. I pulled my belt off and slammed it on the redwood picnic table so hard that both boys jumped. "Now that I have your attention, I have a few things to say," I told them. "It's very bad to take what isn't yours. You start with caps and toys, then you go on to motorcycles and cars, and the next thing you know, you're in jail. But that's not going to happen to you boys. I'm not going to let it happen. I'm going to whip you. If it happens again, I'm going to whip you twice as bad. I don't want to whip you, but I have to." I asked them which one wanted to be first. Neither volunteered, so I took Dusty, who was bigger, and bent him over my knee. I whapped him, but he was a tough little fella and he didn't want to give in, so he bit his lip and refused to cry. After about half a dozen good slaps, he wailed. Sandy was next, and he was wailing practically before he got his first swat. But I gave him a few more, just to make the punishments equal. It was hard to do, and when I was through, I took both boys in my arms and hugged them. "I'm your daddy," I said. "I have to show you right from wrong."

One thing is for certain, back when we were making movies and the TV show it was a whole lot easier to give kids rules that they could live by. These days, everybody talks about life being shades of gray, and how there isn't really right and wrong. It seems most folks are afraid to say what's good and what's bad because they're worried about stepping on someone's toes. Too many people keep their mouths shut instead of teaching children good and honest rules of life.

I reckon that the Roy Rogers Riders Club that we started back in the 1940s and the Safety First Awards that we gave out to schoolchildren in the 1950s would now be considered pretty corny; and I imagine that there would be plenty of smarty-pants who'd poke fun at them. That's too bad, because I know for a fact that they helped a lot of kids grow up to be better adults. The Roy Rogers Riders Club was open to any child that sent us his or her name and address. When we received it, we sent them back a "Rogersgram" that looked just like a Western Union telegram, except this one was sent by "Trigger Express." Each member of the club got a membership card with these rules to live by:

1. Be neat and clean.
2. Be courteous and polite.
3. Always obey your parents.
4. Protect the weak and help them.
5. Be brave but never take chances.
6. Study hard and learn all you can.
7. Be kind to animals and care for them.
8. Eat all your food and never waste any.
9. Love God and go to Sunday school regularly.
10. Always respect our flag and our country.

Dale and I still believe that life for a child is a lot easier if the rules are all spelled out nice and easy, and that is just what we did for the little ones who saw our movies. I get so mad at the lack of manners people have today! Recently I saw two guys walking down the street three feet ahead of the girl they were with, and when they got to the door they just walked on in ahead of her and slammed it in her face. I wanted to say, Where the dickens were you guys raised? It was obvious that no one taught them the rules! Aside from manners, it seems kids don't learn much common sense in school like they used to. Not too long ago it was considered important that children learn basic things like not to play in traffic or to wash their hands before they ate dinner. I guess compared to all the talk about gangs and drugs and AIDS these little things don't seem too important, but I can tell you they provide a basis for learning how to take care of yourself for the rest of your life.

When our TV show was on the air the National Safety Council got in touch with me to see if there was a way we could work together to help kids. We came up with a yearly contest in which some 30,000 schools all over America participated. We awarded a big golden statue of Trigger with a ruby-jeweled saddle and bridle to the school that won, based on its safety program. Kids used to send in slogans that they made up about safety. They were so great, I've saved many of them to this day. These are a couple of my favorites:

Cross at the corner. In the middle is the coroner.

—JIM KENDELL, AGE 10½

Safety's the other fellow's business . . . and I'm the other fellow!

—DONALD ROY DYAL, AGE 7

Because the Safety Council promotion went so well, we held a Roy Rogers lasso contest for kids to send in letters about their good deeds. The winners got a special Roy Rogers lasso with my picture on it. I guess I'm sentimental, but I hung on to boxes and boxes of these letters, too. One little girl wrote, "My good deed is I gave $1.00 to the orphans' home. I gave some of my clothes to children who didn't have much." Another one wrote to say, "When I see a little girl left out of games on the playground I always go up and ask her to play."

At Christmas the Ideal Toy Company would load up a plane with thousands of dolls and toys and I would fly down to South America and hand them out in the orphanages in Buenos Aires, Lima, and Panama City. My movies were real big down in South America, where Trigger was known as Tigre, as they were in Japan and most of Europe, too. It always makes me laugh to see the dubbed version where Gabby

Hayes and I are talking Spanish or Japanese. One thing that stayed the same no matter where I went was crowds of people wanting to meet me. I remember going down to Lima, Peru, to make an appearance at a theater that was showing one of my pictures. When I arrived, 250,000 people were waiting in the city streets. The police thought it would turn into a riot and wouldn't let me perform because they were afraid people would be crushed in the crowd. Another time Dale and Trigger and I went to Scotland and arrived at our hotel around 10:00 p.m. to find a mob outside. Six streets full of people had converged and they all stood pressed up against one another as close as the hairs on your head. At 2:00 a.m., they were still chanting so loud no one in the hotel could get any sleep. Finally we stuck our heads out the window, waved, thanked them for coming, and hollered the lyrics to "Happy Trails."

My popularity was helped by all those products we were selling with my name on them. Even kids who had never seen me in a movie or heard me sing might be carrying a Roy Rogers lunchbox or sleeping under a Roy Rogers blanket and reading comic books featuring me, Dale, Dusty, Trigger, and Bullet.

Dale and I had so many kids of our own that we knew we couldn't approve of any toy that would break easily or hurt someone, so before we agreed to let our likeness appear on a product, we had samples sent home for the Rogers family torture test. Magazine advertisements for our merchandise carried a pledge from me to parents, saying that everything had been "tested in one of the nation's largest testing bureaus," and that was true; but there were no testers more severe than my two boys: "If these things can survive you guys, they'll work for everyone else," I told them. So they slept under Roy Rogers bedspreads, carried Roy Rogers wallets and lunchboxes, took pictures with a Roy Rogers box camera, wore a Roy Rogers mask at Halloween, brushed their teeth with a Roy Rogers toothbrush, and drank their milk from Roy Rogers glasses. The glasses were marked to encourage kids to drink all their milk: a quarter glass down, they were a tenderfoot, halfway down they were a posse leader, three-quarters made them a deputy, and if they drank it all they made sheriff.

My son Dusty now has a good sense of humor about what it was like to have to be surrounded by products bearing his parents' faces, but back then I think it drove him a little crazy. Only recently, he confided to me that one of his fondest dreams as a kid was to have a Gene Autry or Hopalong Cassidy lunchbox. In fact, Dusty had a real thing going about his lunchbox. To hear him talk about it, all the other kids had handsome Gene Autry lunchboxes that were filled to the brim with neatly made sandwiches and loads of cookies and Twinkies all wrapped in shiny aluminum foil. In our home, Dale packed the kids' lunchboxes. Like me, she is a thrifty soul, so she used leftover wax paper or old bread wrappers for the sandwiches instead of foil; and she hand-cut the cheese or bologna for the sandwiches, so it was uneven and lumpy-looking. She also packed lots of healthy things like carrot sticks, carrot cookies, and hard-boiled eggs. Dusty used to pitch a fit about how all the other kids had Kool-Aid to drink while Dale packed thermoses of raw milk from our own cows. Today Dusty is a strapping man well over six feet tall, but he still likes to complain dramatically about his lunchbox deprivations.

In truth, being Roy Rogers, Jr., was no picnic for him. He remembers all too well what it was like to go to school and have the teacher call out his name during roll call the first day and see all the other kids' heads swivel in his direction. Dale told him that he had to learn to deal with it or he would wind up in a mental institution by the time he was twenty-one. It took him awhile to separate who he was from his famous name and to learn how to share his mom and dad with 25 million other kids, but he sure did a great job of it. He pretty much runs the show around here now.

Seeing children in sick wards and orphanages was never easy for me to do, but I loved to do it and I think I've played every children's hospital in America. Does that sound strange? I guess maybe it is, but I reckon I never left one of those places without an ache in my heart and a feeling that I wanted to help every kid along the trail. And I remember 'em, too; I remember so many of those kids like they were here now, or like I saw them yesterday, even if it might've been near fifty years ago. In Aberdeen, South Dakota, we went to sing some songs in the polio ward of St. Luke's Hospital in the winter of 1950. We were feeling bad when we started that trip: worried to death about our little Robin at home. How clearly I recall the faces of the little ones in that sickroom, and how they began to cry when we said we had to leave. It has always been extra hard to say good-bye to children, I guess because I feel that they are so much a part of me. I'm not just saying that; I mean it, because, you know, if it wasn't for all of them, there wouldn't be a Roy Rogers.

Back in 1946 I played at a burn hospital run by the Shriners. I saw what they did for kids for no charge at all—like building them new ears and noses after they were terribly burned in fires. It was just unbelievable what the surgeons could do to reconstruct their faces and bodies. When I came back from the hospital I was speaking to a good friend of mine, Joe Espalier, telling him about all the great work they were doing and raving about the Shriners. I told him that one of these days I wanted to become a Mason, because first you become a Mason, then a Shriner, and you can really help the kids. "You're talking to the right guy," Joe said, telling me that he was a Mason himself. He arranged for me to join. Harold Lloyd was the Imperial Potentate in those days. Gene Autry joined up about the same time I did. In fact, many years later Gene, I, and President Gerald Ford all became thirty-third degree Masons, high as you can go, in ceremonies on the same night.

No amount of fame or money can equal the feeling of watching sick children's faces light up when I visited them in their hospital rooms. When I went around to see them, I often took Trigger with me, and he was as well-behaved in a sickroom as he was on a Hollywood sound stage. We outfitted him with nonskid leather and rubber boots so he could walk down slick hospital corridors safely. He went right into elevators and up staircases; nothing ever spooked him. Some of the kids we visited were so bad off they couldn't even raise their hands, but they had smiles all over their faces when they saw us. There was a time I remember visiting a group of children who had been blinded in accidents; but they could see with their hearts, and they could hear us, too. I told each of them to reach out and I walked Trigger around and had him bend down his head so they could run their hands along his mane and his face. He wriggled his soft nose and whinnied gently when they touched him; then I sat down and sang them songs about the cowboy life.

Word was out in the medical community about how much children liked us to visit. One day I got a phone call from a doctor at the Virginia Mason Hospital in Seattle who told me about a boy suffering from a very serious kidney disease. His name was Russell Rogers—no relation to me, just a sick little guy who loved Trigger and my cowboy movies. Rusty, as everyone called him, was not doing well at all. He was not responding to treatment and was losing ground by the day. "Roy," the doctor said, "all he talks about is you and Trigger. Do you think you could make a phone call and see if that would help?"

I called Rusty in his hospital room and talked to him for a long time. "I'll tell you what," I promised him. "If you get well, I'll bring you down to California, and you can ride Trigger, and I'll be with you the whole time."

"Really?" he said.

"Yup," I answered.

Wouldn't you know it, he got better! I suppose it goes to show how much your mental attitude makes a difference in getting well, because this boy really wanted to ride ol' Trigger. In 1953 we brought him down to our home in Chatsworth and put him up there in the saddle. Boy, oh boy, was he a cute kid! When Ralph Edwards did my story on "This Is Your Life" three years later, Rusty—who was then nine years old and healthy as you please—came zooming out from behind the curtains like he was jet-propelled and jumped right into my lap. He was even wearing a little cowboy outfit! I never saw him after that, and have often wondered what became of him.

Rusty, if you happen to read this book, I sure hope you'll give me a call.

CHAPTER 10

Dale's Story

I pulled a gun on Dusty and Sandy only once: at the ranch, late Saturday in the fall of 1953.

We were living on a ranch in Chatsworth now. The boys were adolescents, but very boisterous ones—chasing each other, wrestling on the floor in the living room, knocking over things. Roy was away and I was home alone with the children. I had spent a very busy day, and the lady who helped with the children was off. I was very tired. The noise generated by Dusty, Sandy, Debbie, and Dodie was getting the best of me.

"Enough's enough!" I hollered. They were too busy to hear. "Knock it off!" I shouted as they ran past so fast papers flew off tables in their wake. They still didn't hear. I got up and went to the couch where they had taken pillows to swat each other in the noggin. "I SAID STOP IT!" They dropped the pillows and somersaulted over the back of the couch, tearing across the floor like twin cyclones. They stopped in place, then suddenly launched into a screaming match to see which of them could deafen the other one first.

I walked away, got out my stage pistol, loaded it with blanks, and fired it into the air six times. Those were the loudest explosions those boys had ever heard indoors. They were frozen in their tracks, paralyzed with fear. I looked at

209

them with murder in my eyes. I only had to whisper, "I said stop it," and they stopped, but now that I had their attention, I drew a deep breath and in a stage shout nearly as loud as my pistol, I flattened them: "NOW BE QUIET!" And for a precious short while, they were quiet.

Dusty had been suspicious of Sandy when his new brother came to live with us. The first morning after Sandy arrived, we discovered Dusty hiding all his favorite toys under the bed. We explained to him that Sandy only wanted to be his friend. By the time they came back from their first fishing trip with Roy, the two of them had become inseparable. Dusty realized that Sandy wasn't going to spoil his fun at all; he was going to double it. At last, he had a partner in crime!

There were times I swore that those two boys had been born for no reason other than to make my life miserable. If there was trouble anywhere, they found it; if they couldn't find it, they invented it. Merely going shopping in the car was an adventure. As far as they were concerned, the backseat was not for sitting; it was for bouncing, wrestling, and issuing war whoops as we traveled through Los Angeles traffic. Whenever I went on errands, they came along. I carried a good-sized switch by my side in the front seat so I could reach back and cool down their bouts when necessary. They'd shout, "Hit the deck!" and duck when I started swinging, but one time I connected pretty good. I heard a yelp, then Dusty—more humiliated than hurt—leaned into the front seat and announced, "Mom, we are leaving home."

"Fine! Good!" I said. "As soon as we get back I will help you pack." There was a strange silence from the wrestling pit.

Two minutes later, Dusty quietly announced. "Maybe we'll wait a year."

One morning I was getting ready to leave the house for the Iverson ranch, a location where we shot many Western scenes. I was fully dressed in my Queen of the West attire—

boots and buckskin fringe skirt, fancy embroidered blouse and Stetson hat, and heavy leather belt. I kissed the boys good-bye and sent them on their way to school. A few moments later, Ginny, the boys' nurse, called to me: "Dale, you will not believe what they are doing. Take a look out the window."

We had a good view of Amestoy Avenue, where I could see my two little cherubs gallivanting along a few houses behind the mailman as he made his rounds. They stopped at each mailbox and pulled out the letters and the magazines, replacing them with rocks, dirt, trash, and other people's mail. Oh, they were having a jolly time!

I ran outside, jumped in my car and screeched out our driveway, slamming on the brakes when I got to the mailbox they were currently plundering. I hit the brakes, threw the door open, and flew out after them, yanking my belt off my waist as I ran. It was a sight to behold: one very angry cowgirl charging down the avenue snapping a belt in the air like a bullwhip as the two fugitives stampeded to avoid my wrath. When I caught up with them, I paddled them all the way back home and made them put the mail back where it belonged.

I reckon their antics are the kinds of things that happen in a lot of families, just a normal part of growing up. Only after he had become a responsible adult did Dusty reveal some of their more heinous activities: their dirt-clod fights with Rex Allen's boys just down the street; how they used to spend summer days catching flies and eating them; and the time they discovered a nest of baby rats in the barn and fed the squirming little rodents to our housecat. I suppose those two were living, breathing, yelling, mischief-making proof that boys will be boys. Come Sunday morning, though, they sat by my side in church, a pair of sinless little saints sprouting wings.

Roy, who had never had a brother of his own, delighted in

the way they took to each other, and he was tolerant of most of their rowdy antics. One time, however, he went through the roof. I knew something was wrong when I heard him roar from the shed where he kept the racing boat of which he was so proud. Someone had pulled every inch of rubber from its dashboard. He had a pretty good idea who the culprits might be. Court was held in the living room for three days running. Roy cross-examined, cajoled, pleaded, and threatened them with everything up to and including the electric chair, but neither of the two prime suspects cracked. On the third day, His Honor announced, "I know one of you did it. If the guilty party does not fess up, I will have to give you both a good licking." He started to remove his belt. Both boys gulped. And finally, Sandy piped up, "I did it, Dad." Sandy was like that. He always came through; and he'd do anything for Dusty.

The way our kids learned to stick up for each other was heartwarming, but on occasion it could make me boil. One day I caught the boys with their pockets full of coins that I knew they hadn't earned. Roy and I were careless about leaving change around the house; Sandy and Dusty figured nobody would miss it. I decided I would take the opportunity to teach them a lesson. "Boys," I said, "do you know what happens to people who steal?"

They looked at each other, then at me, and shrugged, waiting no doubt for a scolding or, at worst, a spanking.

"People who steal go to jail!" I informed them. "In jail they eat nothing but bread and water." I grabbed Sandy by the hand and Dusty by the ear and marched them out to a cabaña we had by the swimming pool. I put them in and locked the door, returning from the kitchen with two hunks of dry bread on a plate and two glasses of water, which I passed to them through the porthole of the little dressing room. Their sentence: a day in jail without lunch.

A little later when I checked on them it didn't seem to me

they were suffering much from their strict regime. Let me tell you, those boys loved to eat, and to deprive them of even a single meal should have been torture. When they were released from their incarceration midafternoon, however, they had big grins on their faces and above each of those grins was a milk mustache. Then it dawned on me: their sister Linda had spent the day smuggling milk and cookies to the jail-birds.

On one occasion, Roy's threat of jail turned out to be more effective than mine. He lowered the boom after the boys decided they had had enough of my unfair rules about not screaming and yelling and wrestling twenty-four hours a day. Dusty was the instigator this time. When the boys were about eight he convinced Sandy that the two of them were getting a bum deal in a houseful of girls where they had to be polite all the time and wash their hands before supper and awful things like that. He had figured out that the two of them would have a much better life if they ran away and spent all their time fishing and swimming and stomping in mud puddles. They piled some toys in a wagon and set off to seek their destiny. They got to the top of a hill near the ranch, when Dusty realized it was lunchtime. When they suddenly remembered that neither of them had packed any food, they started to cry. Meanwhile, Roy was conspiring with Ginny to bring them back. He sent her out in her green Chevrolet, and when she found them she said, "You boys are in a heap of trouble! Your daddy's gone and called the sheriff!" She told them they had one chance to escape the long arm of the law: if they hid under a blanket in the backseat of her car, they might manage to sneak back to the house before they were nabbed in the dragnet.

"The coast is clear!" she whispered to them when they pulled up. They scampered from the car back to their rooms. "Quick, get under your beds!" Ginny hissed as they ran past. There wasn't time to separate, so both boys crawled under

Dusty's bed, where they thought they were invisible. At this point, Roy tramped into the boys' room pretending to look for them with a friend he had enlisted in his plot.

"All right, Roy," the stranger said. "Where are those two outlaws?"

Roy then delivered his line with utmost sincerity: "Gosh, sheriff, you know I'd help you if I could. I just don't know where they are."

"Roy, if I ever catch those two boys running away from home again, they're going to jail for the rest of their natural days."

They never ran away from home again.

In February 1954 Roy and I went to Great Britain. Billy Graham had come to speak at a meeting of the Hollywood Christian Group at our house the previous fall and said that he had been invited to conduct a Crusade for Christ over there. But the invitation had been extended by only a few small churches, so he was worried about attendance. Roy said, "I have a big fan club in the British Isles. Why don't we go over there ahead of you? We'll take Trigger and the whole show, do some performances to pave the way, then join you in London the first week you're there." We had never done an overseas tour, but Roy had the biggest fan club in Britain before the Beatles.

Those fans were enthusiastic, let me tell you! Getting off the plane in Glasgow, we were engulfed by thousands of them screaming, "We want Roy, we want Dale! Sing us a song!" They pressed so hard to be close to us, it was frightening. At one point a lady with an eight-month-old baby pushed close but couldn't break through to us, so she threw her child over some heads in the crowd into Roy's arms. We managed to return the child to its overenthusiastic mother, but by the time we got to our hotel, we were bruised and battered from shaking hands and from people grabbing hold of us.

Roy was killed on opening night . . . according to a rumor that the press picked up for a while. What actually happened was that one of the guns being used by our singing group, who dressed as outlaws and pretended to shoot at Roy when he rode out on stage, wasn't loaded with blanks as it was supposed to be. Instead, it had birdshot cartridges that were intended for use in a sharpshooting act later in the show. Roy rode out and the boys started blasting away. Trigger flinched, Roy started to duck. He went to the microphone with his face streaming blood. "They've been shooting at me for twenty years, and this is the first time they hit me," he told a crowd that sat there amazed by the realism of our special effects. The birdshot was picked out of Roy and Trigger that night and they were fine, but somehow a telegram was sent to Art Rush, who was coming over on the *Queen Mary,* informing him, with great regret, that Roy Rogers was a goner.

It was six cold and rainy weeks of shows throughout the British Isles, and in Liverpool at one point both of us came down with a raging European flu. The doctor put us to bed and injected us with sulfa and penicillin, but there were some newspaper people who were convinced we were faking it to avoid a press conference. They somehow managed to get Glenn Randall, our horse trainer, to lead Trigger up to the hallway outside our hotel room, where they stuffed a get-well bouquet of daffodils in his mouth and knocked on the door. When it opened they peeped in and saw our ashen faces; two of them actually managed to put their hands on our foreheads to confirm that we had a fever. When they realized our illness was no joke, they retreated; Trigger dropped the flowers and nickered his own genuine get-well, then was led away.

But that wasn't the end of it. When word spread that we might be too sick to make a scheduled performance, disbelieving fans started gathering outside our hotel. At one point there were hundreds of them milling underneath the win-

dow, chanting for us to show ourselves and to sing some
songs. At that time we were both in bed, barely able to move
let alone perform. Luckily, our singing group, the Whippoorwills, were able to stage an impromptu recital in the street,
accompanied by Trigger doing some of his tricks, which ap-
peased the crowd. Two days later, we did manage to shuffle
on stage for our show. I remember clinging to the curtains to
keep from falling down.

Toward the end of every show we sang "God Save the
Queen," talked about the Bible a little, and invited everyone
to come see Billy Graham in London. Then we closed with
"Happy Trails." The agency that booked us over there heard
that we were telling people about Billy and he warned us
that if we tried such stuff when we played Dublin, we were
likely to have rotten potatoes thrown at us. They don't go for
evangelists there, he said. I told him that Billy was the reason
we came in the first place. And don't you know, when we
sang "How Great Thou Art" in Ireland, we got a standing
ovation. Afterward the usher asked me if I would come back
and meet the chaplain of the Abbey Players, Ireland's famous
national troupe of actors. The man of the cloth came close
and he said, "You don't have to answer if you don't want to,
but I'd like to ask you a very personal question. I would like
to know: what kind of man is Billy Graham?"

"Sir," I responded, "he is the most utterly dedicated, committed Christian I have ever met in my life."

The chaplain fixed me in his sights and gave me a message
to deliver: "You tell Mr. Billy Graham that I said God bless
him." I will never forget the sincerity in that man's voice
when he said those words.

While touring Scotland, we did what we did in America
whenever we traveled: we went to children's hospitals and
orphanages. In Edinburgh we found a home called Dunforth,
where we met a thirteen-year-old girl named Marion Fleming. Both her parents were alive, but they had divorced when

she was two, and she had lived in the orphanage ever since. British law made a child with living parents nearly unadoptable. I was feeling pretty low when we visited: we had been away from our own home and children so long, and we had missed Dodie's first birthday. Marion was a tiny girl with a haunting voice. She sang us an old folk song—"Who Will Buy My Flowers?"—about a hungry orphan child on the streets of London. I wanted to grab her on the spot and make a run for the door.

We invited her to our show the next day. She sat on Trigger, then came to our hotel for lunch. We were smitten and agreed that we wanted her, but we soon discovered that in order to be eligible to adopt her, we would have to live in Britain for two years. Instead, we invited her to come visit us in California. Later that spring, we all went to the airport to greet her: Roy, me, Cheryl, Linda, Dusty, and Sandy. I remember Sandy's reaction best. When he watched her walk down the stairs from the plane, he broke into a broad grin. He marched right up to her and held out his hand in welcome. That handshake of his sure was something special. Dusty loved to hear her say all our names with her lilting Scottish brogue and spent hours with her in the yard building leaf houses on the ground. She taught Cheryl and Linda how to do the Highland Fling. We called her Mimi, and after a short while it began to seem that she had always been part of us.

That summer, a week before she was scheduled to go back, I found her in the corner of our breakfast room, weeping. We managed to extend the visit to Christmas so she could attend an American school for a semester. By then, her Scottish brogue was disappearing and in its place came American slang (I think I preferred the brogue!). At Christmas, we extended her visa once again to the end of the school year. In June she became our ward—a permanent member of our family. I was in heaven, surrounded by all these children. I told

Roy that we had better stop visiting orphanages or we'd soon have to move to a hotel.

In 1954 we did move to a place much better than a hotel—a 133-acre ranch in Chatsworth, near Canoga Park. It had a lake and ponds, a ranch hands' house, a barn, corrals for horses, coops for Roy's pigeons, and shelters for his hunting dogs. The main house was a big one, made of brick, secluded on the property by big shade trees and shrubs. We added wings on either end to make room for everybody, installed an intercom system to call from one end to the other, and laid down industrial (childproof!) carpeting everywhere. The kitchen was immense, with a walk-in refrigerator, walk-in freezer, and meat locker. When our cook Leola was off-duty, I made southern fried chicken in that kitchen and skillet-cooked cornbread on the side, with black-eyed peas and mustard greens. The boys loved that! Of course, the boys loved just about anything, except liver. In the morning, the first thing Sandy said when he came for breakfast was, "Mom, what's for supper?" Whatever I said (unless it was "liver"), his answer was always the same: "Good!"

The idea we had when we bought Chatsworth was to make room for all of us—kids, animals, and all the stuff Roy liked to collect; but we also bought the ranch with an eye to shooting movies and TV shows there, as well as renting the location to other companies. Sure enough, shortly after we moved in, along came the crew from television's "Brave Eagle"—a Western told from the Indians' point of view. One morning Dodie came flying into the kitchen, crying hysterically. She had looked out her window and seen a group of men on horseback. They were wearing feathered headdresses and war paint, practicing their most blood-curdling yells. It took some time to explain to our own little Indian that they were only actors, just like Mommy and Daddy.

Poor Dodie: she was beginning to seem like a sort of odd-girl-out in our family. Dusty and Sandy, five years older than she, were a terrible twosome, so close they needed occasional prying apart; Marion and Linda became bosom pals and swam together every day; and Cheryl was so interested in boys she didn't need a friend at home. Dodie, who was just three and a half, had Bullet, our German shepherd, whom she declared her property, not to be abused, harmed, or harassed by any of the other children; but we began to feel she would be happy if there were a girl her age among us. We found one, thanks to Dr. Bob Pierce of World Vision, a Christian group that helps children all over the globe. He sent us a picture of a three-and-a-half-year-old Korean War orphan named Lu-Ai Lee. She was part Korean and part Puerto Rican, unadoptable in her homeland because of her mixed parentage. Her eyes were big and brown; her hair was cut into a Dutch bob, and she seemed to have a very, very serious expression on her face. The Rogers family fell in love as soon as we saw her picture.

She arrived in June 1955. When Dr. Pierce carried her off the plane at Los Angeles airport, the little girl nestled into Roy's arms right away, hanging on to him for dear life. She was Daddy's girl from that moment on. We named her Deborah Lee.

Debbie had a lot to learn. English, first of all. She knew *Mama* and *Daddy, milk* and *sleep,* but the first day at the dinner table, when she didn't eat very much and I tried to ask her if she was all right, she could only look at me anxiously and speak a few timid words in Korean. I looked blank. World Vision had given us a pamphlet with some Korean phrases, but it wasn't any help. She repeated the words, looking desperate. When I still didn't respond, she addressed Linda and Marion. They didn't know how to answer. Debbie appeared distraught. Finally we figured out that Debbie was asking to be excused from the table to go to the bathroom. For weeks after that whenever she spoke to any of us in Korean, our first reaction was to pick her up and take her to the potty.

At first Debbie didn't seem to understand about the language. When she and Dodie played together, she would jabber in Korean and Dodie would answer, "What you say? What you say?" When I left for work in the morning, Debbie cried, and there were no phrases in the pamphlet we had gotten to explain to a little child not to worry, that Mommy would be home soon. One morning, after several frustrating weeks of noncommunication, the little girl took my hand and led me out to the driveway. She waved her arms wildly, pouring out an excited stream of Korean words, trying with all her might to get through to me. I bent down, put my hand on her shoulder and said, helplessly, "Honey, Mommy can't understand you." At this, Debbie stopped talking, put her hands on her hips, looked me up and down with utter hopelessness, and turned away to go back to the house. From that moment on, she spoke no Korean. Almost overnight she began to pick up phrases that the children used, and within six weeks she spoke as well as Dodie.

Every night after we tucked Debbie in, she climbed out of bed and rooted for the floor, where she had spent her nights in Korea. Even when I put a guard rail on her bed, she clambered over it or through it to get to the hard wood floor. She constantly caught colds there, but even so, somehow she felt that that was where she belonged. It took Debbie six months to learn to sleep in bed. It took her even longer not to be paralyzed with fear around Bullet. The first time that sweet dog came rushing up to her, looking for a pat on the head, Debbie screamed a howl of terror. Where she had come from, big dogs like Bullet were used as weapons, trained to hate everyone but their master.

Our family dinner table was something special. It was made of oak by our friend George Montgomery and it was huge: it had to be! It was round, with plenty of room for all of us, and had a lazy Susan in the middle; people could turn it and get what they wanted. Before we ate, we prayed; and while we did so, each of us closed our eyes and clasped our hands together below our chin. However, one night Sandy— the bottomless pit—figured out a way to make certain that he always got to the mashed potatoes first. He opened his eyes during prayer and very gently used his clasped-together index fingers to ease the lazy Susan around so that at the sound of "Amen" he was already piling them on his plate like Mount Whitney. Dusty, who could eat almost as much as his brother, figured out the game, and pretty soon he had his eyes open and fingers out, trying to get the potatoes around in front of him. Then Marion caught on, and by the time I opened my eyes to see what the commotion was about, the lazy Susan was spinning like a gyroscope. "Children," I announced, "it is time we started a new family tradition. From now on, when we pray we will all hold hands around the table. And nobody lets go until Daddy says 'Amen.' "

With six healthy kids around it, there were times when that big, wonderful table was the scene of wholesale confusion. Food fights, spitballs, pinching, kicking: all the rowdy things children do that can make a parent want to tear out her hair, or maybe theirs. There was one night in particular when Sandy and Dusty were going at it good, using spoons to launch peas across the table at the girls and goading each other mercilessly. Sandy had a way of teasing Dusty to the point of distraction. They were making faces, kicking under the table, and generally raising havoc. Despite my warnings to knock it off, Sandy got in a lick at Dusty every time I turned away. "Sandy," I said, "if Dusty beats the tar out of you I am not going to do a thing to stop him. You are asking for trouble. This is your last warning!" We had a dairy cow at Chatsworth, and we had just brought in a big container of milk and filled a pitcher on the table. I said, "Sandy, if you don't behave, I am going to drown you in this milk."

Sandy dared me: "Aw, Mom, you would never do that!" Then he laughed and stuck his tongue out at Dusty.

I took the dare. I stood up, lifted the pitcher of milk from the lazy Susan and poured it over his head. He began to wail and I continued to pour, all the way to the last drop. "Young man, when I make a promise, I keep it!" Then I ordered him to go to his room.

In the summer, when the children were out of school, the whole Rogers family toured together, performing at rodeos and state fairs. Cheryl and Linda usually sang a song with Roy and me, something like "The Bible Tells Me So"; Dodie, our little Indian, came out in a squaw dress and did a solo of a little song I wrote called "Chicky-Wicky Choctaw"; and Debbie, wearing a spangled cowgirl costume, sang "Jesus Loves Me" in Korean, solo. Roy then introduced the boys, dressed in their own little cowboy suits, and we all stood on stage together and sang "Oh, Be Careful, Little Hands, What You Do," then "Happy Trails." The kids didn't always get their part in the show right, but that only added to the fun. Debbie never quite learned the words to "Oh, Be Careful . . . ," ending her verse with a loud and sonorous "what *it* do" instead of "what *you* do." Sandy couldn't carry a tune, and the time we gave him a line to deliver, he got it all twisted up. Midway through, he gave up trying to say what he was supposed to say, pulled his little cowboy hat way down over his head, and bawled, "Mawm! I goofed!"

Whereas life at home was merely hectic, life on the road was sheer chaos. Weeks before leaving the house, I tried to organize the tour like a general planning an invasion. We had to have show clothes made for everyone; then I made lists of exactly what each child was responsible for taking: how many pairs of socks and what color they should be, even the exact number of bobby pins the girls were allowed. At each hotel, every child was expected to take inventory of his or her clothing and equipment before we left. In transit, the older children shepherded the younger ones through airports, and they were shepherded by a lady helper from our church in Chatsworth.

For the boys, being on the road presented countless new opportunities to get in trouble. They had a pair of big white rats, which only two boys could love, that they took along in a bird cage, then let loose in hotel rooms. This, of course, thrilled the hotel staff! After a while, when Dusty and Sandy started having trouble getting the bird cage past desk clerks, they exchanged it for an inconspicuous shoe box. On the way home after one show, they stowed their box under the seat in the airplane. Midflight, there was a sudden outburst of squeals coming from the floor. When the stewardess walked past, Dusty and Sandy began squealing to camouflage the sound, but pretty soon the whole cabin was trying to figure out what was going on. The boys picked their box up off the floor and removed the top. To the delight of all the other passengers, out scampered a passel of newborn baby rats.

On another occasion when we were in a plane flying to a show, Dusty decided to play a trick on his brother. "I'm thirsty," Sandy declared.

Dusty volunteered to go to the restroom and get him a drink. He came back with a balloon full. "Here, Sandy," he said. "It's got soda pop in it."

Sandy put the balloon to his mouth and squeezed a big gulp out. Soapy water spurted from the balloon and began to foam all around Sandy's mouth. He sputtered and coughed and moaned. Dusty was jubilant at the sight.

Roy leapt from his seat, grabbed Dusty by the nape, and took him to the bathroom, where he tanned his hide, then washed *his* mouth out with soap. Naturally, by the time the plane landed the boys were best friends again.

Sandy was a fearful little fellow. As an infant who had been beaten, abused, and neglected, he had learned some terrible lessons about what he should expect from life. At night in bed, he often saw shapes and shadows in the bedroom that terrified him. Usually Dusty was able to reassure him, but one night on tour when we were staying in an old hotel somewhere, Sandy ran out of their room screaming. We all awoke and came into the hall, trying to calm him down. Roy led him back into the room to show him there was nothing to be afraid of. As the rest of us waited in the hall, suddenly pandemonium broke out and there was a racket in there that you could have heard in Peking. Sandy came running out again. This time, he wasn't imagining things. There was a bat in the room, and Roy was going after it with a coat hanger. By the time he came out, triumphant, the entire floor was awake and out of their rooms to see what the commotion was about: just another normal night with the the touring Roy Rogers family!

Roy turned Sandy's fears into a good story about both boys that he often told to audiences during our show. "You know, pardners," he'd say. "The Rogers family always goes to church and Sunday school. The children like Sunday school, but they don't always understand everything they hear. Last week the minister was speaking about the part of the Bible that says, 'From dust thou art, and to dust thou shalt return.'

"When they got home, Dusty and Sandy were playing in their bedroom when they noticed some dust under one of the beds. They came tearing down the stairs.

" 'Daddy, Daddy,' Dusty shouted. 'There's somebody under my bed, and I don't know if he's comin' or goin'!' "

Sandy was a bed-wetter. I didn't know it at the time, but the problem stemmed from his brain damage. I thought it was a matter that could be cured by will power alone, so I tried everything. I bought a pad for the bed that sounded an alarm at the first sign of moisture. It woke up everyone but Sandy. I took him to every medical specialist under the sun. I woke him every two hours. I tried rewarding him with presents if he stayed dry. I tried shaming him. The night on tour he fell asleep in his stage clothes and soaked them, I lost it. I ripped off his costume and went chasing that poor boy up and down the hall. To let you know just how desperate I was about the situation, I will admit that I actually tried an old folk cure. I had been told that the country way to cure bed-wetting was to catch a field mouse, skin it, make a stew of it, and feed it to the boy. Sandy didn't ask what was in the stew our cook made for him—so long as it didn't have liver in it, he ate anything—and he gobbled it up with glee; but that night, as usual, he wet his bed. After that I tried to accept the problem; and Sandy, shamed as he was, came to terms with it, too. In the army, he woke up every morning before reveille to make his bedroll so no one would know.

When we were on the road, I always planted myself between Dusty and Sandy at the dinner table to try to keep them from combusting. Still, they managed to rile up each other behind my back. One night before a show in Ohio we all went to a very elegant restaurant. The boys started in and heads in the dining room began to turn. I think they thought that because we were in public, Roy and I wouldn't pour a pitcher of milk on their heads or shoot off blanks. I asked them nicely to please do their dad and me a favor and sit still and behave themselves, but this night I could see that they were going to push us to the limit. As Roy and I were trying to have a conversation, I reached down under the table with both hands and grabbed a fistful of each boy's leg just above the knee. I squeezed. They stopped their teasing. I squeezed harder. Sandy started to moan. I kept squeezing. He moaned louder and Dusty joined him in a long, mournful howl of pain. Every single person in the dining room turned to see where these unholy sounds were coming from. As far as anyone could tell, Roy and I were sitting opposite each other at the table having a pleasant chat. The boys next to me were caterwauling for no apparent reason. I lessened my grip just enough so they quieted down. With a sweet, motherly smile on my face, I said softly, "I told you boys to be quiet. Now will you?" Mollified, they nodded yes.

When we first took Debbie with us, she was so young, and so new to America. She was sitting on my lap when our plane landed for an appearance at the Ohio State Fair. A huge crowd was at the airport waiting for us, and as soon as the plane stopped, they rushed it, screaming and shouting for Roy. Debbie, who wasn't long out of wartorn Korea, looked out the window and saw the throngs of people and police trying to control them. A look of horror came over her face and she fell into hysterics, hiding her face from the crowd all the way to the hotel. It took a lot of explaining before that frightened little girl understood that the people didn't mean us any harm.

Debbie soon became our family extrovert; she could talk to anybody—one-on-one or in front of the crowd at the Calgary Stampede. She went trout fishing with Roy and the boys; she made friends with girls in the neighborhood and got so caught up visiting with them that she came home long after dark. How I went into orbit over that! Oh, I harped on her for all sorts of things: for snitching cucumbers, peppers, and celery from the salad (was she part rabbit?); for raiding my clothes and perfume; for leaving peanut shells and apple cores in front of the TV set. When I scolded her, she pouted; she clamped her lips and stalked off to her room; but I couldn't stay mad at her for long, and she couldn't pout for long, either. After a few moments of glowering at me, her eyes would start to twinkle, and she couldn't help but soften her expression.

Debbie was so much like Roy in the way she cared for animals, especially those that were hurt. I recall the time she brought home an injured sparrow she found on her way home from school. She got an old bird cage for him from the laundry room, gave him water and moistened bread crumbs, and after a few hours he perked up. Oh, she was so happy when he stood chirping on his perch. Late that afternoon she carried the cage up the mountain behind our house and opened it, laughing out loud as the sparrow flew up into the sky.

Just before Debbie's twelfth birthday, Roy had to have a serious operation on his neck. Eight years of hard riding on his speedboat, as well as years of galloping on that horse of his, had injured his discs, causing three vertebrae to jam together and cause him severe pain. The operation lasted five hours and left him in a temporary neck brace, battling complications from an agonizing staph infection. Debbie was so anxious when Daddy went into the hospital that she came to me nearly every hour for reassurance that he would be all right and would come home soon. From the first moment, eight years earlier, when she came off the plane and curled up in his arms, Debbie and Roy had an extraordinary affection for each other. She was the first to run out and greet him when he came home from work; she took off his boots, rubbed his aching neck, and brought him coffee. She and Dodie delighted in taking turns combing his hair when he read the paper, sitting in his lap and trying different hair styles, making him look silly. He adored the attention, and when one or both of those two girls were fussing over him, even if it did distract him from his paper, Roy Rogers looked like the happiest man in the world. How he beamed when Debbie came to visit him at the convalescent home in Bel Air the day after her twelfth birthday! His little girl had won a little blue stuffed animal at Pacific Ocean Park on her birthday; she was dressed in her new stretch jeans and patchwork print top, and finally too grown-up to sit in Daddy's lap.

Two days later, on August 17, Debbie joined her friends on a church bus trip to deliver presents to children at an orphanage in Tijuana. On a two-lane section of Interstate 5, the bus blew a tire and the driver lost control, veering into oncoming traffic. The bus hit a station wagon. Debbie, who was standing at the front because she wanted to look at the road ahead, was thrown through the window and killed.

I had asked Debbie not to go on the trip. I wanted her to wait until Dodie got over a stomach flu and could go with her. Maybe when Roy was home and life was back to normal, we could all go to the orphanage. I was feeling troubled just then about many things: Roy's operation, Dodie's illness, and . . . I wasn't sure exactly what. Debbie pleaded to take the trip because her friends Joanne and Kathy Russell were going, and it would be part of her birthday celebration. I gave in and allowed her to go on her errand of love. The day Debbie left, as I drove back from Roy recuperating in Bel Air, I felt so distressed that I started to pray for God's help. It was a hot, restless afternoon, and as I watched the wind blow leaves across the sky, I asked for tranquillity. I was tense and I desperately needed to relax. By the time I got home, I did feel good. I felt that God had blessed me with His peace. I noticed a strange thing as I pulled in the breezeway: Debbie's red bicycle had fallen off its stand to the pavement.

Ruth Miner, our housekeeper whom the children knew as "Granny," waited at the door of the house with a strange expression as she watched me park the car. "Dale, I have to talk with you," she said, taking my arm and leading me into the living room. I felt blood draining from my face, thinking that something had happened to Roy. "The bus had an accident," she said. "Debbie and Joanne Russell are with the Lord."

It took a moment for the news to register. *"With . . . the Lord?"* I wondered to myself. Then I knew. It felt like a sledgehammer falling on my brain. I screamed, "No! No! Not my baby, not again!" I pounded my fists, I writhed, I tore at my clothes. "Jesus! Jesus! *HELP ME!"*

Dusty, who was then seventeen years old, rescued me from my spiraling despair. He came into the room and sat next to me on the couch. He took my shoulders and made me face him. "Mom!" he said firmly. "Mom, for as long as I can remember, you've told me to trust Jesus. If you meant that, you must trust him, too. Debbie is okay. She is with Him." I put my head in my son's lap and cried. After a long time, he whispered, "What about Dad? I don't think he's strong enough to handle this."

When Roy was given the news by his surgeon, he tore out his I.V. tubes and tried to get out of bed, crying "Why? Why her?" He was put under heavy sedation and rushed back to the intensive care unit at the UCLA Medical Center. I went to visit him there and sat down by the side of his bed. We talked together; Roy couldn't move his head because of the brace; and when it came time to leave, I could not stand up. I was too weak to get out of my chair. Doctors gave me a glucose tolerance test and discovered I was spilling sugar into my urine. I had developed diabetes. The shock of Debbie's death had triggered an attack.

This time, the trip to Forest Lawn to make funeral arrangements for my child would be my responsibility. I planned a double funeral for Debbie and Joanne. The coroner strongly advised a closed-casket service because damage to the girls was so severe. No! Since Robin's death, I had lived with the regret of refusing to look, and this time I knew I had to. I needed to touch Debbie's pretty hands once more and smooth her rich, dark hair for the last time.

"They have worked very hard to make her presentable," Art Rush reported to me before the funeral. Her casket was in the Slumber Room at Forest Lawn. My baby looked eighteen instead of twelve. She wore the white dress she had worn at her sixth-grade commencement, with a pink bow in her hair. In her fingers was the blue plush animal she had won on her birthday. I placed three rosebuds from our yard in her hands and a new gold cross around her neck—the cross she usually wore had been lost in the wreck. I felt at that moment she was aware of the tributes being paid her, and I could almost hear her say, "Hey, Mom, what a blast! Is this all for *me?*"

Dodie, who had always been frantic that she would lose her sister and her best friend, came to me and asked, "Mom, why can't I go to heaven, too, and be with Debbie?" I told her that when God was ready, he would beckon.

I fell to my knees and thanked the Lord for the time we had had Debbie. When I reached the house in Chatsworth a friend looked at me and said, "Dale, your face is positively *glowing.* It is radiant. How . . . ?" God had removed me forever from all fear of death.

I wrote *Dearest Debbie,* a book about the time she had spent with us, addressed to her in heaven. It began, *"How lovely you must be in your new halo!* You always looked so pretty in your simple little white headband. . . . You will never be a closed chapter in my book of life, Debbie. You will live in my heart, and I shall go right on singing the Lord's praises until He calls me home, too, to sing in that great choir of the Heavenly Host." Royalties from the book went to World Vision International, the organization that had brought Debbie to us nine years before, when she was a three-year-old orphan.

In January 1965, Sandy told us he wanted to join the army. It had been his dream for so many years. As a tot, he delighted in toy soldiers, guns, and airplanes, promising that one day he would grow up and drive a tank. Soon he developed a nearly fanatical interest in all things military, especially if it was connected to his original home state of Kentucky or the Civil War. As much as he and Dusty complained about strict discipline at the Altadena military school they attended, Sandy delighted in the school uniforms. He had trouble in math and English, but he couldn't get enough military history. He called himself "the Rebel," and on his thirteenth birthday, he asked for a Confederate uniform. He clicked his heels and proclaimed, "The South shall rise again!" as he and Dusty argued endlessly over the merits of General Lee vs. General Grant.

When he asked our permission to enlist—he was only seventeen at the time—we didn't think he would pass the physical. Despite his enthusiasm for life, Sandy's handicaps made it difficult for him to keep up with others. When he and Dusty used to wrestle, Sandy always lost. He went out for Little League summer after summer, but never made the team. Undaunted by his shortcomings, he gladly served as batboy. At touch football, he didn't seem to know which way to run . . . but he always wanted to play. Roy tried to teach him how to drive the Jeep, but he couldn't figure out how to coordinate the clutch and gearshift. When Roy started to take the boys trapshooting, Dusty was a good shot from the beginning. Sandy simply couldn't figure out how to handle the gun. To save Sandy from feeling shamed, Roy stopped taking the boys to the range. He was a boy who failed often, but who never, ever quit.

"I'm not doing well in high school," he pleaded with us. "I want to prove myself. I promise I will make you proud of me." He did pass his army physical, and the day he graduated from basic training at Fort Polk, he was on cloud nine. His captain told me that he had never seen a young soldier try so hard. I was so proud of him; this was a real accomplishment for the young man whose life was such a struggle every step of the way. But my heart was heavy as lead thinking of Sandy being sent into combat. "Sandy will never be home again," I moaned to Ruth Miner. He did volunteer for duty in Vietnam, but superior officers decided that his reflexes were too slow for combat. He was assigned to the tank corps in Germany: his boyhood dream come true.

Late in October 1965, I went to Texas to spend my birthday with my mother. On Saturday night I had a nightmare: a rider was galloping full speed across a wide plain, heading straight for me. His horse stumbled and fell. The horse got up. The man lay in the sand, motionless. I knew he was dead. I woke up screaming.

When I returned to Los Angeles on Monday, the family was waiting at the airport to meet me. Cheryl and Marion approached, with an odd look on their faces. "Do we have a problem, kids?" I asked.

Cheryl replied, soberly and carefully, "Sort of, Mom."

"Who is it?" I asked as my panic level escalated.

Dusty said, "It's Sandy. He's gone."

"What do you mean, *GONE?*" I shouted. "Sandy isn't in Vietnam. He's in Germany!"

Dusty and Roy took me by the arms. Dusty explained: "Sandy was at a party Saturday night. Some guys got him to drink a lot of hard liquor, and it killed him."

Sandy, the boy with the cast-iron stomach, the boy who could devour everything (except liver), to my knowledge had never tasted liquor stronger than beer. He had come back from maneuvers where he earned his first-class stripes and went with his buddies to the enlisted men's club to celebrate. One of the soldiers needled Sandy, saying "So now you're Private First Class, now you're a man. Or are you? Let's see you drink like a man." Sandy fell for it. He drank an unbelievable amount of hard liquor, then ate a steak dinner, followed by two beers. "Come on, Rogers, bottoms up!" his friends shouted. Sandy, who yearned to be accepted as one of the guys, poured it down. He began to vomit and collapsed. His drinking buddies got him to his bunk, thinking he would sleep it off. In the morning he was dead.

Once more, we went to Forest Lawn Memorial Park to say good-bye to a child. Sandy came home in a flag-draped casket. As I looked at him there in the sharply creased, brass-buttoned uniform that meant so much to him, my mind went back in time, thirteen years, to a battered boy who left the Covington orphanage with all of his worldly belongings in a paper sack. I remembered when someone asked the little boy what he had, how he folded back the top and proudly pulled out all he owned—that tattered sweater.

The service was beautiful. Dusty put Sandy's favorite Civil War sword in his hand. Then a military escort led us out the door of the Church of the Recessional as a bugler blew Taps. When the escorts lifted their rifles and fired them toward heaven in a sharp salute, Roy broke down and cried. They folded the flag from his coffin and gave it to me, his mother. I held it to my heart. Rest in peace, sweet Kentucky babe!

At the Chapel in the Canyon near a fountain splashing in the sun there is now a bronze plaque that says:

JOHN DAVID (SANDY) ROGERS

Here he played. Here he prayed.
Here he loved, and was loved by all.

The next summer, in Sandy's memory, Roy and I went to entertain the troops in Vietnam on a USO tour. I wrote a book called *Salute to Sandy*—about that trip and about Sandy's hard struggle to find a place for himself in a world where he didn't get a lot of breaks. Royalties went to the Campus Crusade for Christ.

When we were in Vietnam a young trooper came to me and said, "Ma'am, I was in Sandy's company in Germany."

"Were you there the night he died?" I asked.

"I wish I had been," he replied. "It would not have happened."

"He did try to be a good soldier, didn't he?" I asked.

The trooper said, "Ma'am he *was* a good soldier."

PART VI

Roy and Dale: Just Us Two

*T*HE 1960s WAS NOT an easy time to be icons of truth, justice, and the American way. Cowboy heroes and cowboy ideals were not merely out of style; they became a kind of joke to the counterculture, which was composed mostly of baby boomers who felt a little embarrassed about having grown up in a society with old-fashioned values and heroes who were good guys. Cowboy "heroes," such as they were, no longer upheld the Code of the West. Clint Eastwood as the scornful, unshaven "Man with No Name, " Paul Newman and Robert Redford as Butch Cassidy and the Sundance Kid, and Sam Peckinpah's Wild Bunch were all cowboys who didn't give a fig for traditional principles of right and wrong. Many movie "cowboy" types, in contemporary films as well as historical dramas, were presented as trigger-happy lunatics, such as *Dr. Strangelove*'s B-52 pilot Slim Pickens, who rides an A-bomb like a bucking bronco, or the bloodthirsty cavalry officers of *Soldier Blue;* and there was Paul Newman's Hud, whose lethargy and nihilism was supposed to symbolize the utter death of the West. Perhaps the ultimate cowboy joke of the decade was the pitiful loser played by Jon Voight in *Midnight Cowboy*—the man of the West as a caricature, a hapless hick. John Wayne finally won an Oscar in 1969, for *True Grit*, but it was for playing Rooster Cogburn, a burlesque of all the heroes he had played in decades past.

Despite 1960s cynicism and its iconoclastic legacy, America's cowboy has proven to be one tough hombre. Even though Westerns were pronounced dead once and for all in 1980 after *Heaven's Gate* laid the most expensive egg in box-office history, we Americans have returned once again to the values of the West to renew our souls. Ten years after the *Heaven's Gate* death knell was sounded, Kevin Costner made *Dances with Wolves.* This epic fantasy about a cavalry officer ennobled by his sabbatical with the Sioux corraled gigantic audiences and won a fistful of Academy Awards. The triumph of *Dances with Wolves* wasn't completely out of the blue; the year before, the miniseries made from Larry McMurtry's *Lonesome Dove* had garnered big television ratings for what was a grand-scale, old-fashioned cattle-drive epic complete with a thundering stampede, a bloodthirsty Indian out for white men's scalps, a pretty blond whore with a heart of gold, and Texas Ranger heroes who could ride, rope, shoot, fight, and philosophize as well as any pop-culture cowboy ever did.

By 1990, it seemed that Americans were eager once again to embrace the values of the West. BMWs were traded in on pickup trucks, Rolexes gave way to Wranglers, cowboy boots appeared on feet once shod only by Gucci, and the fashionable address became Montana rather than the Hamptons. Cowboy cool has gained ever more momentum in the 1990s as an antidote to the rampant sleaze of pop culture and the hypocrisy of so many public figures in politics as well as pop culture. Consider America's cowboy hero: you'll never see him ranting about his problems to Oprah or Geraldo; nor will you see him waiting in line at the Motor Vehicle Bureau or filling out a medical insurance claim form. In the movie West of Hollywood's imagination, there are no corporate committees who decide when to saddle up, no accountants prescribing proper amounts of hay for the horses, no middle-management bureaucrats putting up gates and fences, and little in the way of meddling government to obstruct a buckaroo with a job to do. If a cowboy hero kisses a girl who doesn't like him, she knows how to slap him with her hand instead of with a sexual harassment suit.

Is it any wonder Roy Rogers and Dale Evans are popular all over again? Never forgotten by their true fans, the King of the Cowboys and the Queen of the West have come to symbolize a dearly remembered era when pop culture was clean and decent and you got to be a celebrity because you were a good guy.

Modern Nashville royalty including Clint Black, K. T. Oslin, and Randy Travis idolize Roy and Dale as the parents of country music; in 1991 twelve current country stars joined in duets with Roy on an album called *Tribute,* which climaxed with them all singing "Happy Trails." The album inspired a TV special in which Roy sang with the top names in Nashville today. Roy Rogers's imprimatur is golden once again, and you can buy everything from Roy-brand silver-trimmed bridles for your horse to Roy Rogers chocolate candy for your sweetheart. One of the most popular of all souvenirs at the family museum in Victorville, California, is a plaque with all the rules of the Roy Rogers Riders Club written on it. For many Americans who yearn to return to a sense of moral balance missing now from public life, Roy Rogers and Dale Evans represent the best of the West—its ideals.

If you are lucky enough to go to the Roy Rogers and Dale Evans Museum and meet them in person you will not be disappointed. Roy is old now, but in some significant way he has never aged; he still radiates the rapture and eternal optimism of an all-American boy. Ask him about Trigger or bowling or fishing or his kids, or most certainly about his life with Dale, and you will see his famous eyes crease into slits of happiness and an impish grin erase the decades that have stiffened his knees and dimmed his hearing. And when you walk through the very personal and unpretentious halls of the museum, you, too, will be transported back to a time when America was a nicer place. Stroll past the mementos of the lives and careers of the King of the Cowboys and Queen of the West, and you are in a land where every police officer is helpful, where all polite men wear hats—and take them off when the flag passes by—and where children live a charmed life separate and apart from the grim problems of adults. For those of us who grew up in that wonderful imagined America, Roy and Dale are King and Queen forever.

—J. & M. S.

CHAPTER 11

Roy's Story

It was time to slow down. We had run a hard race, Dale and I, and we were tired. My heart hurt—the doctors said I had angina pectoris—and our children were all leaving home. Linda, Cheryl, and Marion had already flown the nest. When Dusty was nineteen, he lit off to find his fate. He traveled from California to a small town in Ohio, the exact opposite of what I had done when I was about his age. He wanted to make his own way, so he found work at a construction company, and in 1967 he fell in love and married Linda Yoder. Many of Linda's relatives are Amish, so it was quite some wedding to see. OLD MEETS NEW, newspapers said under pictures of her "plain people," all dressed in black, meeting Dale and me in our finest Nudie of Hollywood formal wear. Two years later, our youngest, Dodie, married Air Force Sergeant Tom Faro. The Rogers household had shrunk to just us two.

In 1965 we had moved to Apple Valley in the Mojave Desert, where I hoped to do some things that might help heal my heart: spend time with grandkids, play a little golf, go bowling, breed horses, ride the high desert roads on my motorcycle. We didn't exactly quit show business, but we tried to limit what we did to special occasions, like guest appearances on TV shows or with Billy Graham during one of his crusades. We hosted a variety show on ABC for a while in 1962, and appeared on "Hee Haw," "The Muppet Show," and with Oral Roberts, and I did a few episodes of "The Fall Guy." In 1983, I had a little fun finally playing a kind of louse in Kenny Rogers's TV movie "The Gambler—The Adventure Continues." To this day, Dale continues to tape her inspirational TV talk show,"A Date with Dale." Like the nineteen books she's written, that's a program she does not so much because it is a job of work, but because she has so much faith to share with others.

One thing we've always enjoyed was being part of the Tournament of Roses Parade on New Year's, the day after our wedding anniversary. Through most of the 1950s we rode Trigger and Buttermilk; one time I even had a fellow in Wyoming design us some fancy colored plastic saddles for the event because I got so tired of seeing our silver and leather Bohlin saddles get rained on. Those plastic saddles were good, I'll tell you: light, comfortable, easy on the horse and rider. We had 'em made in red, yellow, and blue; but they never caught on with anybody but us, or for anything other than our horses in that parade. Horse-type people are traditionalists, and leather saddles aren't about to be replaced. A couple of years when we didn't ride our horses, we traveled the parade route in a Pontiac convertible that Nudie had customized. It was a doozy! Bright yellow with a hand-tooled leather interior, silver six-shooters in place of the door handles and the gearshift, 339 silver dollars embedded in the upholstery, and a long Continental kit with silver horseshoes and a silver bucking bronco on the tire case.

One year they wanted us to ride on a float that was supposed to look like two great big horses. We had to arrive at the hangar where they were constructing it at four o'clock in the morning, so they could lift us to the top with a crane, literally strap us on so we wouldn't fall off, then trim the float with flowers below and all around us. The folks doing all the work were kind enough to bring us coffee once they wired us in up there. It was cold in that hangar, and I'd say we drank more than a dozen cups. By the time the float was built and the parade was ready to begin, I had a real problem: my bladder was ready to burst! "I'm sorry, Mr. Rogers," they said, "we can't get you down without messing up all the flowers on your horse. There isn't time to unwire you." Dale told me to think of other things, but I was cross-eyed by the time we started waving to the crowds. It was raining hard, and before long my costume was soaking wet. That gave me an idea. Dale looked over at me and saw steam rising up off my pants. "Roy, you didn't!" she said, but the relieved look on my face told her the answer to that question.

I've been away from the movie business for a long, long time. Back in 1959 I did a cameo role in Bob Hope's movie *Alias Jesse James,* where I appeared along with Gene Autry and Ward Bond; and in 1976 I made my last picture, called *Mackintosh and T.J.* I enjoyed that movie: it was a modern Western about an old cowboy in a pickup truck (me) who teaches a few things to a thirteen-year-old boy. Like I said to a reporter at the premiere, "There's no leading lady, no shooting, some fights, but no blood spurting, and that's the way I wanted it." Back then, they also had me host a series of old Westerns on TV called "Roy Rogers Great Cowboy Movies." They were some of the old pictures, the kind kids used to spend a dime to see every Saturday, starring real good guys like Bob Steele, Wild Bill Elliott, Monte Hale, Lash Larue, Tex Ritter, people like that. Heroes like them are out of fashion now, they tell me, and I guess that's so, judging by the movies I've seen recently. When I heard that Bruce Willis called himself "Roy Rogers" as a nickname in *Die Hard,* I thought we ought to go have a look. He may have called himself by my name, but he also used so many dirty words that I found myself sinking lower and lower into my seat as I sat there watching. I was embarrassed! When we had a chance, Dale and I sneaked out the side door. Some of the movies they're making are so bloody and filled with cussing I wouldn't let Trigger see them!

These days Dale and I like to stay home rather than go out to the movies because we have one of those TV sets that is as big as a wall and gets four jillion channels. I watch ballgames, "Dr. Quinn, Medicine Woman," and those nature documentaries about wild animals with their babies, but I suppose my favorite show of all is the soap opera "The Guiding Light." When my great-grandchildren come over, Dale and I sometimes put videotapes of our old movies on for them to see. They scarcely recognize who the cowboy and cowgirl in those pictures are, but they all like Trigger.

There wasn't anybody more surprised than me when a song I recorded in 1974 turned out to be a hit. Long before that I had given up recording for the simple reason that it was so danged much work for me to learn new material. Not reading music, I've got to get everything in my head if I'm going to record it, and I lost my patience with that sometime back in the 1950s. But young Snuff Garrett, the record producer, is a charmer who could just about talk the ears off a wooden Indian. One day when we were shooting skeet, he asked if I would record a song for him, called "Hoppy, Gene, and Me."

"I guess I could do that," I told him. "How does the song go?"

"I don't know," Snuff said. "I haven't written it yet."

He wrote it; I recorded it; and doggone if it didn't get way up there on the country music charts!

I had some fun in 1991 doing an album called *Tribute* with a whole big gang of the country music people around today. I did duets with Emmylou Harris ("Little Joe the Wrangler"), K. T. Oslin ("Tumbling Tumbleweeds"), Clint Black ("Hold On, Partner"), Kathy Mattea ("Final Frontier"), Lorrie Morgan and the Oak Ridge Boys ("Don't Fence Me In"), Willie

Nelson ("Rodeo Road"), Ricky Van Shelton ("When Payday Rolls Around"), the Kentucky Headhunters ("That's How the West Was Swung"), and Randy Travis ("Here's Hopin' ' "); Dusty sang the song he wrote about me called "King of the Cowboys"; I sang a solo on "Alive and Kickin' "; and all of us, including Dale, got together on the finale—which, of course, was "Happy Trails."

One thing I started back in the 1960s that turned out well is the Roy Rogers Restaurants. When we set that up with the Marriott Corporation, they were called Roy Rogers Chuckwagons, and I appeared at a lot of grand openings for them. In the early days, when you went in to place an order for a beef sandwich, the person at the counter was supposed to ask, "Is this for here or are you taking it on the trail?"

For nearly as long as I can remember, I thought about having a museum. I recall seeing the Will Rogers Museum in California years ago when I started in the business and thinking that there wasn't enough stuff in it, just a few odds and ends from his career. I decided then and there that if I ever got famous, there'd be no shortage. Anyway, I've always liked to save things. I guess because I grew up in an area where we didn't have much, I can't get rid of something once I get it. No matter what came my way, whether it was a letter from a boy or girl movie fan or from a President, or a nice shotgun, or an old-time telephone, I stuck it in the basement, or the garage, or in drawers at home. Dale would say, "Honey when are you going to empty those drawers? I can't get anything in or out of them!" When that happened, I'd put everything in a box and call Bekins Van & Storage to come pick it up and keep it for me. Then I started collecting more.

We bought a bowling alley right across from the Apple Valley Inn, which we were running at the time, and converted the lanes into our museum. First thing I did was call Bekins, and they brought over two big truckloads of stuff I had saved—tools my dad had when I was little, some of my mom's scrapbooks, pictures from the early days of the Sons of the Pioneers, all sorts of things that meant something to me.

There were also lots of fun items I have saved over the years just because they interest me. One of the things I've always liked to do is go to flea markets and swap meets. They all know me at the weekend swap meets, and they know I can't resist a bargain, especially if it's something that's been handmade—a lamp, or a ship in a bottle, or anything from the olden days, stuff like that. Most of what I buy winds up on display in the museum, or in the big storage area where we keep things that don't fit on display. Sometimes I get so carried away I have to laugh at myself. I have one case in the museum that holds a bottle filled with murky water and a strange-shaped object. Awhile back we wrote a sign that says "WHAT IS IT?" to tantalize the public, but to tell you the truth, I'm not sure I remember what's in there myself. It must have caught my fancy sometime back, so I saved and bottled it.

In 1976 we moved the museum to nearby Victorville, where we built a bigger building near the interstate highway on forty acres of land. Just a few years back, my ol' friend Gene Autry opened a museum, too, in Los Angeles. Gene and I are different sorts of people, that's for certain, and our museums couldn't be less alike. His is a grand collection of Western history with fine art and antiques that scholars and curators have assembled. Our place isn't really a regular museum like that at all. It's personal—things that Dale and I have done, and the kids and the family and Trigger. Everything we've done is in it. We've got our family dining table there—the big round one with the lazy Susan that Robert Montgomery made for us, where Sandy used to sneak licks at mashed potatoes before prayers were through. It is set up in a display case that looks just like our dining room used to be. We have our old china on it—that real heavy cowboy quality, all covered with pictures of bucking broncos and lariats. Our old parakeet cage is in the corner, along with the family Bible and a picture of Jesus on the wall.

In another glass case, there's a sign that says, "Let's take a look inside Roy's tackle box." That goes back to the fishing trip I took with Sandy and Dusty when Sandy first came to us, and it's got some of my favorite fishing lures; it's even got what's left in the bottle of the bug lotion we used to try to fight off all those mosquitoes! There's a whole case of wristwatches I have worn over the years to keep me on time, and displays to remember those who have left us: Gabby Hayes and Pat Brady; my wife, Arlene; and, of course, our kids—Robin, Debbie, and Sandy. We've got our fancy parade saddles there, hundreds and hundreds of old Roy Rogers comic books, and racks of the fancy clothes, boots, hats, and guns we used to wear in movies and at rodeos. Awhile back we got a piece of the Berlin wall that we put on display.

We're looking forward to expanding the museum. In the next few years, it is going to become part of a theme park called RogersDale. Dale and I like to think that it will be a place for people to come have fun and learn about our lives, and also to remember what America was like not so many years ago. Dusty came back to California, and he is helping us put that together—that is, when he isn't out performing all over the country with his band, the High Riders. He has a beautiful singing voice, and he's the only one of our kids in show business. When Art Rush died a few years back, Dusty took over the job of managing our careers as well as the museum.

One thing Dusty can sure tell you, and that is which exhibit is the most popular one in the museum. It's Trigger, mounted like so many people remember him—rearing up on his hind legs. Nearly everybody who stops by wants to see him, and we've had folks who have come rushing in five minutes before closing time, willing to pay the full four dol-

lars admission charge just so they can run back and see ol'
Trig for a minute or two before we shut the doors.

Trigger retired from show business when we stopped
shooting the TV show. Some years before that, we had come
to call him "the Old Man," but by the time he was put out to
pasture, he really was getting on in years. He got a nice big
stall at a stable near our place and green fields to roam, and
plenty of mares just across the fence to keep him company.
He spent long days grazing in the California sunshine, and I
went to see him whenever I could. When I was unable to
visit, Danny, the stable manager, called to let me know he
was all right.

Early one morning in 1965 I was jerked from sleep by the
telephone. Before I even picked it up, I had an awful premonition. "Danny," I blurted into the receiver, "it's Trigger,
isn't it? He's gone." Danny confirmed what I feared. He told
me that the Old Man had finished his breakfast and had been
turned out to pasture just like always. Danny had watched
him lie down in the field like he was going to take a nap.
When Danny went out to check, he found Trigger dead. The
old horse had passed so gently that he hadn't even kicked up
dirt, and there was no sign of pain or struggle. He just plain
lay down and went to sleep. He was thirty-three years old.

When news got out that Trigger was gone, I heard from
the Smithsonian Institution in Washington, D.C., who
asked if they could have his remains for their collection of
historical Americana. That was nice, but I didn't want my
stallion's final resting place to be so far away from me. Neither could I abide the thought of putting that beautiful
horse in the cold ground. So I came up with a plan to pre-
serve Trigger for myself and for all the other people who
loved him. I thought about the hunting trophies I had col-
lected over the years and I contacted Mr. Bischoff, the famous taxidermist in Los Angeles, to see what he could do.
Dale howled at the thought of mounting Trigger, saying he

deserved a nice funeral and a beautiful headstone, but I re-minded her he was my horse and I wanted him for my mu-seum. "Okay, but when you die, I'm going to put you on him!" she threatened. I told her that was fine with me, just so long as she made sure I was smiling. Bischoff took Trig-ger away to mount him for posterity.

I'm fussy about saying "mounted" rather than "stuffed" when I talk about what we did with Trigger because there's a big difference, as any hunter can tell you. Stuffed means that the animal's skin has been filled with sawdust, then sewn up like a beanbag. Mounted means that an exact replica of the animal's body has been fabricated and the skin stretched over it. Bischoff took great pains to make Trigger look just like he did in life. He got all the proportions right and mounted him rearing up on his hind legs. We put the silver saddle on his back, outfitted him with bit and bridle, and I tell you, he looks good enough to ride.

That heroic image of Trigger is one kids grew up with, and it makes me happy that he is still around today for them to see and to show their kids. In a way, he belongs to them. I really mean that, because back in the early 1950s, I kinda gave him away. It happened when a rich man in Texas of-fered me $250,000 to buy him. Somehow, news of the offer got out and people actually thought that I was thinking of getting rid of him. Well, suddenly the mailroom was over-flowing with envelopes from kids containing dimes and nick-els they wanted me to have so I wouldn't have to sell Trigger. I returned their money along with a note assuring them that Trigger would never be sold. I also included a certificate that gave each child honorary ownership of the golden palomino.

Trig does require a certain amount of upkeep. We call in the exterminator from time to time to make sure bugs don't get in his hide, and we spray his glass eyes with Windex, and Dusty sometimes takes Dale's old crumb brush and grooms his coat. What's really hard is taking care of all those parade saddles of mine. There is so much ornate silverwork on them, it takes Dusty six days to clean six saddles.

Most people who come to visit the museum feel they know Trigger as well as one of their own pets. And they know us, too, not just as movie stars, but personally. I guess that's because they grew up with us. They cried with us when we lost our children, and they shared our joys, too. We have never felt the need or the desire to wall ourselves up the way some celebrities do. In fact, we lead a pretty normal life nowadays—attend church, see our friends, and entertain our kids and grandkids whenever we can. Everyone in the town knows where we live, and there have been plenty of times when Dale and I will be in our bathrobes and slippers when some stranger shows up at the door looking for us. A few of them ask Dale if she is the housekeeper: they can't believe the Queen of the West would be sitting around with curlers in her hair. I remember one time I came downstairs in the morning and found a whole family of strangers sitting in the living room. "Hi, Roy," the man said. "We're from West Virginia and we figured you wouldn't mind us droppin' in." I think I made them a cup of coffee and we yakked awhile.

At home or at the swap meet, I'll wear a baseball cap and Reeboks, but when I go to the museum to meet our fans—which I try to do every morning—I want to dress like Ol' Roy, King of the Cowboys. That's my image; that's who people come to see. So after I have my coffee I put on my white Stetson hat and cowboy boots, fancy shirt and bandana, and a pair of pants Nudie made me some forty years ago. I can still fit into all those movie clothes. If I ever weigh myself and see I've gained a pound, I just cut back on the pancake-and-egg sandwiches I like so much over at Jilly's Cafe in Apple Valley.

Going to the museum each day to meet people can sometimes be a mite dangerous. More than a few times I've been tossed in the air like a rag doll by some burly middle-aged man who forgets he isn't seven years old anymore, and that I'm eighty-three. It always happens, though: when people see me, they become kids again, and I'm still the sharp shootin' childhood hero they remember. I think some of them would crawl right into my lap if I let them. One day a lady with three teenage children thought her husband had gone crazy because he broke down in tears when he saw me. And there are a lot of women in their fifties and sixties who come over and scold me, saying, "Roy, I was so mad at you when you married Dale! You were supposed to wait and marry me when I grew up." One man who shook my hand told me he was a policeman. He said that when he was a boy his parents used to beat him, and the only happiness he had when he was little was watching us on television. Because he had no guidance at home, he said that when he got into a bad situation, he always asked himself, "What would Roy Rogers do?" Today as a law enforcement officer, he said, he still finds himself thinking that way when he feels confused. I like that a lot.

Now I'll tell you something I like to do. Early in the morning before the museum opens, Dale and I go in the back entrance and walk around in private. It's quiet and the only footsteps we hear are ours. We walk past all the glass cases and displays. We see Robin's baby toys and the folded American flag that covered Sandy's coffin. There are fading pictures of Debbie that make us remember how happy she was for the years God let us have her before He called her home. We see the old battered car that took my family out of Ohio to the promised land of California. There's Pat Brady's Jeep Nellybelle, and pictures of Gabby Hayes when he was a serious young actor, and a shot of Art Rush helping me get ready for our wedding on New Year's Eve nearly half a century ago. There's Dale wearing fancy hats for her first photo session, and me, in overalls, standing next to my first horse, Babe. Sometimes we stop to read some of the piles of letters that little pardners wrote us through the years, asking our advice and telling us about the good deeds they did. I get a little choked up when I see ol' Trigger, rearing high and looking down at us when we walk past; his saddle looks so shiny and inviting. We stroll past memories of the good times and the bad times and the hard times, and we think of all that we have shared.

I guess Dale and I know pretty well, like her song says, that "some trails are happy ones and others are blue"; and we also know that when we have to part, it will be only " 'til we meet again." And that time, our happy trails will be for all eternity.